KILLING

THE

LEGENDS

KILLING
THE
LEGENDS

THE LETHAL DANGER
of CELEBRITY

BILL O'REILLY
AND
MARTIN DUGARD

ST. MARTIN'S PRESS
NEW YORK

First published in the United States by St. Martin's Press, an imprint of St. Martin's Publishing Group

KILLING THE LEGENDS. Copyright © 2022 by Bill O'Reilly and Martin Dugard. All rights reserved. Printed in the United States of America. For information, address St. Martin's Publishing Group, 120 Broadway, New York, NY 10271.

www.stmartins.com
Design by Meryl Sussman Levavi
Library of Congress Cataloging-in-Publication Data has been applied for.

ISBN 978-1-250-28330-6 (hardcover)
ISBN 978-1-250-28331-3 (ebook)

Our books may be purchased in bulk for promotional, educational, or business use. Please contact your local bookseller or the Macmillan Corporate and Premium Sales Department at 1-800-221-7945, extension 5442, or by email at MacmillanSpecialMarkets@macmillan.com.

First Edition 2022

1 3 5 7 9 10 8 6 4 2

*This book is dedicated to all the professionals
at the Macmillan publishing group who have helped
us make the twelve Killing titles the most successful nonfiction
book series in history. Pun intended.*

CONTENTS

KILLING
THE
LEGENDS

PROLOGUE I

AUGUST 16, 1977
MEMPHIS, TENNESSEE
1:30 P.M.

The King is dead.

Nobody knows—not yet. Elvis Aaron Presley lies alone on his bathroom floor, his depleted body struck down by years of narcotics and unhealthy living. Death came so suddenly that he could not even call for help or struggle to his feet. Thick red shag carpet muffled his fall from the commode. So, while Presley's girlfriend sleeps peacefully just a few feet away in the master bedroom, she is completely unaware of the corpse on the other side of the bathroom door.

Elvis, as he was known all over the world, was forty-two at the time of his death. He was once widely acclaimed as the King of Rock 'n' Roll. But by this point, the King, as he was still called by legions of fans, was no longer relevant in the music world. Presley had become an oldies act, still performing hits from a decade and a half earlier after being displaced from the Top 40 pop charts by bands like the Beatles and the Rolling Stones. Recently, he was also eclipsed by rising stars like Led Zeppelin and Bruce Springsteen.

Although he still made millions of dollars playing Las Vegas and other concert venues, Elvis Presley was a physical mess. In his early twenties, he was a virile and handsome man, a sex symbol whose hit records and movie roles made him one of the biggest stars on earth. But at the end, that was no more. His slide into debauchery was long and pronounced, and the sycophants who depended on him for money and prestige did nothing to stop his decline. Onstage, Presley, though still charismatic, had become a garish caricature of himself: swollen, obese, and often unable to remember lyrics due to a barbiturate addiction. And while Elvis was still a relatively young man, his drug addiction and gluttony destroyed his overall health and aged his body well beyond its years.

There was a time when the blue-eyed singer was fastidious about his personal appearance, dying his sandy blond hair and eyebrows a deep black to imitate the look of Tony Curtis, his favorite actor. Presley also had his teeth capped and his nose straightened, and he took up karate for exercise. But by the time of his death, that regimen was long gone. In addition to popping amphetamines to maintain his energy during concerts, and sleeping pills to come back down, Elvis gorged on biscuits and gravy, "potato cheese soup," and loaves of Italian bread stuffed with pounds of bacon, peanut butter, and grape jelly. Once svelte, the King now weighs almost three hundred pounds as he lies comatose on the bathroom floor.

In recent years, Elvis overdosed twice, yet he continued taking pills, rationalizing that he was not a drug addict because he didn't purchase the drugs from street dealers. Instead, the narcotics were prescribed by his longtime personal physician, Dr. George Nichopoulos.

But Elvis Presley was, indeed, addicted. In the first seven months of 1977, "Dr. Nick" prescribed more than ten thousand doses of sedatives, amphetamines, and other narcotics to the ailing singer. Truth be told, before his collapse, Elvis Presley was living in an almost constant state of inebriation.

✦ ✦ ✦

Divorced from his first wife, Priscilla, Presley lived with a tall brunette twenty years his junior, named Ginger Alden. The couple resided in his mansion, Graceland, where he maintained a nocturnal lifestyle. The King purchased the thirteen-acre property for $102,500 ($945,000 in today's dollars) in 1957 and decorated it in garish fashion, particularly the "Jungle Room," where he famously shot out a television screen with a revolver because he was bored. For more than two decades, venturing outside during daylight had been a challenge for him. Presley's fame meant he was instantly recognized no matter where he went, so he slept all day and went out only after dark. This led to eccentricities—like a ten thirty p.m. visit to the dentist and a game of racquetball in his private court at four a.m. At four thirty, he sat at the piano singing gospel music, finally calling it a night at five.

As he did most every day, the King ingested a packet of pills in order to fall asleep. The pills did not work. At seven a.m., he downed another packet. This was in addition to the codeine the dentist had given him the night before.

At eight a.m., Elvis Presley took a third packet of pills, this time a drug known as Valmid, used to treat insomnia.

"I'm going into the bathroom to read," the singer, still unable to sleep, told Ginger Alden at nine thirty. He grabbed a book off the nightstand—*The Scientific Search for the Face of Jesus*—and walked into the bathroom. He wore gold pajamas.

"Don't fall asleep in there," Alden called after him, a subtle reminder that the King had done so in the past. He suffered from chronic constipation brought on by his drug use, and as a result, he spent hours in the bathroom.

"I won't," said Presley, uttering his last words.

Ginger Alden, to whom Elvis Presley had proposed but whom he never intended to marry, fell back asleep. She woke at one thirty in the afternoon to find the space beside her in bed empty. Knowing that Elvis needed to catch a seven p.m. private flight to Portland, Maine, for a concert, Alden thought he must be awake somewhere in the house. She phoned her mother, got dressed, and put on makeup. Then, after Elvis still hadn't returned to the bedroom, she went to the bathroom and knocked on the door.

There was no response. Slowly turning the knob, she pushed the door open and screamed. There, head on the floor, posterior in the air, lay an unresponsive Elvis. His gold pajama bottoms were down around his ankles, and his face lay in a pool of vomit. The singer's body was cold, and his tongue was clenched between his teeth, nearly bitten in two. Alden peeled back one of the King's eyelids, only to see a lifeless blue eye framed in blood. Ginger Alden screamed again.

The lifeless body was rushed to Baptist Medical Center in Memphis, where Elvis Presley was pronounced dead shortly after three p.m. Newspaper reporters calling the emergency room to check on Elvis's status were instead directed to the morgue.

News traveled fast. At four p.m., Vernon Presley, the singer's sixty-one-year-old father, stood on the front steps of Graceland to address a crowd of journalists. He had been a steadfast presence in his boy's career and knew firsthand the source of the King's destruction.

A devastated Vernon was succinct in his remarks: "My son is dead."

PROLOGUE II

DECEMBER 8, 1980

NEW YORK CITY

10:48 P.M.

The Walrus has been shot.

John Winston Ono Lennon staggers up the six steps leading into the main security office of the Dakota apartment building. Blood flows from the four .38-caliber hollow-point-bullet holes in his torso: two in the back, two in the shoulder. The projectiles' hollow points expanded upon impact, as they are designed to do, instantly shredding Lennon's internal organs.

"I'm shot," Lennon cries, blood dripping from his mouth. "I'm shot."

The shooter, Mark David Chapman, a twenty-five-year-old security guard from Texas, calmly places his Charter Arms revolver on the pavement and removes his long green jacket—in order to show the police who will arrive that he is unarmed. As he waits to be arrested, Chapman opens a copy of *A Catcher in the Rye*, a book with which he is obsessed. Then he sits down on the curb to read.

"Do you know what you've done?" Dakota doorman José Perdomo screams at a gloating Chapman.

"Yes," comes the answer. "I've just shot John Lennon."

✦ ✦ ✦

It wasn't supposed to be like this.

In the 1960s, John Lennon was famously a member of the Beatles, the most popular pop group in music history. A dry wit and contrarian demeanor were Lennon's trademarks, on display in song lyrics and the group's motion picture appearances, leading one fellow songwriter to label him "the Walrus."*

In 1970, the Beatles shocked the world when they split up, in part because of Lennon's heroin use. However, this detail was kept quiet, and many fans chose to blame thirty-seven-year-old Yoko Ono, who had become Lennon's muse and girlfriend in 1966. The couple's connection was so strong that Lennon legally added "Ono" to his name on April 22 of that year.

John Lennon strayed from the relationship during a period of separation in 1973, taking up with his personal assistant, May Pang. But Ono and Lennon reconciled in 1975. At the time he was shot, the singer was almost totally emotionally dependent on her.

John Lennon is forty years old, five foot ten, and a slender 139 pounds. The brown-eyed John was raised by his grandmother in Liverpool, England, and married Cynthia Powell at the age of twenty-two after she became pregnant. In 1963, she gave birth to a son they named Julian.

The breakup of the Beatles was mourned by fans the world over. Even now, ten years afterward, cries for a reunion album and concert tour are still voiced hopefully by the faithful.

But, at the time of his shooting, John Lennon has no plans ever to reunite the band. He is enjoying life far too much after the pandemonium and celebrity of his Beatles experience. After their breakup, Lennon took a lengthy sabbatical from music, a period that coincided with the 1975 birth of another son, Sean, with Yoko.

Having grown up without a father, John Lennon relished the chance to raise Sean. He ensconced himself in the family's apart-

---

* Don McLean is thought to have made the allusion in his hit song "American Pie."

ment at New York's exclusive Dakota and spent his days parenting. John and Yoko own five apartments in the Dakota, and Lennon has turned one of them into a recording studio. In the late 1970s, when he finally felt like making music again, the singer recorded part of *Double Fantasy*, a two-disc album, in that apartment.*

Released to critical acclaim, *Double Fantasy* officially went gold— that is, it reached sales of a half-million copies—just this morning. In fact, this day is one of the best in recent memory for John Lennon. It began with eggs Benedict and a Gitane cigarette at Café La Fortuna, on Seventy-First Street. Then Lennon agreed to a photo shoot with *Rolling Stone* photographer Annie Leibovitz, followed by a three-hour radio interview to promote the new album. "We're either going to live or we're going to die," Lennon tells interviewer Dave Sholin. "I consider that my work won't be finished until I'm dead and buried."

Shortly after completing the interview, Lennon leaves the Dakota with Ono to go to a nearby recording studio. The time is four thirty p.m. Despite mild December weather, the singer is greeted outside the Dakota's Seventy-Second Street entrance by a fan wearing a long green overcoat, a scarf, gloves, and a fur hat. This is Mark David Chapman. He has traveled to New York from Fort Worth, Texas, with the intention to shoot John Lennon dead.

The portly Chapman hands Lennon a copy of the *Double Fantasy* album cover to sign. Lennon autographs the cover and hands it back, not knowing that Chapman nurses a silent hatred for him. The assassin believes Lennon is a phony for spouting leftist sayings while living a millionaire's lifestyle. He is also offended by Lennon's atheistic stance, particularly his famous 1966 quote "We're more popular than Jesus now."

Chapman is standing right next to Lennon and could shoot him at any time. But the entrance to the Dakota is a popular place

---

* Other famous residents of the Dakota have included Lauren Bacall, Bono, Boris Karloff, Lillian Gish, Jack Palance, and Rex Reed.

for fans to gather, owing to the many celebrities who live inside the building. Rather than pull the pistol from his pocket immediately, and risk someone interfering with his murderous plans, Mark David Chapman prefers to wait. He accepts the autographed album from Lennon with a big smile and then watches as the singer and Yoko Ono step into a limousine and are driven away.

✦ ✦ ✦

It is six hours later when the couple returns.

Chapman is there, a loaded revolver still concealed in his pocket.

Normally, John Lennon's limousine would drive through the gate and into the inner courtyard, but this evening, another vehicle is parked in front of the entrance. So Lennon and Ono's driver lets them out at the curb on Seventy-Second Street. A small crowd of fans is gathered at the Dakota's entrance.

Lennon carries a cassette player as he exits the car. Yoko Ono walks a few steps ahead of him, passing through the main arch of the building and into the courtyard.

"Mr. Lennon," Chapman says as the singer passes by.

Lennon stops. Chapman pulls his pistol, places two hands on the grip, drops into a combat shooting stance, and fires. The first two bullets strike Lennon in the back, spinning him around and destroying the major arteries and blood vessels surrounding his heart. The second two shots hit Lennon in the shoulder. A fifth bullet misses.

"I'm shot," Lennon cries as he struggles to climb the six steps to the Dakota security office.

Yoko Ono wheels around at the sound of the gunshots, but she is powerless to help as events quickly unfold. Dakota doorman José Perdomo and concierge Jay Hastings bend to help Lennon as he collapses facedown inside the security office. Hastings quickly attempts to fashion a tourniquet from his uniform jacket, but upon pushing back Lennon's blood-soaked shirt and seeing the extent of his injuries, he places the coat over Lennon's torso to keep him warm.

New York City police officers Steven Spiro and Peter Cullen

are two blocks away in a cruiser, on Amsterdam, when they hear the gunshots. They arrive at the scene within two minutes, calling for an ambulance before gruffly forcing Chapman to the ground to be handcuffed. Spread-eagle on the pavement, Chapman cries out, complaining that he is being hurt.

As John Lennon continues to lose blood, a second team of police officers arrives. Acting quickly, Officers Herb Frauenberger and Tony Palma lift Lennon into the backseat of a squad car driven by Officer Jim Moran, who peels out for nearby Roosevelt Hospital, siren blaring.

"Are you John Lennon?" the policemen ask.

The rock star tries to speak but loses consciousness instead.

By eleven p.m., John Lennon is wheeled into the emergency room. He has lost 80 percent of his blood. Physicians attempting to transfuse new plasma into his heart are stunned to see the blood simply flow back out of his shredded vessels. The hollow-point bullets did their job.

At 11:07 p.m., Dr. Stephan Lynn, Roosevelt's emergency room director, informs Yoko Ono that her husband is dead.

"It can't be true," she wails, collapsing in shock and grief. Worldwide mourning begins almost immediately.

PROLOGUE III

JUNE 3, 2016

PHOENIX, ARIZONA

9:10 P.M.

"The Greatest" is no more.

Boxer Muhammad Ali is seventy-four years old. Over the course of his legendary career, it is estimated that the heavyweight champ absorbed almost two hundred thousand blows to the head and torso. He has been diagnosed with Parkinson's disease, but in the words of his wife, Lonnie, it is a "little cold" that has sent him to HonorHealth Scottsdale Osborn Medical Center, where he was admitted one week ago. Ali's serious condition was quickly ascertained, and because his body lacked the resources to fight the infection, he was moved to intensive care and quickly placed on a ventilator.

But now Muhammad Ali's pulse slows to nothing. A Muslim prayer leader known as an imam sings words of praise into the boxer's right ear. And even though Lonnie Ali, the boxer's fourth wife, and his nine children are all gathered, the voice of Zaid Shakir will be the last one Ali will ever hear. The boxer has been a Muslim for more than fifty years. In 1964, after three years as a practicing Muslim, he formally joined the Nation of Islam, and in 1967 he left behind his given name of Cassius Clay.

A doctor presses a stethoscope to Muhammad Ali's chest and then declares the time of death.

Ali's body is taken to the Bunker Hill Funeral Home for embalming. Normally, in the Muslim faith, the deceased is buried within twenty-four hours of death and the body lowered into the ground rather than placed in a coffin. But owing to Ali's global celebrity, and the need for the sort of public closure a large funeral provides, several years prior to his death he forged a spiritual solution. His corpse would be embalmed, but only with a solution containing no alcohol or formaldehyde. Undertaker Jeff Gardner, a Catholic from Ali's hometown of Louisville, was hired eight years ago to perform this task. Ever since the Ali family requested his services, Gardner has worn a pager to alert him of the boxer's demise. When news of Ali's hospitalization came, the undertaker immediately boarded a private jet and flew to Phoenix.

Gardner is met at Bunker Hill by Ahmad Ewais, who has been hired to cleanse Ali's body after the embalming. Lighting a stick of incense, Ewais uses soap and water to wash the champ. Ali's body is covered by a towel from his neck to his knees. Then Ewais cleans the entire body a second time, using ground lotus leaves. On the third and final washing, Ewais uses camphor and perfume before covering the corpse in three sheets of linen. When he is done, only Ali's face can be seen.

The boxer is then lifted into a travel casket, placed in a white hearse, and driven to the airport, where the private jet awaits.

Muhammad Ali is going home to Louisville one last time. His burial will take place one week after his death. The memorial service will be held in the city's convention center. Tickets for the service will be gone within minutes.

The cause of death is officially septic shock, with some believing Ali's Parkinson's was a contributing factor. But as with Elvis Presley and John Lennon, the downfall of this legend was brought on by other human beings.

✦ ✦ ✦

A poor boy from Tupelo, Mississippi. A poor boy from Liverpool, England. A poor boy from Louisville, Kentucky.

Ironically, these three legends had much in common despite living vastly different lives.

All three men achieved vast wealth and fame. All possessed talent and charisma. All surrendered their autonomy to others.

And that capitulation sealed their destinies.

PART I

✦

The King

CHAPTER ONE

JULY 22, 1963

LAS VEGAS, NEVADA

1 P.M.

Elvis Presley is Lucky.

The King, playing the role of race driver Lucky Jackson in the film *Viva Las Vegas*, strolls the deck around the Flamingo Hotel's expansive swimming pool. He walks alone, strumming a guitar while singing a love song. Movie extras lounge in the sunshine, pretending to read a book or sip a drink. Elvis keeps singing as he arrives at the door marked "Women's Changing Room," knowing that the woman with whom he is infatuated can hear him on the other side.*

Elvis is twenty-eight, six feet tall, his hair dyed jet black. Inside the "changing room," twenty-two-year-old Ann-Margret, a Swedish-born actress, changes into a swimsuit. Ann-Margret, playing the character Rusty Martin, is a vibrant on-screen presence. As Elvis sings, she slips into a pair of stiletto high heels that match her yellow one-piece and then emerges onto the pool deck.

There, the two stand eye-to-eye as they begin to sing a duet.

"Once the music started, neither of us could stand still," Ann-

---

* Among the extras who will play roles in *Viva Las Vegas* is actress Teri Garr. Singer Glen Campbell will perform on the movie's title track.

Margret will write in her autobiography. "Music ignited a fiery pent-up passion inside Elvis and inside me. It was an odd, embarrassing, funny, inspiring, and wonderful sensation. We looked at each other move and saw virtual mirror images. When Elvis thrust his pelvis, mine slammed forward too. When his shoulder dropped, I was down there with him. When he whirled, I was already on my heel."

The song, "The Lady Loves," is not the rock 'n' roll that made Presley famous but a charming pop tune soon to be forgotten in movie history, overshadowed by the eponymous *Viva Las Vegas* theme song. But the chemistry between Presley, strumming his guitar while wearing a gray sharkskin suit, and Ann-Margret, in her form-fitting bathing suit, is scorching.

It is one week since filming began on location here in Las Vegas. The Flamingo's guests were informed in advance that the pool would be closed this afternoon and tomorrow. Many now watch from the hotel lobby as this highly choreographed scene is repeated over and over. As the couple slowly climbs the pink stairwell leading to the top of the diving board, cries of "Cut!" come from director George Sidney. The cameras must be repositioned. It is taxing work under the desert sun, with the few palm trees landscaping the pool providing little shade to bring down the 106-degree temperature. But neither Elvis Presley nor Ann-Margret shows any sign of exhaustion. Elvis's makeup and black pompadour are touched up after each scene, and his suit coat shows no signs of perspiration.

In fact, the true heat comes from the actors themselves. The on-screen chemistry is no accident, for their off-screen romance is incendiary. Ann-Margret is not married; nor is Elvis. But it is known around the world that the King has a longtime girlfriend in young Priscilla Beaulieu, who just turned eighteen two months ago.

So the affair is kept secret. Barely.

✦ ✦ ✦

Three years earlier, on March 1, 1960, Sgt. Elvis Presley returned to the limelight. The location is Friedberg, West Germany. The time is

9:17 a.m. The twenty-five-year-old singer wears an olive-drab army uniform as he steps into the enlisted men's club at Ray Barracks. The three chevrons of his rank are stitched onto his sleeves. His tie is neatly cinched. More than one hundred reporters and photographers fill the canteen, jostling to get close to the entertainer for questions before he finishes his military service and returns to the United States. More journalists are present today than were for President Dwight Eisenhower's press conferences during his recent visit to West Germany.

Elvis Presley's body has grown muscular in the army. He has learned karate as part of his training and has also developed a fondness for the amphetamines soldiers take to stay awake while on night maneuvers. Elvis sees nothing wrong with the drugs, though they sometimes make him jittery. He believes the "pep pills" elevate his mental faculties and keep him trim, even as he pursues a diet heavy in white bread and potatoes fried in bacon fat. To ensure a steady supply of pills for himself and his friends, Elvis has bribed an army pharmacist. One fellow soldier, Rex Mansfield, will later say that the drugs were so available in the army that it took him five years to kick his own habit.

But there is no evidence of narcotics right now. A toothy smile creases Presley's face as he prepares to take questions. It has been four years since the blues-rock single "Heartbreak Hotel" turned the former Mississippi truck driver into an international star. That hit was followed by "Hound Dog," which eventually sold ten million copies globally, guaranteeing first-name status for "Elvis."

On this day, Sergeant Presley strides through the crowd with poise and command, instantly owning the room. Removing his army-issue cap, he reveals a high pompadour.

Though the United States is not at war, a draft is in effect. When Presley's number came up two years ago, he was offered the chance to perform light duties entertaining the troops. Instead of taking advantage of the "celebrity wimp-out," as his fellow soldiers call that service, Elvis requested a more ordinary path. For the past eighteen months, he has been assigned to Company C, part of the US Army's

Third Armored Division. But now his two-year military service has come to an end, and his fans, who labeled the day of Presley's induction "Black Monday," are eager to know what comes next.

✦ ✦ ✦

Three years later, as *Viva Las Vegas* continues filming around the Flamingo Hotel pool, Elvis Presley and Ann-Margret complete their duet. Newly minted choreographer David Winters has planned every step of their routine, directing the two young stars to walk perilously close to the water's edge without falling in, all the while singing. Another conceit of the pas de deux is that Elvis and Ann-Margret never look at one another, as if playing hard to get.

It is apparent that the young Elvis Presley, who set the world aflame nine years ago with his swiveling pelvis and innocent snarl, has grown up. His early hits—"Hound Dog," "Love Me Tender," "Jailhouse Rock," and "All Shook Up"—are still his bestselling songs, all having charted to No. 1. But now, on this movie set, Presley knows he has to find the magic formula once again. "I hear the music's changed," he confessed as he returned to civilian life. "I couldn't commit myself to saying I'm gonna be, or I'm not gonna be. All I can say is I'm gonna try."

New hits recorded since he left the army—"Return to Sender" and "Are You Lonesome Tonight?"—become instant classics, but they have not matched the amazing sales of his early songs. The same holds true for the King's film career. *Viva Las Vegas* is just one of thirty-one movies he will make in his lifetime, as arranged by his overbearing agent and manager, Colonel Tom Parker. But unlike many of his other pictures, fated to be immediately forgotten, this production reveals that the King has major acting potential.

As per the script, it soon becomes clear that "Lucky" is so smitten by "Rusty" that he is following her, perhaps being led into a peril of his own making. The scenes play well, capturing the sly innuendo of two people attracted to each other. Ann-Margret, who will admit many years later that her sexy on-screen demeanor led her to be typecast as a "female Elvis," enjoys the King's sense of humor. "He would tease me and I would tease him back. We had lots of laughter."

As the cameras roll, the joke appears to be on Elvis. Ann-Margret leads him up the column of steps to the top of the pool's high dive. At ten feet above the water, it's a long way down should the King fall.

Suddenly, Ann-Margret approaches Elvis with mischief in her eyes.

✦ ✦ ✦

It was upon leaving the army that Elvis Presley chose his future.

Originally hailing from Tupelo, Mississippi, Presley found that his easy southern drawl charmed the press in Germany. Sitting at a large table at the German press conference, reporters on all sides, Presley proclaims that he will once more return to singing rock 'n' roll—though without the rebellious sideburns for which he was once so well known. Life in the military has matured Presley, and he now tells reporters he also wants to make "serious motion pictures."

"Has your military experience been beneficial?" asks a writer from *Screen Digest*.

"It has changed both my career and my personal life," Elvis responds. "I learned a lot and made a lot of friends I wouldn't have otherwise. . . . It's good to rough it. To put yourself to the test."

The questions keep coming.

Presley's measured responses are vastly different from the youthful swagger of his pre-army years. He speaks of going home to Memphis for a while and then traveling to California to perform in a television special with Frank Sinatra, eventually becoming a "singing actor." First up, a film called *GI Blues*.

The members of the media hang on every word, some scribbling notes while others man the television cameras. It is the first and only press conference the army has allowed Presley to conduct, so after two years of silence, his words are eagerly anticipated. However, some reporters cannot help but wish for something a bit more sensational.

The moment finally comes. A question arises about a rumor—that Presley has a "sixteen-year-old girlfriend."

Presley well knows that the young woman in question is only fifteen, yet he does not correct the reporter. Sergeant Presley has never been considered a paragon of virtue, but the notion of a man his age dating a high school sophomore has a touch of scandal.

But Elvis Presley does not back down.

"She's pretty," he says of Priscilla Beaulieu, whom he has been seeing since she turned fourteen. The dark-haired stepdaughter of an air force captain is poised beyond her years, but she still has an eleven p.m. curfew on school nights. Elvis has met her parents, Paul and Anna Beaulieu, who have since allowed their daughter to be driven unchaperoned to Elvis's rented three-story stucco home in Bad Nauheim three or four times a week for the past six months.

"She's a very nice girl," Elvis tells the journalists. "Her family is nice. She is very mature for her age."

It is not known whether Elvis Presley has ever considered his Mississippi rival, Jerry Lee Lewis. In 1957, at age twenty-two, the piano rocker married his thirteen-year-old first cousin once removed, a girl named Myra Gale Brown. Lewis had monster hits with songs like "Great Balls of Fire" and "Whole Lotta Shaking Goin' On." At the time of the marriage less than two years ago, Lewis was earning $10,000 a night to give a concert. After the press learned of Myra's age, Jerry Lee Lewis became a pariah, and his concert fee dropped to just $250 per night. Lewis was shamed, and almost ruined. So the revelation that Elvis Presley is dating a girl only slightly older than Myra Brown gives the press a major story.

Four thousand miles away, the man who could have prevented that revelation is seething.

✦ ✦ ✦

The most influential figure in Elvis Presley's life will be Colonel Tom Parker, the business manager who now plots the entertainer's future. But Parker cannot travel to Germany to protect Elvis—for good reason. So the corpulent businessman pulls the Presley puppet strings from afar.

Gone are the rock-'n'-roll days, with Elvis gyrating across the stage. Now the Colonel believes those moves should belong to a younger man. The Colonel is Elvis Presley's Svengali, and just as he has since 1955, he will, until the end of the singer's life, push Elvis relentlessly. An ongoing schedule of recording, concerts, and movie roles will be thrust upon Presley, leaving him exhausted and bitter.

Tom Parker's real name is Andreas Cornelis van Kuijk. He is a fifty-year-old Dutch carnival barker who may have been involved with a murdered woman in Holland.* That suspicion was raised because, soon after she was killed, van Kuijk left town, finding work on a vessel headed for the United States. Eventually, he jumped ship in Mobile, Alabama, and entered the USA illegally. Soon, he enlisted in the US Army, though he had no passport. The sergeant at the recruiting center was named Tom Parker. The name caught Kuijk's eye and led him to change his name legally to Tom Parker.

In 1932, Parker went AWOL and was charged with desertion. He spent several months in a military prison, finally receiving a dishonorable discharge—but not before the army had him confined to a psychiatric hospital, where he was diagnosed as a psychopath.

Upon his discharge from the service, Tom Parker worked in the carnival business, often operating as a con man on the side. One favorite scam was painting sparrows yellow and selling them for a higher price as canaries. Then World War II broke out. With a universal draft in place, Parker, to avoid possibly being forced to return to the military, deliberately gorged himself until he weighed more than three hundred pounds, making himself unfit for duty. Though he would lose some of that weight, he would remain portly for the rest of his life. And like the phony canaries, he would often appear in light yellow, his favorite clothing color.

---

* In May 1929, a twenty-three-year-old newlywed named Anna van den Enden was found beaten to death in a grocery store. The murder took place in the town of Breda, twenty miles outside Rotterdam. Andreas van Kuijk knew Anna, and some considered him a suspect. However, he was never questioned by the Dutch police, and the murder was never solved.

The transition into music promotion, with its demand for bluster and charisma, was an easy one for Parker. Among his first clients was country singer Eddy Arnold, who brought Parker to Nashville, Tennessee, with great frequency.*Another of Parker's early clients, singer Jimmie Davis, would one day leave the entertainment industry and become the governor of Louisiana. In 1948, a grateful Davis bestowed upon Parker the honorary title of "Colonel," a sobriquet Parker instantly adopted.

But it was the 1955 signing of the young Elvis Presley to an exclusive contract as "special adviser" that was the making of Tom Parker. By cleverly pairing new hit singles with movies of the same title, the Colonel and the singer rose to the top of the music and motion picture industries.

Elvis's first film was *Love Me Tender*. The record of the same name sold more than one million copies. Then came the movie *Jailhouse Rock*. That single sold three hundred thousand copies in the first week and eventually also sold more than one million, reinforcing Presley's superstar status.

Then came the draft. At the peak of Elvis Presley's popularity— he had a seven-figure deal at Paramount Pictures and a steady stream of chart-topping hits—the singer would be required to devote two years of his life to the military and would, thus, disappear from the public eye completely. The chances of his emerging from this exile with his career intact were dubious, to say the least.

But where some saw calamity, Colonel Tom Parker saw opportunity. It was the Colonel who insisted Presley perform his service as a regular soldier, sensing that this would become a public relations coup. As the farewell press conference demonstrated before the Priscilla revelation, this was very much the case. During his time in Germany, Elvis regularly appeared outside his rented house to sign autographs. Indeed, a sign posted the hours each evening when he

---

* Eddy Arnold recorded bestselling country-and-western and gospel albums during his long career, singing well into his eighties. He died in 2008 at age eighty-nine.

would make himself available. As Colonel Parker predicted, Elvis Presley remained in the public eye while still enjoying the status of a "regular" GI.

Parker never once visited his client in West Germany, out of fear he would not be allowed to return to the United States; he possessed neither US citizenship nor a passport. Because of this, Elvis would never perform in concert outside North America.

On the morning of March 2, 1960, Sgt. Elvis Presley boards a military flight from Rhein-Main Air Base bound for Fort Dix, New Jersey. Although he has enjoyed ten Top 40 hits since his induction, having spent considerable time in the recording studio prior to reporting for duty, Presley is deeply concerned about his career.*

But Elvis need not worry: Colonel Tom Parker is in complete control—except for one matter.

In June 1963, when she is eighteen, Priscilla Beaulieu moves into Elvis Presley's Memphis, Tennessee, mansion—not as his wife or fiancée, but as his very young girlfriend. However, the world seems not to judge and, instead, awaits the day when Elvis and Priscilla will tie the knot.

Viva Las Vegas begins filming just three weeks later.

✦ ✦ ✦

Atop the Flamingo Hotel high dive, Elvis and Ann-Margret conclude their duet. The King stands at the very end of the board, with his back to the water. Just as it appears that the two might lean in for a kiss, Ann-Margret pushes Elvis into the pool, guitar, sharkskin suit, and all.

But it is not Elvis hitting the water. Just before the push, his stunt double, Lance LeGault, replaced the idol, and a camera angle allowed the perception that it was Elvis taking the dive. But with

---

* The ten hit singles were "Wear My Ring Around Your Neck," "One Night," "King Creole," "Hard Headed Woman," "I Got Stung," "(Now and Then There's) A Fool Such as I," "I Need Your Love Tonight," "My Wish Came True," "Doncha' Think It's Time," and "A Big Hunk of Love."

the King being paid a salary of $500,000 ($4.1 million today) and a percentage of the profits, that was never going to happen.*

Just off camera, Colonel Tom Parker watches the scene. He understands the sizzle between Presley and Ann-Margret and believes it will produce box-office gold.

This makes the Colonel very happy, for he gets 50 percent of every dollar Elvis Presley will ever earn.†

---

* Lance LeGault went on to a long and successful career as a character actor on such television shows as *The A-Team* and *Magnum P.I.* Today, visitors to Presley's Graceland mansion can hear LeGault's voice narrating the audio tour.

† *Viva Las Vegas* was one of Elvis's most successful films, grossing $10 million ($85 million in today's money). Despite titles like *Kissin' Cousins, Clambake, Roustabout, Fun in Acapulco,* and *Girls! Girls! Girls!,* all his movies made money.

CHAPTER TWO

AUGUST 27, 1965
BEVERLY HILLS, CALIFORNIA
10 P.M.

A secret meeting is under way.

Three black Cadillac limousines pull up to the tall wrought-iron gates guarding 1174 Hillcrest Drive in the Trousdale Estates section of Beverly Hills. Built into a hillside, the 5,300-square-foot ranch-style mansion has three bedrooms, walls of glass, and a separate guesthouse. Thick white shag carpeting covers the living room floor in ankle-deep pile.

The arriving guests have been expected.

In the great round room at the center of the house, a party is in progress—blue and red mood lighting, color TV, a jukebox, pool tables, drinks. Elvis Presley and the coterie of friends he calls "the Memphis Mafia" entertain a bevy of young women. The gathering is large and loud, with more than twenty in attendance.

Elvis is quiet, unsure of how the evening will proceed. Few in the room know who's coming over, but ground rules are in place to ensure the visit goes smoothly: no recording, no press, no photos—and above all, the meeting must remain a secret.

Two members of the Memphis Mafia pull open the gates and wave the limousines through. Colonel Tom Parker, who made this get-together possible, rides in the front car. As the vehicles park in the circular driveway, the occupants emerge. Tony Barrow, a twenty-nine-year-old publicist, is among the arrivals. He has worked closely with Parker to arrange tonight's rendezvous, and he now fidgets nervously, hoping everyone gets along.

Barrow is British and has worked this job for the last three years. He signed on with his clients before they were famous—and it was he who coined the moniker that fueled their rise to stardom, "the Fab Four."

Members of the hottest pop act on earth proceed through Elvis's front door: John Lennon, Paul McCartney, Ringo Starr, and George Harrison. Ten years ago, Presley was their idol, inspiring their dream of making it big in the music world. In Lennon's own words, "Without Elvis, there would be no Beatles."

It was the Beatles who requested this meeting. They had tried before, one year ago. But that rendezvous did not come to pass. "We could never get to him," Paul McCartney will remember. "We used to think we were a bit of a threat to him and Colonel Tom Parker, which ultimately we were. So although we tried many times, Colonel Tom would just show up with a few souvenirs, and that would have to do us for a while. We didn't feel brushed off; we felt we *deserved* to be brushed off. After all, he was Elvis, and who were *we* to dare to want to meet him? But we finally received an invitation to go round and see him when he was making a film in Hollywood."*

Now, the shoeless feet of John, Paul, George, and Ringo sink into the deep shag carpeting as the four are led to Elvis's "playpen," in Tony Barrow's words.

John Lennon is thrilled. "It was very exciting, we were all nervous as hell, and we met him in his big house in LA—probably as big as the one we were staying in, but it still felt like, 'Big house, big Elvis,'" Lennon will remember. "He had lots of guys around him, all these

---

*That film was the musical Western *Frankie and Johnny*. Elvis's costar was Donna Douglas, already famous as Elly May Clampett on *The Beverly Hillbillies*.

guys that used to live near him—like we did from Liverpool; we always had thousands of Liverpool people around us, so I guess he was the same. And he had pool tables! Maybe a lot of American houses are like that, but it seemed amazing to us; it was like a nightclub."

However, the excitement quickly turns awkward.

"There was a weird silence," Barrow will remember of the moment Elvis and the Beatles first laid eyes on one another. The King has been plucking at a bass guitar while watching television without the sound on.

Elvis is about six years older than John and Ringo, the two eldest members of the band at twenty-four and twenty-five respectively, but the generation gap seems more like a chasm. The Beatles—along with bands like the Rolling Stones and Herman's Hermits—are part of the music world's raucous "British Invasion." They wear their hair long, with bangs covering their eyebrows and long sideburns. Elvis and his crew, their southern ways transported temporarily to Los Angeles, still prefer a more traditional 1950s pompadour.

Also, the King no longer makes cutting-edge music. His most recent single, "Crying in the Chapel," sold over a million copies but never reached No. 1 on the *Billboard* Hot 100 sales chart. Also, his recent film *Girl Happy* did nothing to stretch his acting chops. Its $3 million gross box office is well below the $10 million of *Viva Las Vegas* just two years ago.

Help!, the second Beatles film, will be released one month from tonight. It will gross over $12 million ($100 million today).

Even more palpable is the "buzz" gap. The Beatles are a sensation. They are at the end of a sixteen-show US tour that began at Shea Stadium in New York City two weeks ago and will conclude here in Los Angeles with two sold-out shows at the Hollywood Bowl. They are spending six nights in a rented Benedict Canyon home nearby, to rest before those final performances. That location was supposed to be top secret, but word has leaked. Fans throng the streets in front of the residence, forcing road closures. Others try to scale the property's walls.

Elvis Presley once owned that level of fame. But while he still needs those wrought-iron gates to keep fans away, the King is no longer a teen idol.

So on one side of the room stands Elvis Presley with his group of revelers. On the other stand the Fab Four. No one knows what to say.

Except John Lennon. The brash guitarist addresses the issue of their parallel careers with two quick questions.

"Why do you do all these soft-centered ballads for the cinema these days?" he asks Presley. And then: "What happened to good old rock and roll?"

Elvis does not respond. The question had to hurt him. But no one will ever know for sure.

✦ ✦ ✦

The truth is that rock 'n' roll is changing dramatically, along with the rest of the world. Traditional groups like the Four Tops, the Righteous Brothers, and the raucous Sam the Sham and the Pharaohs still dominate the charts in 1965, but a darker political tone is beginning to intrude on pop music.*

The emergence of socially conscious artists like Bob Dylan and Joan Baez has been a radical departure from the *Girl Happy* fluff Elvis still embraces. For Presley and the Colonel, history is passing them by. The assassination of President John F. Kennedy, the rise of the civil rights movement, and above all the controversial Vietnam War has music fans seeking new messages in their music.

Even as the Beatles and Elvis meet tonight in Beverly Hills, the impact of President Lyndon Johnson's Gulf of Tonkin Resolution accelerates the cultural change. Thousands of miles away, North

---

* The five bestselling singles of 1965, in descending order of their place on the charts, were "Wooly Bully," by Sam the Sham; "I Can't Help Myself (Sugar Pie, Honey Bunch)," by the Four Tops; "(I Can't Get No) Satisfaction," by the Rolling Stones; "You Were on My Mind," by the We Five; and "You've Lost That Lovin' Feelin'," by the Righteous Brothers.

Vietnamese torpedo boats allegedly attacked two US naval vessels, leading LBJ to order retaliation by US bomber aircraft. As with the war in Korea that ended twelve years ago, the presence of American troops in Vietnam is framed by the US government as an effort to defeat communism.

But unlike with the Korean War, which came at the peak of post–World War II anticommunist fervor in the United States, the US bombings in North Vietnam have many questioning if this is a *just* war. Protests have begun at universities around the country. Many students are aligning with antigovernment opposition through acts of rebellion, like growing their hair long and smoking marijuana—a substance that Elvis Presley, despite his fondness for opioids and amphetamines, considers an abomination.

The intensity of this cultural shift demands that the world of entertainment pay attention. So, while the sophomoric "Wooly Bully" is all the rage in 1965, the future belongs to protest: Dylan and Baez; Crosby, Stills, and Nash; Jefferson Airplane. The Beatles will record their statement songs, too, riding the wave of the popular mood in a way that will take their music from the innocent lamentations of "She Loves You" and "I Want to Hold Your Hand" into the very political "Revolution"—which, in traditional ironic Beatles fashion, protests the act of protesting.

Colonel Tom Parker is violently opposed to Elvis making a similar career alteration. He despises "message" songs and refuses to let Presley record such material. It will not be until 1969 and the song "In the Ghetto"—a record made behind the Colonel's back—that the King will address societal issues. Presley's continued frivolity in 1965 means his reputation as a "serious" artist is slipping away. "Crying in the Chapel" may have sold a million copies, but it has absolutely nothing to do with life in today's America.

It is not known whether Elvis Presley understands what is happening in the world of pop music. He does, however, have a choice: to align himself with a new brand of music or to continue with business as usual. After talking with Elvis, Paul McCartney recalled, "I only met him that once, and then I think the success of our career started to push him out a little—which we were very sad about, because we wanted to coexist with him. He was our greatest idol, but the styles were changing in favor of us."

✦ ✦ ✦

As the meeting with the Fab Four unfolds, Elvis is kind to the Beatles, shaking their hands and exchanging with them stories about life on the road. But that conversation does not last long. "They quickly exhausted their initial bout of small talk, and there was this embarrassing silence between the mega-famous five," publicist Barrow will remember.

The King calls for guitars, which are instantly procured. A short jam session breaks out. "The boys found that they could make much better conversation with their guitars than they could with their spoken word. Music was their natural meeting point, their most intelligent means of communication," Barrow adds.

As per the ground rules, no one takes a picture of this moment. No one turns on a recording device.

Not having drums, Ringo Starr pounds out the backbeat on wooden furniture. Elvis continues playing the bass, which is usually McCartney's instrument. "See, Macca. I'm practicing," the King jokes.

McCartney quickly replies, "Brian Epstein will make a star of you soon," referring to the Beatles' manager.

Publicist Barrow watches the scene. "Everybody was singing," he will remember fondly. "They tried to make light of it and not show too much adoration for their idol, but Elvis Presley was their idol and one of the prime influences of the Beatles' music."

Finally, Colonel Tom Parker has had enough. He enters the room with a pile of Elvis albums, hands them out like presents, and ushers the Beatles to the door. The meeting lasts just an hour.

"Long live ze King," John Lennon shouts in a comedic German

accent as he steps into his limousine. There is talk among the Beatles about whether Elvis took drugs before their visit.

"Elvis was stoned," Lennon insists.

"Aren't we all?" George Harrison quips.

CHAPTER THREE

E lvis Presley is tense.

It is a Monday morning, and Elvis and longtime girlfriend Priscilla Beaulieu pose shoulder to shoulder before Nevada Supreme Court judge David Zenoff in a suite at the Aladdin hotel. They stand together against a backdrop of tall white candles and elaborate white lily wreaths, as Elvis's favorite color is white.

Two wedding photographers work the room—which is difficult; the space is too small for the fourteen assembled wedding guests. Everyone is standing uncomfortably close, including Colonel Tom Parker, who has orchestrated the event.

More people would have been in attendance, but Parker did not want a large crowd—and he specifically banned all but two members of Presley's Memphis Mafia crew, who, at any given time, depending on the singer's needs for bodyguards and company, could number anywhere from six to twenty. This decision angered a number of Elvis's confidants, but the superstar would not go up against the Colonel. His loyalty ran too deep.

Outside the suite, located on the hotel's third floor, members of the press listen through the closed door, waiting for the ceremony to end so they can be the first to see the new bride and groom. Rumors about the top-secret wedding have been circulating for days.

The fortunate invited guests gathered at Elvis's Palm Springs home yesterday afternoon. "By that time," Memphis Mafia member and co-best man Marty Lacker will remember, "the reporters were there by the dozens. When they saw all the people arriving, they knew something was about to happen, and that something was probably a wedding. The reporters were trying to bribe the maids. One was offered five hundred dollars to reveal what was going on, but she didn't do it."

By late afternoon, the guests had all gathered in front of the home. Colonel Parker strode down the long driveway to announce that there would be a press conference. Problem was, the meeting would be held more than two hundred miles away, in Las Vegas. Immediately, the press rushed to relocate.

Even as reporters drove through the night, the wedding party and guests flew to Vegas on two chartered aircraft. The group had been carefully chosen. Elvis's father, the fifty-one-year-old Vernon, and his second wife, Dee; Priscilla's parents; and Joe Esposito and Marty Lacker, who would serve as best men. Priscilla's sister, Michelle, would serve as maid of honor.*

The ceremony begins on time. The marital vows are standard, the same words Judge Zenoff has recited hundreds of times. However, there is one exception: Elvis Presley refuses to say "obey" in his vows. Priscilla will.

A trio consisting of a violin, accordion, and stand-up bass plays "Love Me Tender" as Elvis and Priscilla enter the room. As Judge Zenoff states the vows, the musicians stand ready to launch into "Here Comes the Bride" when the ceremony is complete. The couple appears nervous. Elvis usually enjoys teasing Priscilla, pulling her hair or tugging on her earlobe, but there is no evidence of that behavior now.

---

* Elvis Presley's mother, Gladys Love Smith Presley, died on August 14, 1958, of a heart attack brought on by acute hepatitis.

Presley stands with his hands at his sides, a carnation in his lapel. Priscilla holds a small bouquet of flowers. The King wears a black-on-black tuxedo custom-made for this day by Hollywood designer Lambert Marks, who chose a fabric of paisley silk brocade. Elvis accessorizes with black cowboy boots, diamond-and-sapphire cuff links, and a platinum watch also decorated with these precious gems. His trademark black pompadour is extra tall for this special day, supported by wires that run up the back of his head, hidden under his dyed black hair.

"'Cilla," as Elvis calls his bride, bought her simple full-length white dress with lace sleeves and matching veil off the rack. Her brown hair is also dyed black, to match her new husband's, and is layered high in a bouffant style. Later, one of Elvis's groomsmen will say, "She looked like she had about eight people living in her hair."

Elvis had proposed just before Christmas last year, instructed to do so by Colonel Parker, who recognized that the attention spawned by a wedding might give Presley's tanking career a vital boost. As Parker well knows, the King has not had a hit record since "Crying in the Chapel." His highest-ranking single since then, "I'm Yours," reached only No. 11. And while his 1966 Christmas album would go on to become the bestselling holiday record in history, it is clear that Presley's time as the "King of Rock 'n' Roll" is now a memory. With his own six-figure income on the line, Parker turned his focus to having Elvis make a number of foolish movies, which include soundtrack albums. But that strategy has failed, as both the films and the recordings are mediocre at best. The United States is being pulled deeper into the Vietnam War, and the protest culture around the world is growing stronger. Elvis's pop music and thinly plotted romantic movies belong to a different era. The King finished filming his most recent movie, *Clambake*, just four days ago. It is Elvis's twenty-fifth film and one of the rare times in their relationship that he and Colonel Parker fought about his career path. That rift is still not completely healed as Elvis stands before the judge.

Parker's hope that Elvis would become a crossover star in both movies and music was based on the career of crooner Frank Sinatra, who has successfully managed both. Like Elvis, the young Sinatra hit a career lull, too, in the early 1950s. So the singer switched from lighthearted movies to serious fare. His role as Angelo Maggio in *From Here to Eternity* won him the 1954 Academy Award for Best Supporting Actor. Subsequent roles in *Guys and Dolls* and *The Manchurian Candidate* have also boosted Sinatra's celebrity. Indeed, Frank Sinatra is now just as well known as a serious actor as he is a singer. It is not lost on the Colonel that Sinatra's wedding to Mia Farrow one year ago generated enormous publicity. This is the inspiration for his demanding that Elvis marry Priscilla.*

Frank Sinatra once railed against Elvis Presley and rock-'n'-roll music. But as American culture leaves the King behind, the two stars have become good friends. Ironically, Sinatra's music is enjoying a resurgence even as Elvis's work falls into decline. The fifty-one-year-old New Jersey native's duet with twenty-six-year-old daughter Nancy, a simple pop tune whose official title is "Something Stupid," is now No. 1 on the *Billboard* charts.

Colonel Tom Parker arranged for Sinatra to loan Presley his private jet to make the midnight flight from Palm Springs to Las Vegas. He even set up actor and amateur aviator Danny Kaye to pilot the aircraft.†

✦ ✦ ✦

Elvis and Priscilla will maintain his Memphis mansion, Graceland, as their primary residence. The new bride and groom plan to live in Tennessee most of the year. They have also just leased a five-thousand-square-foot mansion with palm trees and a pool in Palm Springs. The reason for the acquisition is that Colonel Parker lives just a half mile away.

The Colonel's choice of Las Vegas for the wedding is primarily a

---

* Author Mario Puzo modeled his *Godfather* character Johnny Fontaine on Sinatra.

† The fifty-six-year-old Kaye starred in seventeen films, among them *White Christmas* and *The Secret Life of Walter Mitty*. In 1964, Elvis Presley bought President Franklin Roosevelt's old yacht and donated it to Kaye's cancer charity.

business decision. Elvis Presley is closely associated with the city due to the success of *Viva Las Vegas*, and the new owner of the Aladdin hotel, Milton Prell, is a good friend of Parker's. The developer has connections with the local press and can keep things quiet until the time for publicity is ripe. Prell purchased the establishment two years ago for $10 million ($83 million in today's currency) and spent millions more upgrading it, adding a lounge, a five-hundred-seat showroom, and a golf course.

Prell is the casino resort's third owner in five years. Twice, the Aladdin has been shut down for lack of customers. In fact, the hotel is so associated with failure that its nickname is "the Vegas jinx." Maybe Elvis and Priscilla can change its luck. Having the wedding in Prell's personal suite guarantees excellent publicity for the Aladdin and, Prell hopes, a surge of fans who will want to spend a night in the hotel where Elvis got married.*

✦ ✦ ✦

As the couple stands before the judge, there are rumors that Priscilla is pregnant. Just enough billow to the front of her off-the-rack dress to fuel that speculation. Indeed, the timing will prove extremely suspicious, as she will give birth to daughter Lisa Marie just thirty-nine weeks from now.

But the fact is that Elvis got down on bended knee to present Priscilla with a three-and-a-half-carat diamond ring five months ago. Prior to that, he was never in a hurry to get hitched, having lived with Priscilla for four years. In her memoirs, Priscilla will claim that Elvis would not have sex before marriage and that the consummation of their union did not take place until this very night.

This does not mean the King has remained chaste. During this time, Elvis was extremely active in pursuing women. "His list of one-night stands would fill volumes," one biographer will write. In ad-

---

* The jinx will continue. Milton Prell will have a stroke later in 1967 and will be forced to sell the property. The original casino was demolished in 1998. A Planet Hollywood now stands on the site.

dition to Ann-Margret, Elvis has been linked to actresses Natalie Wood, Marilyn Monroe, and Peggy Lipton, among many others.

But it was Ann-Margret who caused the most trouble between Elvis and 'Cilla. In November 1963, after the filming of *Viva Las Vegas* was complete, the Swedish singer was quoted in the Los Angeles media as saying she was "in love" with Presley.

Elvis and Priscilla are staying in his Beverly Hills mansion when the story breaks. Colonel Parker seeks to defuse the situation by immediately sending Priscilla back to Graceland to shield her from the media. But, first, an enraged 'Cilla must know the truth. She confronts Elvis, demanding to know if he has been unfaithful. She has long known about the chemistry between him and Ann-Margret, but he has insisted there was no physical romance.

Caught in a lie, Elvis confesses everything.

Priscilla hurls a vase across the room, narrowly missing the King.

"You tell Ann-Margret to keep her ass in Sweden, where she belongs," Priscilla shrieks.

Yet the affair does not end. As Parker puts Priscilla on a plane to Memphis, the opportunity for Elvis and Ann-Margret—whom the Memphis Mafia refer to as "Thumper"—to spend more time together emerges. But, in time, the affair subsides. "There were other factors in Elvis's life that forced him apart from me, and I understood them," Ann-Margret will write. "Elvis had always been honest with me, but still it was a confusing situation. We continued to see each other periodically, until we had dated for almost a year. Then everything halted. We knew the relationship had to end, that Elvis had to fulfill his commitment."

By mutual agreement, the once-sizzling couple moved on. Just as Elvis now ties the knot at the Aladdin this morning, Ann-Margret will wed actor Roger Smith one week from today, at the nearby Riviera hotel and casino.*

---

* In a private conversation, Ann-Margret, now eighty-one, told Bill O'Reilly that Elvis treated her with the utmost respect. And to this day, she has a genuine affection for him.

But marriage will not end the deep friendship between Elvis and Ann-Margret. Just one month from today, as she opens her first-ever performances in Las Vegas with a lengthy engagement at the Riviera, the King will send a guitar-shaped bouquet and then show up backstage to offer his congratulations. Presley will step inside her dressing room and shut the door. "His smile faded, and his eyes lost their playfulness and turned serious," Ann-Margret will write. "Suddenly, the old connection burned as brightly and strong as it had years earlier." The two will hold hands, and Elvis will even drop to one knee to confess "exactly how he still felt about her."

And while Ann-Margret "intuitively knew he still had feelings for her," the affair is over. She will remain married to Roger Smith until his death in 2017.

"If Elvis would have wound up with Thumper," Marty Lacker will lament after Elvis's death, "this whole story might have wound up differently."

But that was not meant to be. Instead, Ann-Margret and Roger Smith will be among the mourners attending Elvis Presley's funeral.

✦ ✦ ✦

Back in the Las Vegas suite, Elvis and 'Cilla both look nervous. Neither has been married before, and at age twenty-two, Priscilla seems overwhelmed. She nervously clutches the bouquet, her eyes darting around the room.

Elvis, for his part, is stiff. After the ceremony, he will joke, "How can you look happy when you're scared?"

"The Memphis troubadour and his gray-eyed brunette bride-to-be landed at McCarran Airport early Monday morning, and drove with friends to the county courthouse where they obtained their marriage license at 3:30 a.m.," the *Las Vegas Sun* reported. The county clerk's office opened at such an early hour to prevent the press from knowing about the wedding. Indeed, Elvis and Priscilla's secret exchanging of vows will spawn a trend in Las Vegas—the city will soon be awash in late-night wedding chapels where couples will be married by pastors dressed to look like Presley. In fact, couples inspired to wed in Vegas will become so numerous that the city will eventually bill itself as the "Marriage Capital of the World."

The idea to plan the wedding in secrecy belongs, of course, to Colonel Parker. He knows that the clandestine ceremony will keep the press even more intrigued—and he is correct. The Colonel manipulates the media, controlling exactly how the story will be told. "Leave your cameras and your pencils and notebooks outside, please," he informs them, thus preventing any miscue inside the suite from being reported.

Reporters and television cameramen from all over the country comply. Colonel Parker looks on—even hitting one photographer over the head with a cane when he has the audacity to move to a different location for a better shot.

Elvis and Priscilla are then led to a small table at the front of the room. "I guess you're all wondering why we asked you to come in," Elvis says playfully. Then, in full view of the press, he pulls Priscilla to him for a long kiss.

"You noticed it was a sweet kiss full of pride, warmth and affection rather than the usual Hollywood movie type of kiss which anticipates a love scene," Hollywood syndicated columnist May Mann will write. "He kissed her tenderly. But then Elvis is not usual nor does he do the usual, but always that which is most admirable."

Romance quickly turns to business. Reporters fire away: "What made you finally get married? Why did you give up bachelorhood? How long were you engaged? Why this and how that. Elvis and Priscilla handle the questions nicely," according to best man Marty Lacker.

The Q&A lasts just fifteen minutes. Colonel Tom Parker then orders the media from the room.

As they depart, many are struck by the fact that Priscilla does not say much; she defers to Elvis. "You can plainly see who wears the pants in this marriage," one reporter whispers to Mann. "I didn't think they made that kind of woman anymore. She lets her husband do the talking for both of them."

Press conference complete, the couple heads down the elevator for a reception in the Aladdin's ballroom. Comedian Redd Foxx is the only celebrity in attendance, personally invited by Parker. Three swans made of pink ice decorate each table. The wedding cake, filled with apricot marmalade and Bavarian cream, features six tiers and cost $3,200 ($23,000 today). The pastry chef did not add Elvis's name in icing until thirty minutes ago, yet another attempt to keep the wedding a surprise. Twenty waiters in formal attire and white gloves serve suckling pig, oysters Rockefeller, fried chicken, caviar, and lobster.*

And so the marriage begins, the union of Elvis, Priscilla, and Colonel Tom Parker. Till death do they part.

---

* Redd Foxx was an African American comedian who often played Las Vegas. It was there that he met Tom Parker. Foxx used a lot of blue language at a time when that was rare. He would have a long and successful career, the highlight of which was the television sitcom *Sanford and Son*.

CHAPTER FOUR

NOVEMBER 9, 1967
RIVERSIDE, CALIFORNIA
6 P.M.

Elvis Presley is becoming more disenchanted each day.

Although he has no idea, the audience at the Rubidoux Drive-in Theatre is about to settle into their cars for tonight's screening of Presley's new movie *Clambake*. The California sun set an hour ago. Now, popcorn and soft drinks in hand, the folks wait for the trailers to end and for the first show of tonight's double bill to begin. These are the diehard Presley fans, venturing out on a Thursday night to watch yet another formulaic Elvis movie. They have come to see the King sing and dance and then win the girl in the end—as always.

On the screen, the King sings, "Who needs the worry and the strife?" The movie set behind him is designed to look like a sandy beach—grass-roofed huts, lifeguard chair, fire pit. An actor dressed in a chef's toque tends to a spit as young women in midriff-bearing tops and tight pants dance to the beat of a rock band that has magically appeared out of nowhere. Elvis, dressed all in red under a white jacket, picks up an electric guitar. Placing one foot atop a boulder, he fingers the fret board and begins strumming. The scene is ridiculous, by intention, yet another mindless Elvis film bearing no correlation to reality.

But the viewers at the Rubidoux love it—or, at least, *like* it. The truth is, after twenty-five movies in eleven years, Presley's on-screen charm is beginning to wane.

"Life can be a ball," Elvis sings. "Clambake, gonna have a clambake / Clambake, gonna have a clambake."

The movie is ninety-eight minutes of songs and action. The trailer's voice-over narrator loudly states, "It's a bikini bake! Elvis go-gos on water! Elvis go-gos wild!"

Everything about the movie—from the plot to the dancers to the acting—is standard for an Elvis Presley film. But one thing about *Clambake* is different. The movie marks the first time in his movie career that the King had words with Colonel Tom Parker. Elvis wanted to do new things with his life, and *Clambake* was not one of them.

With the singer's $650,000 ($5.3 million in today's dollars) fee being more than respectable, money is not the divisive issue between Presley and Parker. Elvis's father, Vernon, who lives off his son, insisted Elvis take the payday. Indeed, the King signed a new deal with the Colonel on January 2. As a sign of his longtime loyalty to Elvis, Parker will receive an incredible *half* of all profits derived from Presley's movies and records. Legal critics will be mortified, later calling the arrangement "excessive, imprudent, unfair to the estate and beyond all reasonable bonds of industry standards."*

Elvis, who willfully agrees to the new arrangement, remains the Colonel's only client. The Colonel sees no need to take on other entertainers because he makes so much money off the King. Thus, it is in the Colonel's best interest to find new ways to broaden the revenue stream and make sure his client is dependent on him. Presley's fondness for spending lavishly on himself and his friends puts him

---

*These comments were made in 1980 by Memphis lawyer Blanchard E. Tual, a court-appointed attorney representing Elvis Presley's daughter, Lisa Marie, and his ex-wife, Priscilla. The court charged that Colonel Tom Parker conspired to steal millions from Elvis's estate.

constantly in need of cash. Producer Hal Wallis, a Hollywood legend credited for turning the rock-'n'-roller into a movie star, no longer wishes to work with Elvis. Wallis recently turned down a Parker demand for $500,000 per film plus 20 percent of the gross, saying he believed Elvis's film career had run its course.

Parker knows Elvis is in decline. The silly movies exist solely to sell records. The King constantly performed live early in his career, but it has been six years since Elvis sang in concert. His most recent public appearance took place in Honolulu, Hawaii, on March 25, 1961, to raise funds for a new Pearl Harbor Memorial. The fund-raiser was successful, and Parker gained a nice public relations opportunity for his client.

Upon landing in Hawaii, Elvis was mobbed. Famed actor Jimmy Stewart, also traveling on the flight, was ignored by the crowd in their rush to see Elvis. "There is no way to describe the pandemonium. I never saw as many women in my life," comedian Minnie Pearl, a fellow passenger, later marveled. "They were screaming. They were yelling. I was just horrified. I thought, 'They're going to kill him.' And they would have if they could have gotten loose."

The King's concert at Bloch Arena raised $54,000 ($370,000 today) and spurred such great public interest in Elvis that the remaining desired charitable funds were soon acquired. Despite the concert's enormous success, it was the movie *Blue Hawaii*, filmed on location shortly after the memorial show, that was far more beneficial to Presley's career.

And so it was that Elvis Presley stepped away from the stage but continued to make movies.

But without concerts, films are now the only avenue to bring in money for the Colonel and the rock star. Television might be an option, but it is unthinkable to the Colonel. "We do not mix our motion picture career in any way with a television career, especially if we are not in on the profits," Parker has stated to Hal Wallis.

Indeed, the last time Elvis Presley appeared on television was in 1960, as the special guest on *Frank Sinatra's Welcome Home Party* for him shortly after he left the army. The King is just as against television as Colonel Parker, still upset by an appearance on *The Steve Allen Show* in 1956 in which he was forced to wear a tuxedo and sing "Hound Dog" to an actual hound dog.

But while the Colonel sees Elvis making a living on the mindless *Clambake*s of the movie world, the singer himself is angry. Elvis's formal education ended with his graduation from Memphis's Humes High School in 1953. Until now, the King has shown little interest in expanding his intellectual horizons, and the Colonel has relied on Presley's lack of curiosity to maintain power over the singer and direct his every move. But all that may be changing.

In the days leading up to the production of *Clambake*, Elvis took up reading as a new hobby, much to Parker's chagrin. The books are mainly spiritual in nature, dealing with religion and the afterlife. The Colonel insists that Elvis stop his new path of self-enlightenment, even demanding that members of the Memphis Mafia discourage the King from reading during the filming of *Clambake*. "I don't want him reading any more books; they clutter up his mind," states a furious Parker. "Some of you may think maybe he's Jesus Christ and should walk down the street wearing robes and helping people. But that's not who he is."

Fourteen years from now, long after Presley's death, court proceedings looking into the singer's estate will indicate the depth of Parker's control. "Colonel Parker knowingly violated Elvis's trust and continued to abuse it until Elvis's death," Memphis attorney Blanchard Tual will state, adding that Parker is guilty of "collusion, conspiracy, fraud, misrepresentation, and overreaching . . . these actions against the most popular American folk hero of this century are outrageous and call for a full accounting of those responsible. . . ."

"Elvis was naive, shy and unassertive. Parker was aggressive, shrewd and tough. His strong personality dominated Elvis, his father, and all others in Elvis's entourage."*

---

* This statement was part of Priscilla Presley's lawsuit against Tom Parker, wherein she tried to regain control of the estate following Elvis's death.

✦ ✦ ✦

The book reading continues. Now, in Priscilla Presley's words, this newfound fascination is leading Elvis to do some "soul searching." This is natural for a newly married man whose wife is four months pregnant. There is still an insecure divide between the couple, with Priscilla afraid even of letting her husband see her without makeup. But as the King settles into marriage and ponders the nature of the Almighty, he is beginning to see that his future must be different from his current reality.

But this introspection has made the King depressed. The King is usually upbeat, so this morose display is a new facet to his personality. Elvis spent the months leading up to *Clambake*'s production at his ranch outside Memphis, so upset by the poor script and weak songwriting that he added 30 pounds to his 170-pound frame. Even though he plays a waterskiing instructor, Elvis will not take his shirt off in the movie.

Now that *Clambake* is on the big screen, theatergoers can see for themselves that Elvis Presley is not the same. They can also see that the King is no longer cool, his clothes and pompadour out of place during the emerging hippie movement that will eventually become known as the "Summer of Love."

The movie's title scene is symptomatic of Presley's decline. Everything about the make-believe clambake is false. It starts with the party itself: as Elvis plays guitar and even bounces on a trampoline, chicken is roasting, and actors feast on hot potatoes, yet there is not a single clam in sight. The phoniness continues: Elvis gingerly plants a foot atop a boulder, which soon gives way because of its papier-mâché construction. Also, the electric guitar Elvis strums has no cord and could not possibly be plugged into sand. The setting is Miami Beach, but Southern California oil wells and coastal mountains can be seen in the background. In one scene, the sun even sets over the "Atlantic" Ocean.

Yet the biggest flaw appears to be Elvis himself. His weight gain is obvious. Depressed about playing yet another singing bachelor with romantic feelings for his leading lady—in this case, Shelley Fabares from *The Donna Reed Show*—the King barely goes through the motions.*

On-screen, he looks noticeably puffy as well as pudgy. Tabloids are reporting that production was shut down for two weeks when Elvis fell inside his Los Angeles home, suffering a concussion. What the press did not report—because it did not know—was that the accident occurred when the singer's cocktail of uppers, to stimulate weight loss, and downers, to help him sleep, went awry.

It is clear Elvis Presley is in trouble. *Clambake* will rank No. 15 in box-office gross for its nationwide opening weekend, lagging well behind Disney's *The Jungle Book*, a rerelease of *Gone with the Wind*, and the movie musical *Camelot*.

For all Colonel Parker's determination that Elvis become a true movie star, it is clear he is no match for heartthrobs like Robert Redford and Warren Beatty. Their respective films, *Barefoot in the Park* and *Bonnie and Clyde*, are performing solidly at the box office, with Academy Award consideration.

Elvis longs for that kind of respect, but Parker is only too happy to point out that audiences don't care if Presley can act. In 2022 money, the combined box-office gross of all the King's films is more than *$2 billion*—an astounding number that does not even include the soundtrack albums. As to Parker's point, *GI Blues* and *Flaming Star* both came out the same year, 1960. But while the lightweight *GI Blues* soared at the box office, the serious Western *Flaming Star* did not. No. 15 is as high as *Clambake* will go. In just one week, it will drop completely off the list of top-grossing films. By Christmas, it will be out of theaters altogether.

The *New York Times*, which does not normally deign to review

---

* Shelley Fabares, a teen idol in her own right, starred in three movies with Elvis. The first being *Girl Happy*, in 1965; then *Spinout*, the following year; and *Clambake*. According to one member of the Memphis Mafia, Elvis was smitten with Fabares. Yet, despite the natural chemistry between the singer and the actress, according to long-time Elvis friend and bodyguard Sonny West, Fabares refused to let the relationship advance beyond the purely professional.

Elvis movies, smells a disaster and happily feasts on the debacle. "*Clambake*," reviewer Howard Thompson writes, is "a silly, tired little frolic that could have used a few clams."

✦ ✦ ✦

Even though it's his fault, Colonel Tom Parker knows he needs to do something—and fast. So he decides to embrace the unthinkable.

Elvis Presley will go on television.

But there are many problems with this—and the shrewd Colonel is not sure his pliant client can pull it off.

CHAPTER FIVE

Elvis Presley is ready.

"Let's go," the King says to Steve Binder, producer of his up-coming NBC television special. The two are standing in the thirty-four-year-old Binder's office above Sunset Boulevard. The young producer has been in charge of the teen music show *Hullabaloo* and specials by singers Petula Clark and Leslie Uggams. He is a Beach Boys aficionado, not a Presley fan. Although Binder enjoys Elvis's company, he has bluntly informed the star that his career is "in the toilet." As proof, he challenges Elvis to take a walk down this crowded street to see how women react to him. It takes a few days of convincing, but the stroll is about to happen.

"Let's go where?" the singer asks. "Downstairs."

Several of Elvis's bodyguards jump to their feet and prepare to follow him out the door.

"No, no. Only Steve and I are going down there," Elvis com-mands. "But we're goin' down there, you know, to see what it's like on Sunset Boulevard."

It is the peak of rush hour. The legendary boulevard is bumper to bumper with traffic. Elvis and Binder step out onto the sidewalk and begin making small talk. Presley is now thirty-three and fit, having spent several months getting himself in shape through karate and dieting. He is suntanned and rested after returning from two weeks in Hawaii.

"He was awesome looking," Binder will remember. "I mean, I'm heterosexual. I'm straight as an arrow, and I got to tell ya, you stop, whether you're male or female, to look at him. He was that good looking."

Yet not a single pedestrian or driver notices Elvis Presley.

"After a while, it got uncomfortable," Binder noted. "And Elvis pretty soon was trying to draw attention to himself. He was kinda waving at cars, and some kids were coming from Tower Records, and they bumped into us. They didn't even lift their heads up to see they had bumped into Elvis. . . . And, we stood out there for like ten almost embarrassing minutes, trying to draw attention to *Hey, this is really Elvis Presley*."

The two men walk back inside. Elvis is not angry; he is determined.

His comeback is about to begin.

✦ ✦ ✦

In October 1967, just as *Clambake* is coming and going from theaters, Colonel Parker reaches a deal with the NBC television network. Elvis will tape a Christmas special to be shown during the 1968 holiday season. In return, he will receive $250,000 ($1.7 million today). NBC will also put up $850,000 ($5.8 million today) toward the production of Presley's next film, *Change of Habit*, in which he will costar with television actress Mary Tyler Moore.

NBC announces the deal on January 12, 1968. Rehearsals will begin in June, with taping at the end of the month.

There's just one catch: Steve Binder doesn't want to do a Christmas special. He believes it is a stale format. Instead, the producer has a different concept in mind for Elvis, and he appeals to the singer that this is his chance "to do something really important." Binder envisions the show retelling the story of Presley's musical career, introducing him to new listeners while inspiring old fans. There will be no guest stars—just Elvis and his songs.

Parker hates the idea, remaining insistent on taping a traditional Christmas special, with musical guests and comedy skits in the variety show format.

"From that first meeting, I knew he was champing at the bit to prove himself again," Binder will recall of the King. "Elvis asked me, 'What happens if I bomb?' I said, 'Elvis, you'll still be remembered for your movies and all your early hit records. If it's successful, every door that was closed to you will reopen.'"

Elvis sides with Binder, not Parker.

In a tense meeting, Elvis and Parker argue about the special. The singer wins, but the Colonel does get one yuletide carol. And so the production moves ahead. In public, Elvis Presley continues to support the manager, but as the meeting wraps up and Parker leaves the room, Presley pokes Binder in the ribs.

"Fuck him," Elvis says.

✦ ✦ ✦

Rehearsals begin on June 17 in Los Angeles. Elvis is so taken with the process that he literally moves into his dressing room, sleeping there each night. He often jams into the late hours with drummer D. J. Fontana and guitarist Scotty Moore, his original sidemen from the days when he used to tour. He is eager to prove himself, although a bit insecure: in addition to singing, there is elaborate choreography to conquer and a number of costume changes. Presley involves himself personally in every aspect of the show, dedicated to making the special *very* special. Binder notices how much Elvis enjoys a playful interaction with the other musicians between takes and decides to show this fun side of Presley as an improvised addition to the show.

As rehearsals continue, Elvis reveals more of his true personality. The introspection and reading that began during *Clambake* continue, but with greater meaning. Presley is not immune to the national grief brought on by the assassination of Sen. Robert F. Kennedy here in Los Angeles. That happened less than two weeks ago. Also, there was the murder of Martin Luther King Jr. in Presley's hometown of Memphis.

New songs are written for the special to reflect this new maturity. Elvis even confides to Binder that he will no longer make movies or perform music that doesn't matter to him. "If I Can Dream" is written at Elvis's demand, reflecting his personal sadness about Kennedy and King. "Write the greatest song you've ever written to put at the end of the show," he asks songwriter Walter Earl Brown Jr.[*]

"If I Can Dream" will replace Colonel Parker's hoped-for Christmas carol. Elvis prerecords it for the special; he will lip-synch during the taping. While singing the recording, Presley does something very unusual: he lies alone in the fetal position in a darkened recording studio. When the song is done, he loves it so much, he orders it played back more than a dozen times.

The show takes shape quickly, bringing the listener along through Presley's musical evolution, with country and western, rhythm and blues, and some gospel numbers. The King grew up on gospel, and during breaks between rehearsals, he can be found with singer Darlene Love and a group called the Blossoms, harmonizing spiritual tunes.

"He was in such good shape," guitarist Mike Deasy remembers of one night as the band rehearsed the Jerry Reed song "Guitar Man." "He was into karate, and he was physically very cool.

He's taller than you thought, but he was out there doing this dance while we were playing, and it was a super connection. It became bigger than the music itself."

Finally, it is time to take the stage.

✦ ✦ ✦

---

[*] Brown was formerly a member of the pop group the Skylarks. He also wrote music for Frank Sinatra and "Mama" Cass Elliot. During his long show business career, Brown worked in television as vocal director for *The Andy Williams Show* and *The Carol Burnett Show*, among others. He died in 2008 at the age of seventy-nine.

On June 27, the six p.m. filming time approaching, Steve Binder is in a panic. Colonel Parker is supposed to be in charge of distributing tickets, but he has failed to do the job. No one is waiting in line to see the show. "We sent somebody over to Bob's Big Boy to ask customers eating hamburgers and [drinking] malts to come over to see Elvis Presley," Binder will remember. "And we somehow pulled together with enough people at NBC who were there, calling their friends and families and what have you to get these audiences in there."*

At first, the crowd is not enthusiastic about watching a washed-up Elvis Presley tape a special.

This quickly changes.

They will all long remember what takes place this evening.

The King is back. Lean and cut, he strides onstage in a black leather jacket and pants. He is visibly nervous at first but soon finds his groove. "We played a couple of songs, and it got loose after a while, and it turned out fine. He just had been out of the public eye for a long time," drummer Fontana will remember.

"That's Alright," "Love Me Tender," "Heartbreak Hotel," "Guitar Man," "Trouble," and even the ballad "Memories"—Elvis sings them all. He even throws in "Blue Christmas" at the last minute, for the Colonel. The gospel sequence with Love and the Blossoms is transcendent, an integrated choir singing along with Elvis. The audience is so enthralled that they boo when Presley announces the closing song.

"Man, I just work here," the King responds in trademark Elvis drawl.

✦ ✦ ✦

It is December 3, 1968, when the Elvis special finally airs. Singer Sewing Machines is the sponsor. The show will go down in history as "The Comeback Special" and will be the No. 1 broadcast of the year,

---

* No one knows for sure whether Parker attempted to sabotage the special. Doing so would have gone against his financial interests. However, he was enraged that he was losing control of Presley. To this day, the situation is undefined.

capturing 42 percent of the national viewing audience. The show's soundtrack album will go platinum, and "If I Can Dream" will reach No. 12 on the *Billboard* charts.

The King is definitely back.

Long live the King.

CHAPTER SIX

It is *Viva Las Vegas* all over again.

The showroom here at the International hotel is packed with 2,200 fans—the biggest audience in Vegas history. Elvis rises from the couch in his dressing room, aware that his knee's nonstop bouncing will give away his severe case of nerves. Members of his core band are with him and can't help but notice his shaking hands. Presley paces backstage, already perspiring through his dark-blue two-piece karate costume: bell-bottom pants, a blue sash, a dark multicolored scarf. The King's shirt is open almost to his waist, and his collar reaches high around his neck. It's been eight years since his last live performance, and the next ninety minutes will be crucial to his future.

Elvis Presley is quiet as he begins his stage preparation. The stakes are enormous.

One member of the band, guitarist John Wilkinson, seeks to calm Elvis. "If you get lost, just turn around and we'll start playing louder," Wilkinson said, making a veiled reference to the possibility that Elvis will forget some lyrics. Comedian Sammy Shore, dressed in a beige suit with dark brown trim, warms up the audience. Shore's humor is sometimes blue, and he uses a tambourine as a prop. At

age forty-two, the longtime stand-up was carefully chosen as Elvis's opening act because he is well known in Vegas cabaret circles
and would not do anything to distract from the main event. More
important, he makes Elvis laugh. And for that reason, Shore will
soon be named Presley's permanent opening act. The comedian's mic
went dead when he first came onstage tonight, making it impossible
for the raucous crowd to hear him. A new microphone was quickly
brought onstage. After his thirty-minute set, Shore exits, and the
house lights darken. Anticipation builds throughout the showroom.

The International bills itself as Las Vegas's first "megaresort," a
thirty-story hotel and casino larger than any establishment not only
in the city but in the entire state of Nevada. It is less than a month
since the resort opened. Singer Barbra Streisand was the first headliner, performing for four weeks until Elvis was ready to go. Her
initials are still imprinted on the stage floor in marker, indicating the
spot where Streisand's microphone was placed each night—causing
Elvis to make many a "BS" joke during rehearsals.

Presley and his backup group are scheduled to perform fifty-
seven shows at the International this year, and every single one is
already sold out. To make it easier to get to work each night, Elvis
lives in the hotel's five-thousand-square-foot penthouse suite. He
is being paid $100,000 per week ($750,000 today) for this four-week
run. Two performances a night—a dinner show at 8:15 and another
set at midnight—seven days a week. Ticket sales stand at $2 million
($15 million today), an enormous profit for the new hotel, which
is already struggling with debt. By the end of the month, Elvis will
have performed for 101,500 fans.*

✦ ✦ ✦

It has been four months since Elvis Presley finished his thirty-first
and final movie, *Change of Habit*, with Mary Tyler Moore. Moore will

---

* The International hotel became the Hilton in 1971, which it remained until 2012. It is
now known as the Westgate Las Vegas Resort and Casino.

not make another film until *Ordinary People* in 1980, for which she will receive an Academy Award nomination. However, she will soon be cast in the lead role of *The Mary Tyler Moore Show*, which will begin its seven-year run on CBS in 1970. It is on the set of *Change of Habit* that the actress meets Edward Asner, who plays the role of Lt. Moretti. Asner would go on to create the character Lou Grant in Moore's show.

On the subject of Elvis Presley, Mary Tyler Moore said this: "He could not have been more charming. He had a big crush on me. . . . It was not a very tangible thing, it was a pedestal from afar. He would call me 'ma'am' if he wasn't paying attention, pawing at the ground like a teenager. He was older than I was, but he was very much taken with me."

Nothing came of that flirtation, and nothing good came from *Change of Habit*, either. The film did not do well at the box office, confirming to Elvis and Colonel Parker that the days of foolish movies were over. Both men realize the *real* money is in live performing. So Colonel Parker was only too happy to broker a deal with International owner Kirk Kerkorian for Elvis to perform an extended run of shows.

✦ ✦ ✦

It's showtime. Elvis Presley walks to the stage, going over the set list in his head. He hears the first notes from the orchestra, chosen by him to bring a big Las Vegas sound to his performance. Also onstage is Presley's personal band, TCB (for "Taking Care of Business"), comprising five musicians.

The showroom is packed with fans and celebrities from all over the world: Cary Grant, Sammy Davis Jr., Fats Domino, former California governor Pat Brown, Phil Ochs, Barbara Stanwyck, Sonny and Cher, Paul Anka, Donald O'Connor, Henry Mancini, Dionne Warwick, Johnny Rivers, Lou Adler, Mac Davis, and Herb Albert. Ann-Margret sits at a table with her husband.

In the wings, Elvis peers out at the sixty-foot-wide stage. He is shielded from the audience by a five-ton gold lamé curtain. Crystal chandeliers hang from the showroom ceiling, almost obliterated by cigarette smoke. The audience sits at small tables. On top of each rests a complete copy of the set list plus a program, an Elvis calendar, and one copy each of the albums *Elvis in Memphis* and the soundtrack for the Comeback Special.*

Priscilla Presley sits in the front row. She wears a dress with a plunging neckline, her long black hair cascading down. Her eyebrows are knitted in tension. On the surface, the Presley marriage has grown stronger since the birth of their daughter, Lisa Marie, one year ago. But last year, while taking private dance lessons, Priscilla had a brief affair with her instructor. She regrets the indiscretion, but she will also write that "I came out of it knowing I needed much more out of my relationship with Elvis."

Her husband has no idea. Priscilla has seen a new side to Elvis since the NBC special. He has spent the entire month of July out of the public eye, a musician once again, not spending his time making frivolous movies. Instead, Elvis has rehearsed with his band and trained hard with a karate expert, getting into the best shape of his life. He has lost fifteen pounds and is drug free for the first time in years.

There is no formal introduction to the show. As the musicians onstage begin to play, a visibly nervous Elvis strides out, microphone in hand, acoustic guitar hanging from one shoulder. Elvis vamps for a moment, basking in the applause of the full house.

From her seat up front, Priscilla Presley is dazzled. She knows her husband is nervous—that much is clear from the way the microphone shakes in his hand. Still, he stands tall and poised, defining the word *charisma*. This is certainly not Woodstock. It is retro Elvis, a classic throwback. The audience rises as one, filling the room with

---

* The set list for the opening show: "Blue Suede Shoes," "I Got a Woman," "One Night," "Love Me Tender," "Medley: Jailhouse Rock/Don't Be Cruel/Heartbreak Hotel/All Shook Up/Hound Dog," "Memories," "Can't Help Falling in Love," "My Babe," "I Can't Stop Loving You," "In the Ghetto," "Suspicious Minds," "Yesterday," "Hey Jude," "Johnny B. Goode," "Mystery Train," "Tiger Man," and "What'd I Say."

a roar. The standing ovation goes on for almost a full minute. The crowd treats Elvis as a long-lost friend, shouting his name, calling out songs they hope to hear.

Without waiting for the applause to die down, Elvis launches into "Blue Suede Shoes," one of his first hits. Though she can see he remains tense, Priscilla also recognizes that her husband is enjoying the crowd and feeding off their energy. Hips swaying, Presley kicks into overdrive. Though everyone in the room has heard "Blue Suede Shoes" multiple times, the thirteen-year-old rock tune sounds brand-new with the backing of the TCB Band and the Bobby Morris Orchestra.

Elvis Presley personally selected every musician performing on the stage tonight. He also hired a male vocal group known as the Imperials to sing backup, and the Black female quartet the Sweet Inspirations to fill the sound with women's voices.

The audience never sits down. All through the opening number, they call out to the stage, glorifying Elvis.

After the opening number, the band tears into "I Got a Woman." Presley leans into the microphone stand as the rockabilly beat fills the room. The audience claps along, lost in the moment. "Well, I've got a woman way across town / she's good to me," he sings, hitting the big notes at the finish, left leg tapping with the beat. The King works the room, kissing as many women in the front row as possible. Priscilla doesn't seem to mind.

And so, the show continues.

This is Elvis Presley at his best. Karate kicks punctuate the beat. He jokes with the crowd between songs, building a relationship with the audience. "Welcome to the big, freaky International hotel, with those weirdo dolls on the walls and those funky angels on the ceiling," he says before one number. Then he spies a friend in the crowd.

"Hiya, Mac," Elvis calls out to Mac Davis before launching into the songwriter's composition "In the Ghetto."

Davis will later recall Elvis and that night fondly: "He was physically beautiful at that age, just a specimen. You couldn't take your eyes off the guy. Women rushing the stage, people clambering over each other. I couldn't wipe the grin off my face the entire time."

Onstage, Presley never stops sweating. He quaffs water and Gatorade to cool down. Women in the audience, noting his drenched face, throw handkerchiefs onto the stage.

Rolling Stone and the *New York Times* both give the show extraordinary reviews. But perhaps the best critique comes from the teen magazine *Tiger Beat*. "I saw the Beatles at the Hollywood Bowl, and the Rolling Stones at the Cow Palace in San Francisco," wrote editor Ann Moses. "But there was something about that night that was so special. Everyone was dumbstruck and didn't want the night to end. It was one of the greatest shows I've ever seen."

The standing ovation at night's end is thunderous. Myram Borders writes in the *Nevada State Journal* that it was "one of the rare occasions when a Las Vegas standing salute was sincere rather than rigged with a few cronies of an entertainer planted down front to stamp and scream approval."

Priscilla Presley is just as taken. "It was magical," she will later write. "The energy was incredible. He was like this tiger on stage that was unchained with this magnetism that drew everyone in."

Elvis Presley's first live show in Las Vegas is an overwhelming triumph.

And even though he has no idea, it will be all downhill from here.

CHAPTER SEVEN

FEBRUARY 27, 1970
HOUSTON, TEXAS
2 P.M.

Elvis Presley stands and waves to the crowd from a jeep as he is driven into the Houston Astrodome. Just three nights ago, he finished his second monthlong engagement in Las Vegas, selling out every show. The final midnight performance extended to three a.m.—Elvis was so pleased with the crowd that he did not want to leave the stage. In fact, his banter with the folks included Colonel Tom Parker: "He's not only my manager, but I love him very much," Presley said.

Fully in control, the Colonel now seeks to monetize his client in a brand-new way. Elvis is not the headliner at today's Astrodome performance. That honor belongs to horses and pigs. Houston's annual Livestock Show and Rodeo is taking place inside the five-year-old indoor stadium. Admission: $4.50.

Elvis leaves his orange vehicle and strides to the stage at one end of the arena. He wears a white shirt, white bell-bottom pants, and white boots. Above him, a billboard flashes "Elvis, Elvis, Elvis." Competitors from the chuckwagon race are just leaving the dirt floor. A calf-roping contest will take place immediately after the concert; then Elvis will return to the stage for an evening show. Despite the low cost of admission, little more than sixteen thousand people fill the seats—an appallingly low figure for a venue that seats more than forty-four thousand.*

The TCB Band waits on the rotating stage. The Sweet Inspirations stand behind them, ready to sing backup vocals. Event organizers tried to ban the four Black women from the concert, but Elvis made it known that he would not perform in Houston if they were not onstage.

Up in the press box, Colonel Parker watches the proceedings with nervous intensity. He wears a Stetson hat and smokes a long cigar. After Elvis finished that late show in Las Vegas a few days ago, it was just a matter of hours before the singer and band were flown to Houston on a private jet. Elvis is nocturnal, covering his hotel room windows in aluminum foil to block the daytime sun. With such little sleep, he showed up for the press conference looking bloated, with deep circles under his eyes. Priscilla is nowhere to be seen. Elvis insists that she stay home in Memphis with Lisa Marie rather than travel with the band. He is not bothered by her absence, but he often grows bored when alone in his hotel suite and fills some of the time with casual dalliances.

Elvis is noticeably chubby as he appears before the Texas press. What the press can't see is that he has begun using drugs again. His personal physician since 1967, Dr. George Nichopoulos, is prescribing him amphetamines and other narcotics on demand.

The Astrodome shows are supposed to top the Vegas performances. No longer confined to showroom audiences of twenty-two hundred, tonight Elvis, Parker anticipates, will sing to tens of thousands. But Presley is visibly disappointed upon landing in Houston, joking with the cowboy hat–wearing dignitaries about the small size of the city's airport: "I thought we were going somewhere, man."

Yesterday's sound check was a debacle, Presley and the band unable to keep in synch with the acoustic blend of stadium steel, con-

---

* Attendance was low because the first show took place during a weekday afternoon. Also, marketing was weak, and people were confused that Elvis Presley would be in a "rodeo."

crete, and horse manure. "Just go ahead and play," Elvis tells the band, sensing disaster.

This afternoon's show confirms his fears. A nervous Elvis cannot make it work. He even apologizes to the audience before leaving the stage. Shortly afterward, a despondent Presley lies down for a nap in his hotel room.

"Well, that's it. I guess I just don't have it anymore," he says.

✦ ✦ ✦

Colonel Parker calls for reinforcements. Like Elvis, Priscilla Presley does as the Colonel tells her. An example of Parker's influence could be seen last year, when a fit and happy Elvis returned with Priscilla from a Hawaiian vacation. The singer enjoyed the travel so much that he immediately began planning a European trip that would include several family friends. But Parker said no. With no passport, he cannot leave the United States and therefore could not control any such trip. After all, the Colonel's main function in life is to keep Elvis Presley totally dependent on him. The singer's book reading has expanded greatly, becoming a regular habit, which continues to frustrate Parker. Using his manipulation skills, Parker tells Elvis it would be insulting his fan base if he traveled to Europe before scheduling an American tour. So Priscilla, Elvis, and the Memphis Mafia travel to the Bahamas instead, where a hurricane keeps them locked inside their hotel the entire stay.

Thus, Priscilla does not say no when Parker arranges for her to fly to Houston to quiet rumors of a growing rift in the Presley marriage. She will attend the Sunday-afternoon performance in a black see-through outfit.

Changes are made to the arena. Nothing can be done about the rodeo, but Parker orders that the rotating stage be slowed to permit Elvis surer footing. The acoustics are tweaked, allowing the band to hear one another without a big echo. When Elvis takes the stage for his second of six shows, he is more relaxed. He cavorts about with confidence, karate-kicking and strutting his stuff. But with the crowd seated so far away from the stage, there is little of the audience banter of the Las Vegas shows.

By the end of the weekend, the shaky Astrodome shows have turned positive. Audience size grows with every performance. More than two hundred thousand people will see the King in person. The thankful rodeo, which has never seen such attendance numbers, gifts Elvis with a solid-gold Rolex wristwatch in thanks. The King jokes with the local media about wanting to get out of town as soon as possible—and quickly makes good on his word, jetting to Los Angeles without Priscilla, where a rumored paramour awaits.

✦ ✦ ✦

Meanwhile, Colonel Parker looks away from the warning signs of Presley's personal decline. The ruthless manager has to see the change in Elvis's appearance, his paranoia over his personal security, and his penchant for carrying a handgun. Also, there is the infidelity, drug use, terrible diet, and a growing rift with his band.*

The Colonel, it seems, couldn't care less about all the turbulence. He seizes the moment, negotiating a new deal with the International hotel for a third appearance starting in August. A feature-length live-concert documentary is in the works, along with a pay-per-view appearance to be broadcast in movie theaters. Parker talks openly about an Elvis Presley Summer Festival in Las Vegas, where in addition to the nightly performances Elvis posters and souvenirs will be sold.

What Presley does not know is that his manager is losing big at the Vegas roulette tables. It is said that Parker drops more than a million dollars a year in gambling losses. Even so, the Colonel cannot wait to get back to the tables.

✦ ✦ ✦

---

* Some members of the TCB Band wanted more money. That was not going to happen with Parker, so Elvis was caught in the middle.

It is August 10, 1970.

The great Elvis Presley stands backstage at the Showroom International, the International hotel's two-thousand-seat performance space, the world's largest, surrounded by fawning acolytes. Entertainer Sammy Davis Jr., dressed in a flashy jacket with wide lapels and oversize pockets, a shirt with an open collar, and a long scarf, laughs at Elvis's bad jokes while holding a lighted cigarette. Presley's third monthlong engagement is about to begin.

He now wears jumpsuits onstage for greater ease of movement. Recently, he split his trousers a few times, forcing the TCB Band to cover for him as he left the stage to get new ones. Presley also now wears long sideburns and bangs almost down to his eyes. To some, it is a bizarre look.

But Elvis is still Elvis. Joe Guercio, the newly hired arranger for the International shows, has sparred with Presley during rehearsals. Guercio does not like some of the King's music. But opening night proves the arranger wrong, and he admits it. "I've been onstage with a lot of stars," Guercio will recall of this hot August night. "But they have no idea what a star is. . . . If you want to talk about going out and grabbing people—Elvis Presley was a happening, and what he had going will never be again."

✦ ✦ ✦

As 1970 unfolds, Elvis Presley, despite his unique success, is becoming increasingly isolated and unhappy. Only Colonel Parker can control him—and that's just in the professional area. Otherwise, Presley is an emotional mess: aging rapidly, drug-dependent, and self-destructive. His adoring public has no idea, and his entourage continues to indulge him for fear of losing a paycheck. The most famous singer in the world has no confidant.

So it is that the once-charismatic, polite young man from Mississippi has put aside discipline and reason. He now lives totally in a world of excess.

He is thirty-five years old.

CHAPTER EIGHT

SEPTEMBER 21, 1970
MEMPHIS, TENNESSEE
1 P.M.

E lvis Presley may be ill.

Dr. George Nichopoulos inserts a needle into the singer's arm, about to draw blood. The doctor is mystified by Presley's inflamed left eye. Yet the swollen orb is not the only ailment concerning "Dr. Nick" since his arrival here at Graceland today. The personal physician is not taking any chances. Nichopoulos believes something else lurks beneath the surface.

The King complains frequently about headaches. Dr. Nick first saw Elvis in 1965, but he became his regular doctor on February 27, 1967. Elvis was thirty-two years old. The singer was suffering from saddle sores on his legs and backside from too much time on horseback at his Circle G Ranch, outside Memphis. Having treated Elvis these past few years, the doctor has a baseline for the singer's fitness. The only maladies Elvis presented at that time were back pain, insomnia, and vertigo brought on by an ear infection.

But *Clambake* changed everything. To Dr. Nichopoulos, the injury sustained by Presley when he tripped and hit his head on a porcelain bathtub in his Beverly Hills home somehow changed the singer's mental and physical health. Elvis was knocked out cold. When he eventually revived, he began cursing, and a golf ball–size lump swelled from his forehead. The next day, he was so despondent from the head injury that it was decided he should return to Graceland to heal. There, Elvis began phoning a Memphis deejay to request Tom Jones's "Green, Green Grass of Home." He also claimed to see his dead mother standing at his bedside.

At the time of Presley's fall, Dr. Nichopoulos diagnosed post-concussion syndrome.

Symptoms include headache, dizziness, and problems with concentration. Elvis was also known to have suffered traumatic blows to the head several times in the 1950s and during his army service. Those occurred during fistfights and in a roller-skating accident.

Presley stayed off the *Clambake* set for two weeks. Erratic and impulsive behavior is another aftereffect of a hard blow to the head, both of which Elvis has displayed since the fall. Dr. Nick has taken note. He is unsure whether to blame the singer's strange actions on head trauma or on his pampered lifestyle.

For now, Presley's weight is swinging in the right direction: he is a svelte 163 pounds. He drinks little alcohol, because it can make him fly into a rage, and he has never been a smoker, but there are many ways to be unhealthy. Dr. Nick is well aware of the singer's high-fat, high-carbohydrate diet and chronic lack of sleep. Bacon is a staple for Presley, whether eaten on peanut butter and banana sandwiches or wrapped inside meatballs. Breakfast is a high-fat extravaganza: sausage, bacon, potatoes, eggs, and coffee. Soda is Presley's drink of choice, whether Pepsi, Nesbitt's Orange, or Shasta Black Cherry. Also, he never gets tired of cheeseburgers or coconut cake.

He has eaten this way for almost twenty years.

And then there are the narcotics. As the man writing the prescriptions, Nichopoulos is well aware of the King's pharmacological consumption.

So Dr. Nick is conducting a complete analysis of Presley's physical fitness: blood panel, liver function tests, urinalysis, and even a venereal disease test focused specifically on syphilis.

The results come back negative.

Dr. Nick doesn't accept them.

Something is wrong with Elvis Presley. The physician knows it.

✦ ✦ ✦

It has been one week since Elvis returned from his first national tour in thirteen years. The Colonel is again changing the way Presley brings in revenue. First it was movies, then the extended runs in Las Vegas, and next, big venues like the Astrodome. Now Parker wants Elvis hitting the road, playing in a different town every night like other rock stars. The small concert venues of the 1950s have been replaced by convention centers and arenas capable of seating more than ten thousand fans, and the Colonel wants to cash in. The first cities booked were Phoenix, St. Louis, Detroit, Miami, Tampa, and then closing night in Mobile, Alabama.*

The Colonel has already booked a second tour for November: Oakland, Portland, Seattle, San Francisco, two shows at the L.A. Forum, San Diego, Oklahoma City, and closing night at the Denver Coliseum.

If all goes smoothly, Parker envisions Elvis touring in this manner for years to come.

The experiment begins on September 8. Time and money weigh heavily on Parker's mind, so he makes drastic changes to the typical Elvis performance. There are no preshow press conferences—the Colonel believes the singer needs to save his energy for the show. There are also no free tickets for the press, as in the past—writers and photographers have to purchase theirs from the box office, just like any other audience member. And rather than pay for an entire fifteen-piece orchestra to travel with Elvis, Parker hires local musi-

---

*Ticket prices were $10, $7.50, and $5. The average Presley show brings in $75,000 after expenses—$450,000 in today's dollars.

cians. The Sweet Inspirations will still provide female backup vocals, but the Imperials will not be included this time.

A bomb threat delays the start of the Phoenix concert for two hours. A pair of opening acts warms up the crowd before Elvis hits the stage in a white jumpsuit. He has just finished his third series of shows at the Intercontinental and flown in from Vegas only this afternoon. "Elvis, looking as sexy as a thirty-five-year-old can look, sauntered onto the stage," one audience member will write for the fan magazine *Strictly Elvis*.

But even as the screaming women in the audience swoon to hear the King sing his old hits mixed with a collection of new standards, Parker sees that something has changed. Presley's fans from fifteen years ago are in the house, but they are now closing in on middle age. Back in the fifties, almost 90 percent of Presley's audience were teenagers. The Colonel now sees men with neatly trimmed hair, dressed in coats and ties; women in their thirties and early forties wearing nice dresses and salon-styled coiffures.

And yet, Elvis is such a cultural phenomenon that half the crowd in Phoenix definitely comprises teenagers. And the girls among them scream for Elvis even louder than the grown women. No other act in rock 'n' roll has yet reached across generations like this.

The sound system is horrible—Elvis and the band can't hear one another—and the late start brought on by the bomb threat does not help the energy level. But Elvis knows his audience. One particularly vocal teenage girl is publicly rewarded for her enthusiasm. The King throws her one of the green scarves he wore onto the stage tonight. The crowd roars their approval. A new Elvis tradition has begun. From now on, Presley will throw multiple scarves to his favorite females at each performance.

The tour is a smash hit. Parker gets busy booking new dates.

✦ ✦ ✦

Among Elvis Presley's favorite females in the fall of 1970 is a young woman living in Washington, DC, named Joyce Bova. The brunette

is a congressional staff member assigned to the House Armed Services Committee. Like Elvis, she was born a twin.* The two met in
1969, during his first run in Las Vegas. Bova was in town on vacation. She very much resembles Priscilla. In fact, Elvis pressured Bova
to wear the same beehive hairdo once favored by his wife. Bova will
later tell of their steamy three-year affair, which included trysts in
hotel rooms; a visit to Graceland, where she came face-to-face with a
portrait of Elvis and Priscilla; and raucous parties filled with famous
celebrities. When Bova asks Elvis about the growing divide between
him and Priscilla, he responds, "A woman isn't attractive in that way
once she becomes a mama."

Which is why Bova will later claim she aborted Presley's child,
not wanting their relationship to end.†

✦ ✦ ✦

It is nearing Christmas 1970 when Elvis Presley flies to Washington,
DC, for a rendezvous with Bova. The trip is impulsive, the sort of behavior Dr. Nick has been monitoring. In fact, the physician's diagnosis
is correct. A condition brought on by head trauma is causing swelling throughout Presley's body, attacking each organ, including the
brain. But in 1970, "autoimmune inflammatory disease" is still a set of
symptoms with no name. Elvis Presley will not be diagnosed with this
life-ending condition until decades after the inquest into his death.

The genesis of the DC trip is strange. In Memphis, Elvis spends
$100,000 on thirty-two handguns. He also buys some cars. Con-
fronted by his father, Vernon, a man just as fond of spending his
son's money as Colonel Parker, Elvis abruptly leaves town, flying

---

* Elvis was born on January 8, 1935, thirty-five minutes after his stillborn twin, Jesse
Garon Presley. Jesse was buried the next day in an unmarked grave at the Priceville
Cemetery in Tupelo, Mississippi.
† Although the authors of this book cannot verify Bova's claims, she did write a memoir
and produced some evidence of the abortion allegation. However, there is no indica-
tion that Elvis knew anything about it.

commercial to Washington in order to avoid another confrontation with his father.

After visiting with Bova, Elvis then flies to his Los Angeles home. Over the years, Presley has built a collection of handguns and police badges. He travels with them during these impulsive adventures, believing they offer power against anyone who would question him on his drug use. While examining his badges, Elvis decides that one is missing: the one for the Bureau of Narcotics and Dangerous Drugs. "The narc badge represented some kind of ultimate power to him," Priscilla will write in her memoir. "With the federal narcotics badge, he could legally enter any country both wearing guns and carrying any drugs he wished."

The singer then decides to fly back to Washington.

On the midnight red-eye flight, he puts pen to paper. The intended recipient of his letter: president of the United States Richard Nixon.

"Sir, I can and will be of any service that I can to help the country out," Presley writes. He tells the president about his hope to receive a federal agent's shield and then informs Nixon that he will be staying at the Washington Hotel under the alias "Joe Burrows."

"I will be here for as long as it takes to get the credentials of a federal agent."

It is six thirty a.m. when Elvis's letter is left with the White House guard. The temperature is just above freezing, and the forecast calls for wind, rain, and snow.*

The King doesn't have long to wait. A call to his hotel room from the White House offers him the chance to meet Nixon at noon. Elvis and his small entourage arrive on time. The singer plans to present Nixon with the gift of a .45-caliber pistol, but the weapon is immediately confiscated by the Secret Service.

President Nixon has expressed an interest in meeting some "bright young people outside of the government." He feels that Elvis

---

* The six-page note, on American Airlines letterhead, is the property of the Richard Nixon Presidential Library and Museum in Yorba Linda, California.

Presley might be just such an individual, to which top aide H. R. Haldeman responded in a note written across the top of the memo: "You have got to be kidding."

Elvis enters the Oval Office wearing a purple jumpsuit, a gold belt buckle, and amber sunglasses. His black hair, which he dyes every two weeks, is worn down to his neck and swept off his forehead. He shakes hands with the president. The two pose for a picture. An earnest Elvis Presley tells Nixon of his need for a narcotics badge, adding that the Beatles, in particular, are a subversive force in American life. Their open drug use is a form of anti-American protest. Elvis talks of Communist brainwashing and of the use of marijuana. He talks of being accepted by hippies and Black Panther radicals alike and says he is happy to "go undercover" to help Nixon.

"I'm on your side," Elvis sincerely informs the president.

Nixon turns to an aide. "Can we get him a badge?"

An excited Elvis spontaneously throws his left arm around the president of the United States and wraps him in a hug.*

✦ ✦ ✦

For the next two years, until 1973, Elvis Presley will earn a living just as many rock stars do. He will tour the United States, singing to sold-out houses, including at Madison Square Garden in New York City. Elvis is paid handsomely for these performances, but his expenses, both professional and personal, do not allow him to accumulate many assets. And unbeknownst to the financially naïve Presley, there is danger brewing in that area.†

---

* The meeting lasted for thirty-five minutes and—because the press loathed Nixon and would make a mockery of a conversation with Presley—was kept secret. The story did not come out until January 27, 1972, when Jack Anderson broke it for the *Washington Post*.

† Elvis will also meet with future president Jimmy Carter, backstage at the Omni Arena in Atlanta, while Carter is still governor of Georgia. The date is June 30, 1973. In 1977, while Carter is president, Presley will phone the White House late one night and inquire about a criminal pardon for a friend. Of note: Jimmy Carter and Elvis Presley are distant cousins.

CHAPTER NINE

The show is about to go on—but all is not well.

The *2001: A Space Odyssey* theme plays as the lights go down and the King takes the stage for his first concert broadcast outside the United States. The Honolulu International Center is filled with screaming fans. Elvis wears a special white jumpsuit with an image of an American bald eagle on both the front and back of the garment. A heavy waist-length cape decorated with sixty-five hundred precious stones is draped around his shoulders. The show's late hour was chosen specially so the performance could air during primetime in Asia, where it is being broadcast live.

Aloha from Hawaii via Satellite has Presley excited. Once again, he got himself in top shape. His standard regimen of karate, protein shakes, and diet pills worked off twenty-five pounds in just one month. The King and Colonel Parker will split the $900,000 payday ($5.85 million today)—money Parker now desperately needs. The Colonel is a regular at the Las Vegas gaming tables, sometimes losing more than $100,000 ($620,000 today) a night. Over the years, he has gone deeply in debt, and only Elvis can save him.

British promoters are dangling an offer of six shows for $500,000

($3.1 million) in London, but Parker continues to ignore opportunities for Elvis to tour outside the United States. He tells the singer that European arenas are too small to satisfy his many fans. Once again, Parker's status as an illegal alien without a US passport continues to affect when and where Presley performs.

But Parker's financial problems are not the only concern. Even though he looks good in Hawaii, Elvis is a mess. The long days and nights on the road, along with his increasing fondness for the celebrity lifestyle, have ended his marriage to Priscilla.

Writing about the breakup, Priscilla will state, "This was not the gentle, understanding man I grew to love. He was under the influence. And with my personal growth and new realities, he had become a stranger to me."

So Priscilla Presley has moved out of Graceland, legally separating from Elvis on July 26, 1972, about six months ago. Almost immediately, she takes up with her karate instructor.

Elvis is already dating Linda Thompson. The twenty-two-year-old sister of a Presley bodyguard is a blond beauty queen and so enamored of Elvis that she endures his drug use without a word. As does Colonel Parker.

As does *everyone* in Presley's entourage.

✦ ✦ ✦

Elvis Presley has never been a financial wizard. He lives from day to day, has no investment portfolio, and doesn't pay much attention to what his manager is doing. This will prove extremely harmful to the singer. Also, Presley is not tuned in to what is happening in the country. Nineteen seventy-three is a defining year in the history of rock 'n' roll, with new acts—Pink Floyd, David Bowie, the Eagles, and Bruce Springsteen—once again changing the world of music. Record albums are increasingly more important than singles. Artists prefer to create one major album per year, with a couple of songs chosen for airplay on the radio.

But Parker still believes in the old, 1950s style of making records, where a singer pumps out several albums per year—quantity over quality. And to make sure he benefits personally, the Colonel allows Presley to record only those songs of whose publishing rights he owns a percentage. The result is a series of poor records that mirror the shallow songs Elvis recorded during his movie days. Presley, who once found the studio a creative release, now, in the words of Marty Lacker, a longtime member of the Memphis Mafia, finds the sessions "drudgery."*

Aloha from Hawaii promises a chance to once again elevate Elvis's career. However, when announcing the show, Presley slurred his words, and his eyes appeared glazed during the press conference. To be fair, Presley was rightfully exhausted after yet another monthlong run in Las Vegas. The Colonel, in his desire to make as much money as possible, continues to book Presley for an incredible fourteen shows a week. The grind is so great that no other act comes close to his. Without narcotics, Elvis would likely be unable to keep up the withering pace.

✦ ✦ ✦

The Hawaii show is a smash hit.

The broadcast will reach 1.4 billion viewers in thirty-six countries, making it the largest audience ever to see a concert. The worldwide reaction is profound. The live double-album recording will go to No. 1 on the *Billboard* charts—knocking Pink Floyd's *Dark Side of the Moon* from the top spot. This is Elvis's first time in the album Hot 100 since 1965.

But *Aloha* will also be Presley's last album.

✦ ✦ ✦

The King of Rock 'n' Roll is about to suffer betrayal. And he has no idea.

Behind his back, Colonel Tom Parker, again desperate for cash,

---

* Colonel Parker bought songs directly from musical people he knew. He usually paid cash, thereby controlling what happened to the song after Presley recorded it.

is planning an artistic coup. In addition to his enormous gambling losses, Parker is struggling with weight problems of his own and suffers a heart attack. At the same time, his wife, Marie, is sliding into dementia at the age of sixty-five. Her monthly nursing bills are enormous.

To raise money, Parker secretly begins negotiating with RCA Records. He believes that Elvis will go along with any deal he makes. The singer regularly ignores his lawyers and accountants, preferring to trust the Colonel in all matters. So, although Elvis's current contract with RCA is not due to expire until 1975, Parker wants to abort the agreement and replace it with a pair of audacious deals that will forever restrict Presley's income but enhance his own.

Six years hence, a successful lawsuit filed on behalf of twelve-year-old Lisa Marie Presley by her court-appointed guardian will charge Parker and RCA with "collusion, conspiracy, fraud, misrepresentation, bad faith, and over-reaching." In 1983, the suit will award Lisa Marie $1.1 million ($6.2 million today) to be paid by RCA. The Memphis decision will strip Parker of all power concerning the Presley estate, and he will be forced to sever all ties.

But that is in the future.

Now Parker arranges a new seven-year contract with RCA in which Elvis Presley is required to provide two LPs and four singles per year. The royalty in the United States will be ten cents per single and fifty cents per album sold. Overseas, that figure is ten cents per album. As usual, half the contractual money will go to Elvis and the rest to Tom Parker. What Elvis is *not* told is that other top recording artists such as the Rolling Stones and Elton John earn double that amount in royalties—and they don't pay a 50 percent management fee.*

At the end of the seven years, RCA will pay Elvis a bonus $100,000 ($620,000 today)—once again, to be split evenly with Parker.

---

* Standard management fees in the music industry range from 15 to 25 percent.

Meanwhile, Parker's company, All Star Shows, will arrange the singer's public performances and will be paid by RCA $675,000 ($4,185,000 today) over seven years. Parker will also be compensated for "planning, promotion, and merchandising." Additionally, for reasons unknown, the conniving Colonel will get another $675,000 from RCA and a consulting fee paid over five years.*

But perhaps the worst part of the deal with RCA is the deletion of the "audit" clause. That means Elvis can never legally challenge what is stipulated in the contract. Thus, the singer will have no idea what RCA and the Colonel are receiving in his name.

Nevertheless, Presley signs the contract without hesitation.

In Lisa Marie Presley's subsequent lawsuit, there was this allegation: "The executives at RCA had to have realized that the side deals to Colonel Parker were in effect a payoff to Colonel Parker not only for the buyout, but for keeping Elvis under control in future years with no audit. . . . RCA realized that after these agreements were executed it had carte blanche to do whatever it wanted, knowing it would never have to account to Elvis."

The lawsuit goes on to say the following: "[Elvis Presley] did not have the mental capacity to evaluate carefully any of the agreements he signed, acknowledged, or approved. . . . Colonel Parker had to have been aware of Elvis' mental and physical deterioration. He made the conscious decision to make as much money as he could from Elvis before his inevitable premature death."

Court documents will also note that Parker had a separate side deal with the Hilton hotel. He would be given a year-round suite, food and beverages for his home in Palm Springs, and free transportation back and forth to Las Vegas.

All this, in exchange for Elvis appearing onstage at the Hilton

---

* Some believe this was a bribe to Parker for delivering Elvis to the company at an undermarket price, but this has never been proven.

for $130,000 per day ($780,000 today), a figure already surpassed by acts of "far less commercial value," the court filings add.

On March 1, 1973, RCA and Tom Parker complete one of the biggest heists in entertainment history.

✦ ✦ ✦

But this was still not enough for the Colonel. According to Alex Shoofey, president of the Hilton, "the Colonel was one of the best customers we had. He was good for a million dollars a year [in losses]."

Therefore, Parker was not done making deals.

Again working with RCA Records, Parker sells Elvis Presley's music catalogue for a paltry $5.4 million—the equivalent of $33 million in 2022 currency. A musician's catalogue comprises all the musical compositions created by the performer and includes copyright ownership. Sale of the catalogue means the artist forfeits all rights to royalties and control over how his music can be presented to the public. This includes allowing other artists to record and interpret Presley's music without compensation and using Elvis songs in television commercials and on movie soundtracks.

All told, Elvis will sell a billion records. But after 1973, he will no longer receive a penny in royalties. Presley had sixty-six *Billboard* Top 20 hits before waiving the rights to his catalogue. After March 1, he had only two other successful singles. He is currently thirty-eight years old. By contrast, in 2021, at the age of seventy-two, Bruce Springsteen will sell his own catalogue for $550 million.*

✦ ✦ ✦

After splitting the monies from the new deals evenly with Colonel Parker, Presley is left with just $2.7 million ($12 million today). His

---

* Among other artists who have recently sold their catalogues are Bob Dylan, Paul Simon, Neil Young, ZZ Top, Stevie Nicks, Lindsey Buckingham, and John Legend. As the music industry continues to evolve, these catalogues will become highly profitable for use by streaming services.

tax bracket is 50 percent. Combining management fees and taxes, Elvis is left with $1.25 million ($6.3 million today). Priscilla will receive about half that when the divorce becomes final in October, plus thousands more a month in spousal support.

Obviously, this is one of the worst deals in music history. But, once again, Elvis Presley signs on the dotted line.

✦ ✦ ✦

Two months later, a despondent Elvis appears onstage at the Sahara Casino in Lake Tahoe. He has gained back the weight lost for *Aloha* and added five pounds more. "Elvis Presley is neither looking nor sounding good," reports *Variety*. "Some 30 pounds overweight, he's puffy, white-faced and blinking against the light."

Apparently disappointed with his life, Presley has taken to swallowing pills right out of the bottle, opening his mouth and pouring them in. The singer is also experiencing heart pains—so much so that he is rushed to the hospital and must cancel some of his Tahoe shows. His personal physician, George Nichopoulos, will state that Presley's bowel movements are becoming affected and that he is impotent. While on tour, Presley pays the doctor $800 a day to write prescriptions. When Nichopoulos is unavailable, Elvis pays other physicians up to $1,000 a day to ensure the flow of narcotics.

In a bizarre twist, Nichopoulos has taken to dressing like Elvis, wearing rings and bracelets and unbuttoning his shirts to the middle of his chest. He frequently dons a gold medallion—a gift from Presley that marks Dr. Nick as a member of the Memphis Mafia.

Upon Elvis's return to Graceland after his hospitalization in Nevada, five-year-old Lisa Marie watches in alarm as her father ingests yet another mouthful of pills. Elvis and Priscilla share joint custody of their daughter. Unlike his ex-wife, who can be a strict disciplinarian, the singer indulges Lisa Marie's every whim. The two often stay up until three in the morning watching television and playing records. They then sleep well into the afternoon.

Later in life, Lisa Marie will remember her father as mischievous and prone to laughter. But not today.

"Daddy, Daddy, I don't want you to die," she says.

"Okay. I won't," Elvis replies. "Don't worry about it."*

---

* These words come from several interviews Lisa Marie gave in 2020.

CHAPTER TEN

E lvis Presley is in the hospital.
   Again.

The world has no idea. The thirty-eight-year-old's admission to Baptist Memorial Hospital under a fake name is a closely guarded secret. Just the Colonel, Vernon Presley, and the singer's close friends know of his dire condition. It is not pretty. The singer lies on his back, his bloated body hooked up to monitors. A central venous pressure line drips fluid from a glass bottle nearby. A clipboard hangs from the end of the bed, soon to be filled with handwritten notes on Presley's condition. A nurse presses a mercury thermometer into his mouth to take his temperature. The King is not capable of walking around the room.

It is just six days since his divorce from Priscilla became final, but two beds are being set up in the King's private room. One for him and one for girlfriend Linda Thompson. She will stay here as long as Elvis is a patient.

That may be a while. Dr. Nichopoulos originally thought Presley's breathing difficulty was an isolated incident, and he sent nurse Tish Henley to Graceland to be with the singer. But it rapidly became clear that Elvis needed to be in a hospital. The King's face is jaundiced; he has severe respiratory distress and toxic hepatitis; his abdomen is distended; and he weaves in and out of consciousness. Presley's current condition began a week ago in Los Angeles, when he passed out in front of Linda Thompson. Panicked, Thompson called Dr. Nick, who immediately ordered that the singer be flown back to Tennessee. There, his condition continued to deteriorate, leading to his current hospitalization.

Dr. Nick orders an extensive battery of tests. Baptist Memorial is a massive institution, as large and tall as a Las Vegas casino, with some of the best medical technology in the South. Nine other physicians are called in to consult on the bizarre symptoms exhibited by Presley. The first concern is his heart, but results show that his cardiac condition appears fine. However, liver function is limited, with the hepatitis a likely culprit.*

Also, blood screens for the stress hormone cortisol point to an adrenal insufficiency, gastric tests find a bleeding ulcer, and detailed blood analyses pinpoint the specific drugs the singer has been abusing.

Elvis Presley is not yet forty years old, but his body is in a catastrophic state.

The primary question going forward is: What will kill him?

✦ ✦ ✦

Everything.

Elvis lives in chaos. It is not just Tom Parker's nefarious business dealings, or the 168 live shows the singer will perform this year, or his divorce. It is all that combined and more. Nineteen seventy-three is an emotional grind for Presley, and he is abusing drugs to get through it.

✦ ✦ ✦

---

* Elvis Presley's hepatitis was believed to have been caused by excessive use of the steroid cortisone, which lowers inflammation.

There was hope at the beginning of the year, just after the *Aloha* special wowed audiences around the world. Many of his fans believed Elvis would rebound. In fact, he had the good fortune to meet a man just like him—someone who understood the daily pressures of being surrounded by sycophants, traveling the world as king of his personal domain.

That man was Muhammad Ali.

The date is February 14, Valentine's Day. Elvis has always had a thing for boxing, having tried and failed to make his high school team. In the 1962 film *Kid Galahad*, he played a fighter, enjoying the physicality of the role. So he makes a point to engage the thirty-one-year-old Ali when the boxer arrives in Las Vegas for a fight. The two men have met before, when "the Greatest" came backstage after one of Elvis's shows. "All my life, I admired Elvis," Ali will remember. "It was a thrill to meet him."

Like Elvis, Ali is struggling. He lost the heavyweight championship fight to Joe Frazier two years ago and is trying to get another shot at the title. Tonight's fight, at the Vegas Convention Center, is against Joe Bugner, a relative unknown whom Ali must defeat on his road back to the top. Should he win here, Ali will go on to fight another contender, Ken Norton, just a month from now.

Elvis arranges to meet the boxer in the hours leading up to the Bugner fight. The two get together in Ali's hotel suite. Both are known for their charisma, showmanship, and wit. They pose for photos—Elvis with his fists up in a fighting stance, the boxer feigning annoyance. Despite Presley's six-foot-two height, the six-foot-three Ali seems to tower over him.

When all the posturing for the cameras is done, Ali presents Elvis with a pair of autographed boxing gloves. Presley returns the favor, handing the fighter a custom-made robe. On the back, in fake gemstones, is written "The People's Choice." The wording is a faux pas on the singer's part—he does not know that Ali prefers to be called the people's *champion*.

No matter. Ali wears the robe from Elvis as he steps into the ring, then goes on to defeat Bugner by unanimous decision. The boxer now considers the robe a good-luck charm and will wear it into the ring against Ken Norton. For the rest of Elvis's life, he and Muhammad Ali will remain friends.

✦ ✦ ✦

Days after meeting Ali, Elvis Presley finds his world descending into the surreal. On February 18, while the singer is performing in Las Vegas, four men climb onstage, apparently wanting to shake his hand. But the singer recoils; he fears for his safety. Presley immediately assumes a karate stance. In a surprising show of his martial arts training, he subdues the lead intruder. The audience is unsure whether this is part of the act, but they cheer as security guards finally usher the trespassers away.

An out-of-breath and angry Elvis then addresses the audience. "I'm sorry, ladies and gentlemen. I'm sorry I didn't break his goddamned neck, is what I'm sorry about."

Although Elvis Presley had a perfect right to defend himself, the incident indicates the presence of rage. Despite Presley's public stance that he is at peace with his divorce, he is extremely upset that Priscilla had an affair and has continued the relationship with her paramour.

Presley believes the onstage attack is the work of his ex-wife's new beau, karate instructor Mike Stone. So Elvis decides to break the law. He gives Memphis Mafia member Red West an M16 automatic rifle from his personal gun collection and orders him to travel to Los Angeles to murder Stone. "He has no right to live, Red. Find someone to wipe him out."*

The thirty-six-year-old West, a longtime friend, is an original member of the Memphis crew and will do anything for the King. As his nickname implies, his hair is deep red. West is known to be good with his fists and, on occasion, has fought on Presley's behalf.

---

* This quote is from Red West's book, *Elvis: What Happened?*, cowritten with two other members of the Memphis Mafia.

Red West does not say no to the King's order. Using his connections in the world of organized crime, he inquires about the logistics and cost of a contract killing. Meanwhile, he hopes that Presley will calm down.

And he does.

"Forget it," Elvis finally tells a relieved West. "It's too heavy."

✦ ✦ ✦

On February 23, less than one week after the onstage attack, Ann-Margret attends Presley's Las Vegas show. It is a decade since their romance, and she is happily married. In an homage, the King orders Lamar Fike, the lighting director, to aim a spotlight where Ann-Margret is sitting, illuminating his former lover for the rest of the show.

"Keep the spotlight on her, man. She's beautiful. I want to look at her," Elvis says from the stage so everyone in the audience can hear.

✦ ✦ ✦

And then there is Vernon Presley, Elvis's fifty-seven-year-old father. He is close to his son and works out of an office in Graceland. Vernon was raised in poverty. His own father was a sharecropper, barely able to support the family. When Elvis's mother, Gladys, died in 1958, Vernon quickly married a woman named Dee Stanley. The singer did not like that his father remarried so quickly, and there was tension between the two men.

Nevertheless, Vernon is a constant in Elvis's life, basking in the reflected glow of his son's celebrity. He often travels to concerts, and Elvis is fond of introducing him from the stage. When home in Memphis, Vernon Presley patrols the gates of Graceland to greet guests on his son's behalf. By associating closely with Elvis, he has all the luxuries life can afford.

But the tension remains.

In a bizarre series of events, Vernon seeks to break out of his son's shadow. He writes a song called "Don't Close Your Door," recording it in the secrecy of his Graceland office.

The song goes nowhere.

But Elvis is aware of it, and so are some of his friends, who whisper that Vernon Presley is an opportunist.

Which may be true.

✦ ✦ ✦

As Elvis lies in his Memphis hospital bed, certain facts come to light. The pieces in the jigsaw puzzle that is Presley's health start to come together. Earlier this summer, while living in Los Angeles, the King began to see a spinal specialist. At the time, Dr. Nichopoulos was not informed. The unnamed West Coast physician prescribed a cocktail of highly addictive Demerol and the steroid methylprednisolone. The latter powerful drug can lead to a disease known as Cushing's syndrome, which caused the puffiness in Elvis's face. This malady will persist in some form for the rest of Presley's life.

Another persistent condition is a headache brought on by post-concussion syndrome. Amazingly, that night long ago during the filming of *Clambake*, when Presley fell and slammed his head into a bathtub, still haunts him.

Monitoring the singer in the hospital, Dr. Nichopoulos—at the behest of Colonel Parker—prescribes methadone and phenobarbital to mitigate Elvis's drug withdrawal. To fix the many ailments coursing through his system, Presley continues to ingest a small pharmacy: Lasix, Mylanta, Colace, Dulcolax, Valmid, Vistaril, and Darvotron.

Barely able to function, he is released from Baptist Memorial on November 1, 1973—though not before being diagnosed with glaucoma. On top of the swelling face, constipation, and headaches, Elvis is slowly losing his eyesight.*

---

* Elvis was given a prescription for special sunglasses to mitigate the damage from his glaucoma. For the rest of his life, he would remain in the habit of wearing gold aviator sunglasses in public and onstage to prevent the pain that came from strong sunlight and bright stage lights.

But no matter what condition Elvis Presley is in, Colonel Parker continues his deal making. He signs contracts for Elvis to kick off 1974 with another grueling round of Vegas performances.

After all, the show must go on.

CHAPTER ELEVEN

APRIL 16, 1975

LOS ANGELES, CALIFORNIA

MORNING

Elvis Presley's drug addiction continues, but hope may be on the way.

The top-secret negotiations are now public: "Will Elvis Be Barbra's Next?" wonders the headline in this morning's *Los Angeles Times*. Hollywood insider Joyce Haber's Wednesday column goes on to describe the behind-the-scenes discussions now taking place for Elvis to costar with Barbra Streisand in a rock musical with the working title *Rainbow Road*.

The film also goes by another name: *A Star Is Born*.*

"Is Elvis in?" Haber asks. "I can tell you he's interested. Jon [Peters, Streisand's hair dresser and then-romantic partner] and Barbra recently flew to Las Vegas, where the famous one-time Pelvis—he's still overweight—was playing the Hilton. Elvis says he's always wanted to work with Barbra."

Haber's sleuthing is correct. Elvis is once again unable to sell

---

* This is the third time *A Star Is Born* is being made. The first film was released in 1937, starring Fredric March and Janet Gaynor. A 1954 version featured Judy Garland and James Mason. A fourth remake will take place in 2018, with Bradley Cooper and Lady Gaga.

records; his last top single, "Burnin' Love," was released three years ago. Presley turned forty on January 8, and was so despondent that he locked himself alone in his bedroom at Graceland all day. His spending continues unabated—in January, he bought his first jet, a Boeing 707. This raises his monthly expenses to $500,000 ($3.1 million today). Also, he just spent two more weeks in Memphis Baptist after overdosing on prescription drugs. Girlfriend Linda Thompson notes that he is so overmedicated that sometimes the singer will actually fall asleep while chewing his food at the dinner table.

But perhaps the biggest reason for working with Streisand is that Elvis *really* likes her. He once surprised the singer backstage after one of her Vegas shows, entering her dressing room as she was painting her fingernails. Streisand focused on her nails as they began speaking, too nervous to look Presley in the eye—whereupon Elvis got down on his knees, took the bottle of polish from her hands, and actually painted her nails. "You've got a great voice, Barbra," the King told Streisand, "but you keep putting your hand in front of your face, and it's distracting."

More recently, Streisand and Peters attended Elvis's March 28 show at the Hilton. The couple came backstage afterward to formally offer Presley the lead male role in *A Star Is Born*. This will be a return to moviemaking at the highest level for Elvis, his name above the title, the "serious" screenwriting team of John Gregory Dunne and Joan Didion doing the script, and a chance to work with one of Hollywood's top leading ladies. At nearly thirty-three, Streisand is just coming off the enormous box-office success of *The Way We Were*, with Robert Redford. Her new film, *Funny Lady*, opened two weeks ago, to rave reviews, confirming her place as one of the world's top film stars.

And Elvis Presley is *perfect* to play the role of run-down rock legend John Norman Howard. Streisand will later explain why: "His career was slightly in decline, he was overweight, and I thought he was perfect to play the part."

The meeting lasts two hours. Fine points of the deal still need to be worked out, but Streisand and Peters, working in conjunction with First Artists, initially offer Elvis $500,000 ($3.1 million today) and 10 percent of the film's profits.

Jerry Schilling of the Memphis Mafia is in the room as Streisand and Peters pitch the role to Presley. He has known Elvis since the age of twelve and is familiar with the King's moods. "After they left, I could tell [Elvis] wanted to do it," Schilling will remember. "But, as with so many of the things he wanted to do at that point in his life, he expected people would try to stop him."

Presley is too veteran a performer to agree to the deal on the spot, but as Streisand and Peters leave his dressing room, he is ecstatic. Left unsaid is that his latest Las Vegas stand has been a triumph. After his overdose, Dr. Nick assigned a full-time nurse to administer Presley's medications, leaving him mostly alert and coherent. Elvis has once again lost weight—he is not down to his ideal 160 pounds, but he has lost enough that the media has made note of his improved appearance.

A Star Is Born is likely Presley's last chance to regain prestige in Hollywood—and he knows it.

But Colonel Tom Parker could not care less.

The Colonel has many reasons to be alarmed by Elvis returning to movies. If successful, Presley could be traveling down the same career path as Frank Sinatra, forsaking the cash cow of constant touring to make films and record the occasional album.

Parker also is aware of how much Elvis is spending. The singer needs to bring in an even million a month just to remain solvent. The eight weeks required to film *A Star Is Born* would eliminate $130,000 ($700,000 today) per night, if he were instead performing on the road. Parker gets half that. Also, because the Colonel sold Elvis's catalogue to RCA two years ago, the days of Presley paying his bills with royalty checks are over.

The truth is, Parker is no longer looking out for Elvis Presley's career goals. Instead, he frames every deal for the singer in terms of what is best for his own wallet. "I guarantee you they'll turn the contract down, because I'm going to request top billing," Parker tells Elvis.

On April 14, two days before Joyce Haber's *Los Angeles Times* column makes the potential film role public, bringing with it a huge public outcry in support of Elvis taking the role, Parker responds with his counteroffer. Calling Streisand's negotiation a "cheap deal," he tells First Artists that Elvis will not make the movie unless he receives $1 million in salary, soundtrack rights, and half the box-office profits. Also, as promised, Parker demands top billing for Elvis over Streisand.

The counteroffer is so ludicrous that Parker and Presley never even get a response. Eventually, the role goes to Kris Kristofferson, who achieves great success when *A Star Is Born* is released.

Members of the Memphis Mafia will later recall that Elvis is secretly relieved when the negotiations break down. "At the time, we figured that Barbra never intended to use Elvis anyway," top Elvis assistant Joe Esposito will write in his book, *Good Rocking Tonight*. "I can't imagine Elvis and Streisand lasting one week on set together. . . . It was over with, and we never heard another word about it."*

✦ ✦ ✦

On April 17, Elvis buys another aircraft. This plane—fitted with gold-plated toilet fixtures, a queen-size bed, and the initials "TCB" on the tail—will become legend. He names it the *Lisa Marie*. Total cost: $1 million plus $750,000 ($10.6 million today) in renovations. This is followed four days later by another large purchase: a home near Graceland for Linda Thompson, on whom Elvis frequently cheats. By October, their relationship will be over. By November, Elvis is taking out a $300,000 ($1.8 million today) loan on Graceland to cover his outrageous expenses.

He is now in the habit of acquiring airplanes (six in 1975 alone),

---

*The consensus among Presley's entourage was that the insecure and dominating Streisand would have driven the distracted Elvis crazy on set with excessive retakes.

buying Cadillacs for strangers (more than fourteen in 1975), and giving out his personal jewelry from the stage.*

✦ ✦ ✦

Elvis's personal life becomes even more bizarre. He actually refuses to bathe, fearing he might fall down in the shower or bath. Instead, he begins to take what he calls a "whore's bath," swiping a washcloth over crotch and armpits. Open sores cover his body. He treats them with pills specially ordered from Sweden that claim to cleanse from within.

But it is while he is performing live that the unraveling of Elvis Presley can be most clearly seen. He angrily throws guitars into the crowd, looks at his watch as if bored, appears exhausted, and sometimes lies down onstage to sing. "A physically and artistically sub-par Elvis Presley walked out on a strange concert performance for half an hour here Sunday night, but eventually returned," *Variety* writes of one show in Baltimore. "A Civic Center spokesman attributed the vet rock and roll singer's murmuring, swearing and unscheduled hiatus to the reported intestinal problem that had kayoed Presley from an earlier portion of his tour."

Elvis's erratic behavior includes his waving a small handgun around his dressing room; he finally fires a shot that barely misses Dr. Nick. He also insults his band from the stage, one night telling the audience that backup singer and onetime girlfriend Kathy Westmoreland will "take affection from anybody, anyplace, anytime. In fact, she gets it from the whole band."

During the same July 20 show, he tells the crowd that the aroma of "green peppers and onions" is wafting across the stage, leading him to believe that his all-Black backup group had been eating catfish before the show. Clearly ill at ease, the singers hide their discomfort by

---

* Presley's fleet of jets is based in Memphis and used by him, his father, his band, and his entourage during the frequent tours. On one occasion, Presley flies daughter Lisa Marie from Memphis to Colorado just so she can see real snow; the two return home the same day. The aircraft the *Lisa Marie* is currently on display at Graceland.

looking down at their shoes. "If you don't look up, I'm going to kick your ass," Elvis commands. "Sorry for any embarrassment I might have caused, but if you can't take it, get off the pot."

Stunningly, the Sweet Inspirations leave the stage, letting Elvis finish the concert without them.*

✦ ✦ ✦

Elvis Presley's deterioration is obvious. The nickname "Fat Elvis" is now being used to describe his physical appearance. He is heavy-lidded onstage. His singing voice is thin. Many of his self-destructive miscues are right out of the *Star Is Born* script.

The King's decline is so well publicized that an old friend calls him on August 30 to commiserate. At the time of the call, Elvis is back for another two weeks in Memphis Baptist, complaining constantly of headaches, insomnia, "general pain, hurting all over"—all symptoms of traumatic brain injury.

Presley takes the call from his hospital bed. The old friend was once president of the United States, but a year before, he resigned from office after the Watergate scandal. There is no better man to comprehend the public embarrassment Presley is suffering.

Richard Nixon wishes Elvis well, hoping that everything will be okay.

It will not be.

---

* After Elvis apologized profusely, and they accepted, the Sweet Inspirations came back to perform the next night. But backup singer Kathy Westmoreland (not a member of the Inspirations) quit the tour that night. Presley will later explain the incident by saying he thought it was funny. Westmoreland will eventually rejoin the band.

CHAPTER TWELVE

JUNE 26, 1977
INDIANAPOLIS, INDIANA
10 P.M.

The man with seven weeks and four days to live is onstage again.

Market Square Arena is packed. Despite widespread public awareness about Elvis Presley's weight gain and erratic performances, an audience of eighteen thousand fills the aging venue. As the lights go down and the anthem "Also Sprach Zarathustra" booms over the loudspeakers to announce his entrance, a large sign flashes, "Welcome Elvis."

Then those bulbs switch off, bathing the arena in complete darkness.

The crowd goes wild. Delirious applause and screams. Fans have waited a long time for this. The license plates in the arena parking lot show that the crowd has driven from more than a dozen states to be here. Thousands stood in a line stretching around the arena this afternoon to buy the last of the $15 tickets ($68.60 today) for places behind the stage. There's not an empty seat in the house.

The concert begins at eight thirty with ninety minutes of opening acts featuring singers and a comedian. In addition, Elvis's stage announcer, Al Dvorin, reminds the audience to visit the souvenir stands in the concourse.

"The big question was, of course, had he lost weight?" writes Rita Rose of the *Indianapolis Star*. "His last concert here, nearly two years ago, found Elvis overweight, sick and prone to give a lethargic performance. As the lights in the arena was [*sic*] turned down after intermission, you could feel a silent plea rippling through the audience: 'Please, Elvis, don't be fat.'"

Backstage, Presley adjusts his jumpsuit. Bodyguards surround him in red waist-length bowling jackets with "Elvis" emblazoned on them in white letters. The King sips Gatorade from a Coca-Cola cup. Despite his years of performing, he looks nervous. He jokes with his crew, accepts a quick shoulder rub, and then steps alone toward his audience.

The drummer counts time, and the band begins to play. A spotlight cuts the darkness. Presley enters stage left wearing a playful grin. Announcer Dvorin stays quiet—the King needing no introduction. Flashbulbs pop throughout the auditorium as fans capture the moment for their scrapbooks.

Presley is not fat. The singer's face is puffy from steroids, but he once again looks trim in his white jumpsuit. A little spread around the middle, but otherwise not so bad. Many forty-two-year-old men would be pleased to look this good. He wears an enormous gold belt buckle, spangled white bell-bottom pants, a high-collared shirt open to the navel. His hair is jet black, his face framed by muttonchop sideburns.

Elvis straps on an acoustic guitar, strolls to center stage, and goes to work.

CBS is filming tonight's show for a television special. Interviews conducted outside the arena this afternoon show the dedication of Presley's fans. Men and women—though, mostly women—speak in excited tones about the chance to see "the King," as almost everyone interviewed refers to the singer. Their ages range from teenage to geriatric. Their eyes gleam with happiness as they talk about the chance to witness Elvis live. "I'm so excited. I just can't wait" is the standard refrain.

The band is tight: two guitars, a bass, drums, horns. Elvis vamps as the crowd cheers and squeals, and then he launches into Ma Rainey's blues classic "See See Rider." The audience stretches upraised hands toward the stage like penitents at a revival meeting.

June 26 is a seminal date in Elvis Presley's life. June 26, 1954, was the first time a young Elvis got the phone call that would change his life, an invitation to make a record at the legendary Sun Studio in Memphis. June 26 is Colonel Parker's sixty-eighth birthday. Elvis's father, Vernon, will die of a heart attack on this date two years from now. And on June 26 of last year, a starstruck Elton John came backstage in Landover, Maryland.*

And this June 26 evening will mark a very special event as well, as this will be Elvis Presley's last concert.

✦ ✦ ✦

Much has happened to the singer over the last two years, most of it bad. Elvis's health continues to falter. He has developed a condition known as chronic obstructive pulmonary disease, whose related conditions include emphysema. COPD is most often found in smokers. Presley does not often use tobacco, but his years of singing in smoke-filled showrooms exposed him to the dangers.

Also, the singer's liver disease continues to worsen. As with the COPD, he does not seem a likely candidate for such a condition: liver problems appear most often in heavy drinkers. Though the singer doesn't even like alcohol, his use of pills and his consumption of a diet high in fat are putting a strain on that vital organ.

And, as always, Presley's chronic constipation is wreaking havoc on his colon. His heart, liver, and bowel issues become so severe in the waning months of 1976 that Elvis completely shuts himself off

---

* Elton John was escorted backstage before Presley's show. Their meeting was warm, and John took a photograph with a very young Lisa Marie. Elvis complimented John on his work, and the two discussed doing a recording together. Before heading back to his seat for the performance, John requested "Heartbreak Hotel," but Elvis could not comply, given the tightly rehearsed set list.

from the world. He is so large during his December appearances in Las Vegas that some believe he is wearing extra padding beneath his jumpsuit.

Upon returning to Graceland, Elvis only gets worse. He mostly stays in his bedroom, watching TV and listening to the radio in his pajamas. He lives on a diet of cheeseburger platters and Dr. Nick's pills—Amytal, Dexedrine, Percocet, Hycomine.

New girlfriend Ginger Alden, whom Elvis met on November 19, 1976, quickly tires of the King's behavior. By January 1977, the dark-haired model convinces Elvis to rejoin the world. The singer rewards her affection with a Hawaiian vacation and an 11.5-carat diamond engagement ring.*

But by April 1, 1977, Elvis is back in Memphis Baptist for the fourth time. In addition to his other health issues, he is now anemic. Also, his glaucoma is getting worse—he is inconsistent about wearing the sunglasses that might prolong his eyesight—stealing his vision a little more every day.

✦ ✦ ✦

On May 21, in the singer's Louisville, Kentucky, hotel suite, Dr. Nick works to resuscitate a semiconscious Elvis, injecting him with drugs that will allow the singer to take the stage that evening. When this fails, the doctor dunks Presley's head in a bucket of ice water. Apparently, the singer took too many pills and is having trouble righting himself.

Colonel Parker enters the room. The manager is currently said to be $30 million in debt to the Las Vegas Hilton ($137 million today). "You listen to me," he shouts after watching Nichopoulos try to revive his client. "The only thing that matters is that he's on that stage tonight!"†

---

* The two never marry, with Elvis refusing even to set a date.

† The figure of $30 million comes from *People* magazine's March 5, 1984, issue. The authors of this book were not able to independently verify the gambling debt.

Finally, Elvis awakens fully, slips into his jumpsuit, and heads for the venue.

✦ ✦ ✦

As bad as his health is, Elvis Presley's greatest concern is not his heart, lungs, liver, or any of the maladies coursing through them. Utmost on his mind are three members of the Memphis Mafia. One year ago, Elvis instructed his father to fire Red West, Sonny West, and Dave Hebler. The elder Presley, who nursed a well-known personal disdain for his son's inner circle, did so eagerly.

Elvis's reasons for the purge are many. He and Vernon claim it is a cost-cutting move designed to lower the singer's overhead. Not only did the bodyguards need to be paid and fed for their services, but they were also a liability in terms of lawsuits: the three men were known to be overzealous in the physical methods they used to deal with fans. Getting rid of the three will lessen the need for legal payouts.

The bodyguards have another story. They claim they were fired because they confronted Presley over his drug use. The truth is difficult to ascertain, but the three men are out for revenge.

It is normal for Elvis to fire entourage members, but he is also known to miss them once they're gone and to quickly hire them back. But not this time. So the three have coauthored an "as told to" book on life with Presley, a tell-all entitled *Elvis: What Happened?* The publishing date is five weeks away. Even though he does not know which sordid details will appear in the book, Presley is furious. He demands that Colonel Parker stop its publication, but nothing can be done. Advance copies are already being circulated. The British press in particular has begun printing some of the disparaging tidbits from it.* Also, another rift is growing between Elvis and Parker.

---

* *Elvis: What Happened?* was written by Australian journalist Steve Dunleavy based on three hundred hours of interviews with the three former members of the Memphis Mafia. With an initial print run of four hundred thousand copies, the book arrived in stores on August 1, 1977, and became a bestseller. But it received mixed reviews, and Elvis's fan base saw it as a betrayal. Red West would later express regret for his part in its publication.

Presley insider Larry Geller will later insist that Elvis "was adamant about firing the Colonel." The *Nashville Banner*, in turn, runs a story in late April stating that Parker is trying to sell Elvis's management contract in order to cover his gambling debts.

Yet the relationship continues.

Elvis is still on the road, making millions of dollars for himself and Parker. He tours constantly, selling out wherever he goes. Critics point to his pale skin and strange ramblings from the stage as a sign that he is a sick man. But no matter his social miscues or the growing innuendoes in the press about his eccentric behavior, Elvis's audience is utterly loyal. One show in Dearborn, Michigan, draws a record 62,500 fans. So far in 1977, Elvis has toured five different times. After finishing the Indianapolis show, the singer will have the entire month of July off before hitting the road again in August.

In the meantime, Elvis is becoming a bit more introspective. He is noticing more of the little things. "I'm going to look fat in that faggy little suit," he tells backup singer Kathy Westmoreland one week before Indianapolis, pointing to the new blue jumpsuit he would wear onstage in Rapid City, South Dakota. "But I'll look good in my coffin," he adds.

✦ ✦ ✦

Elvis sings for eighty minutes in Indianapolis—"Love Me Tender," "Bridge Over Troubled Water," "Hound Dog"—just the hits; some of his own, others covered. By the time Presley reaches the final number, "Can't Help Falling in Love," he has delivered a solid night of entertainment.

But then something snaps. Elvis's voice stays smooth and in tune, but he begins speaking gibberish, forgetting the lyrics. The band soars to cover for him; Elvis gets back on track. If anyone in the crowd knows or cares, they do not show it. Hands are still outstretched toward the stage as the house lights come up. Women in the standing-room section up front wave wildly, trying to get Presley's attention—and perhaps one of his cherished scarves. Some cry, caught up in the euphoria. Elvis takes a victory lap onstage, bending down to touch his fans' extended fingertips. He takes a white scarf from around his neck and drapes it over the shoulders of one lucky woman standing front and center.

A short time later, Elvis leaves the stage the way he came on, descending a set of stairs on the left. Immediately, his bodyguards in their matching red jackets cluster around the singer. Even as the band continues to play and the audience clamors for an encore, a smiling Presley is whisked through the cinder-block bowels of Market Square Arena and rushed out the door to a waiting limousine.

Only then does the voice of Al Dvorin echo throughout the auditorium: "Elvis has left the building. Thank you and good night."

CHAPTER THIRTEEN

AUGUST 17, 1977
MEMPHIS, TENNESSEE
NOON

E lvis Presley is gone.

A single white hearse carries his body home. His body was driven first from Memphis Baptist Hospital to the Memphis Funeral Home for embalming. Now it is on to Graceland.

Hot, humid weather under a bright sun. News helicopters circling overhead. Flags throughout Memphis flying at half-mast. Elvis music playing almost nonstop on local radio stations. "The King Still Lives in Our Hearts," reads a sign in front of a Pizza Hut. Reporters arrive from Japan, Denmark, Britain, Australia, Norway, among other nations.

The world is in shock. Fifty thousand grieving fans quickly show up at Graceland, holding one another and crying. They form a long line in front of the mansion and down Elvis Presley Boulevard. Many have driven hundreds of miles; some have brought their families. The mourning fans hold up handmade signs speaking to their love for Elvis. Most don't refer to him as "the King" but instead as their *hero*. Flower arrangements line the gates, hundreds upon hundreds of bouquets piled atop one another, many in the form of guitars and hound dogs.

"We love him" is the phrase of the day.

And it's not just in Memphis. Around the world, mourners gather to celebrate the life of Elvis Presley. On Long Island, five thousand fans will jam the parking lot of the Nassau Coliseum, where Presley was to have appeared next week. In London, an overflow crowd spills out of a church celebrating the singer.

"Rock 'n' roll never forgets," one fan tells a television reporter in Memphis.

✦ ✦ ✦

Things have happened fast since the discovery of Elvis's lifeless body on the bathroom floor yesterday. An autopsy was immediately conducted at Memphis Baptist. The cause of death: the singer's many medical complications. Elvis had gained a significant amount of weight since that last show in Indianapolis, an estimated seventy-five pounds. Had he lived, the public would have seen him in this condition, for Elvis was due to go back on the road, to Portland, Maine, this very day. In the months to come, as the world looks for a scapegoat to blame for Presley's demise, fingers will be pointed not at Elvis himself or at Colonel Tom Parker but at Dr. George Nichopoulos. But for now, the extent of Elvis's chronic drug use is still largely a secret.

Inside the hearse, Elvis lies in a copper casket, just as his mother did nineteen years ago. It has been less than twenty-four hours since he died. In this time of deep sadness, a tearful Vernon Presley has asserted himself. It was Vernon who gave nine-year-old Lisa Marie the terrible news. Elvis's daughter was at Graceland and saw the ambulances, but she still cannot believe her father is gone. Her namesake aircraft was immediately dispatched to Los Angeles to pick up her mother, Priscilla, for the funeral. At first, Vernon did not call his son's former wife. She heard the news from her sister as the tragedy flashed around the world. Priscilla will spend much of the air journey in Elvis's bedroom at the back of the aircraft. "I lay there," she will write, "unable to believe Elvis was dead."

Vernon has specified that fans be allowed to see the performer one last time. So, beginning at three p.m., the public is allowed to pass through Graceland and pay its respects before his open casket.

The hearse pulls up the driveway and parks before the tall white columns framing the front door—the same spot where Vernon announced his son's death to the world at four p.m. yesterday. Longtime friends serve as pallbearers, carrying the coffin inside and placing it in the first-floor entry archway between the music room and living room. For now, a carpet of flowers drapes the coffin. Staff at the Memphis Funeral Home have dressed the King in a cream-colored suit, a silver tie, a blue shirt with diamond cuff links, and a diamond stickpin. Per Vernon's direction, Elvis's hair has been cut, his sideburns trimmed and dyed black. He looks like he's asleep.*

Before the room is opened to the public, family and friends walk past the coffin and offer Vernon their condolences. The funeral will take place tomorrow at two p.m. Then Elvis will be interred in a mausoleum at Forest Hill Cemetery, three and a half miles from Graceland. His mother is already buried there, her grave marked by a large marble monument of Jesus praying before a Christian cross and another featuring the Star of David, in homage to her Jewish heritage. In Gladys Presley's honor, Elvis has long worn both symbols on a chain around his neck. Vernon Presley, knowing Elvis would want to be near his mother, will soon have her body moved to a spot next to Elvis in the mausoleum.

At three p.m., the Graceland gates are opened. Fans begin the slow procession to view the King. Dozens faint in the hot sun. Memphis police wade into the throng, handing out water. One man suffers a heart attack. A pregnant woman goes into labor. Before authorities order the gates closed at six p.m., thirty thousand people will make the pilgrimage.

---

* The pallbearers were the singer's road manager, Joe Esposito; Dr. George Nichopoulos; guitarist Charlie Hodge; Felton Jarvis, a Nashville producer; friend Lamar Fike; former Memphis radio announcer George Klein; cousins Billy and Gene Smith; and Memphis Mafia member Jerry Schilling.

"Why are you treating us like this?" one dejected fan screams as the cops shut the gates.

"We're afraid of a riot," an officer responds.

"You don't understand," the fan replies. "We're not troublemakers. . . . We're family. We came because we love him."

✦ ✦ ✦

Just after the doors are closed to the public, Elvis's casket is moved into Graceland's living room for tomorrow's funeral service. Priscilla and Lisa Marie take one last look. Standing over the casket, they slip a bracelet depicting a mother and child onto Elvis's right wrist.

"You look so peaceful," Priscilla says and then pauses. "Just don't cause any trouble at the Pearly Gates."

✦ ✦ ✦

The crowd will not go away—and some *are* troublemakers. One thousand mourners maintain a vigil outside Graceland through the night. Many have no hotel reservations and sleep on the grass. Some try to charge the gates, only to be repelled by Memphis Police and forty members of the Tennessee National Guard. At four a.m., the crowd still numbers three hundred when a car plows into the mourners, killing two. The drunken eighteen-year-old driver is arrested two blocks away, one lifeless body still on the hood of his car.

✦ ✦ ✦

Colonel Tom Parker is in Maine preparing for Elvis's upcoming concert when he gets the news. His first instinct is not to fly to Memphis but, instead, to board a plane for New York City. There is still money to be made. Parker knows that anything related to Elvis will soon sell out around the world. He travels directly to RCA headquarters in Manhattan to callously demand they immediately increase the flow of Presley music and memorabilia into stores. He also meets top merchandising executives from other companies to facilitate a new line of Elvis posters, ensuring that he will continue to make money on "the boy," as he calls Presley, for many years to come. Parker knows that Elvis leaves this world nearly broke, having mortgaged Graceland on several occasions to cover staff payroll. He will not allow the same to happen to him.

Only after he takes care of business does the Colonel fly to Memphis to pay his respects.

Already, T-shirts with an image of the King and the words "Elvis Presley, in Memory, 1935–1977" are on sale for $5 each in front of Graceland.

✦ ✦ ✦

When he arrives for the funeral, the Colonel does not look like your typical mourner. Dressed in a baseball cap, a casual shirt, and slacks, he carries with him a contract. Quickly finding Vernon Presley, he presents him with a new deal so that he can remain Elvis's manager. "He acted quickly," Priscilla will later write, "fearful that with Elvis gone, Vernon would be too distraught to handle correctly the many proposals and propositions that would be in the offing. Vernon signed."

The Graceland portion of the funeral service starts at two p.m. Ann-Margret is in attendance, as are actor George Hamilton, singer Chet Atkins, and Hollywood actor and football player Jim Brown. *Saturday Night Live*'s Bill Murray will arrive at the cemetery, as will former first daughter Caroline Kennedy.

Televangelist Rex Humbard, handpicked by Vernon, performs the service.*After the service is opened with a prayer, a group known as J. D. Sumner and the Stamps sings "When It's My Time." Then Jake Hess, an Elvis favorite, performs the gospel song "Known Only to Him."

Comedian Jackie Kahane, a frequent Presley opening act, delivers the eulogy at the request of Colonel Parker. All this is followed

---

* Humbard was a fifty-eight-year-old preacher based in Ohio. His *Cathedral of Tomorrow* TV show was broadcast worldwide. He and Elvis never met.

by more singing and preaching. Kathy Westmoreland, the backup singer whom Elvis once insulted, has forgiven him. She performs a beautiful version of "My Heavenly Father."

The final moment arrives.

The pallbearers carry the copper coffin outside to the waiting white hearse. Mourners follow, stepping into line among seventeen white limousines. Escorted by Memphis motorcycle police, the caravan rolls out of the Graceland gates. A female officer snaps to attention and holds her salute until the coffin passes by. As the procession rolls past the estimated eighty thousand people lining the route to the Forest Hill Cemetery, a woman jumps from the crowd and runs into the street, restrained by authorities a moment before she can throw herself atop the hearse.

At the cemetery, pallbearers carry the casket into the marble mausoleum. The lawn outside is covered in floral arrangements. Later, Vernon will allow the public inside to take flowers as souvenirs.

In just two weeks, grave robbers will attempt to break into the mausoleum and steal the King's body. Vernon will then order his son's casket to be relocated to the gardens in Graceland, where it can be protected behind the mansion gates.

There it remains to this day.

EPILOGUE

Vernon Presley died of a heart attack on June 26, 1979. He is buried at Graceland next to his son and first wife, the singer's mother.

Upon Vernon's death, Priscilla Presley was named executor of the Graceland estate on behalf of Lisa Marie, Elvis's only living heir. The King's will stipulated that Lisa Marie not come into her inheritance until the age of twenty-five.* In an attempt to maintain business as usual, Priscilla petitioned a local probate court to allow **Colonel Tom Parker** to continue representing the estate. At the time, all income received was funneled through Parker, who took his 50 percent commission before passing the remainder along to the Presley bank account.

Then things began to unravel.

Suspicious of Parker, Judge Joseph Evans appointed Memphis attorney Blanchard E. Tual to look into Parker's business dealings with the singer. Tual composed a three-hundred-page document detailing the alleged illegality of the Colonel's affairs. He recommended that Parker no longer receive monies from the estate and that all his commissions be placed on hold. In addition, the lawyer, in order to audit the Colonel's financial gains from Presley, asked for Parker's past income tax returns and that an assessment be made of

---

* Priscilla and Ginger Alden, Elvis's girlfriend at the time of his death, were not granted any money in the will.

all dealings between Parker and RCA Records. Despite the deletion of the audit clause from the original RCA agreement from 1973, the court ordered that an accounting take place.

The judge also found Parker's 50 percent commission to be egregious. Tual estimated that the Colonel had embezzled at least $7 million ($40 million today) from Elvis's estate *since his death*.*

Amazingly, Priscilla and her coexecutors (the National Bank of Commerce in Memphis and Joseph Hanks, Elvis's longtime accountant) petitioned the court to *halt* Tual's inquiry, supporting Colonel Parker. Judge Evans, however, was of the belief that attorney Tual was acting in Lisa Marie's best interest. He ordered the investigation to proceed.

In the midst of all this, Parker suffered a severe fall at RCA's Los Angeles offices while stepping into an elevator. He broke his right shoulder and was unable to get up. The elevator door repeatedly opened and closed as he lay in the entrance. Friends would later say this injury aged the Colonel ten years.

Finally, on the fourth anniversary of Elvis's death, August 16, 1981, the court's decision was read aloud in a Memphis courtroom. Judge Evans ordered Priscilla and the executors to file suit against Tom Parker for illegal business practices and not to enter into any other business arrangements with him or anyone else without the court's permission.

To avoid possible criminal prosecution, Parker claims he is not a US citizen and that, therefore, the court has no jurisdiction over him. As his legal proceedings drag on, hotels in Las Vegas rescind the Colonel's gambling credit lines, banning him from high-stakes games. However, they allow him to play the slot machines. Parker's broken right shoulder still pains him, so he is forced to have friends pull the levers for him.

Graceland becomes insolvent—the estate lacks the money to pay

---

* In 1968, a journalist asked Parker about his outrageous commission: "Is it true that you take fifty percent of everything Elvis earns?" Parker's response: "That's not true at all. He takes fifty percent of everything I earn."

its annual property tax bill. Priscilla Presley opens the building for guided tours, an act that both saves the estate and enriches it to this day.

In 1987, Elvis Presley Enterprises buys the contents of four storage facilities Parker owns. All are filled with the singer's memorabilia. Priscilla directs this $2 million purchase. Parker, desperate for cash, accepts.

The Colonel dies on January 21, 1997, at the age of eighty-seven.

✦ ✦ ✦

Dr. George Nichopoulos endures much the same public humiliation as Tom Parker, but his downfall is more dramatic. The Shelby County, Tennessee, medical examiner eventually lists Elvis Presley's cause of death as coronary arrhythmia, an irregular heartbeat brought on by high blood pressure. Toxicology tests also show the presence of codeine, morphine, barbiturates, and the sedatives Ethinamate and Quaalude. This leads investigators to begin looking closely at the relationship between Presley and narcotics—specifically, at who was providing them. In 1980, Dr. Nick is indicted on fourteen counts of "unlawfully, willfully, and feloniously" prescribing narcotics to the singer.

Nichopoulos is acquitted. However, the investigations into Elvis's death do not end. In 1995, the Tennessee Board of Medical Examiners permanently suspends Dr. Nick's medical license. As part of his (unsuccessful) appeal process, the doctor admits to prescribing thousands of pills to Elvis over the years, saying he did so because he "cared too much" about Presley.*

Dr. Nick later worked as a road manager for singer Jerry Lee Lewis. Nichopoulos died on February 24, 2016, at the age of eighty-eight.

---

* Nichopoulos was acquitted of criminal charges because the jury of six men and six women told reporters he could have prescribed the narcotics to treat valid medical conditions.

✦ ✦ ✦

Today, Elvis Presley's memory is dimming among younger people, yet he is still a powerful presence in the rock world. Despite the loss of his music catalogue, his estate generates more than $25 million annually. Graceland was closed for 2020 due to COVID-19, but the Elvis estate still brought in $23 million. Even in death, the earnings from his estate made Presley the fifth-highest-paid celebrity that year.

The money goes to **Lisa Marie Presley**, who was fifty-four years old in 2022. She resides in San Francisco, has been married and divorced four times, and has borne four children. In 2020, her twenty-seven-year-old son, Ben Keough, committed suicide. He is buried at Graceland near his grandfather.

✦ ✦ ✦

Priscilla Presley lives in Los Angeles. She still oversees the business of Elvis.

PART II

✦

The Walrus

CHAPTER ONE

John Lennon is conflicted.

At twenty-eight years old, the world-famous rock star stands five foot ten, weighing 139 pounds, and wears his brown hair down to his shoulders as he meets with his three bandmates at the Apple building in Central London.

The Beatles are trying to decide whether to record portions of a new album outdoors. Their label, Apple Records, and their astute producer, George Martin, would like the band to play music and vamp for a video simultaneously. That would be easier in an outdoor setting.

But the band is divided. Ringo Starr and George Harrison want to continue recording inside the studio. Paul McCartney, who has emerged as the most creative force in the group, likes the outdoors scenario. So it comes down to John Lennon. After some discussion, Lennon utters a simple comment: "Fuck it. Let's go do it."

And just like that, the Beatles set out for the rooftop of their Apple Corps headquarters, located in a five-story Georgian townhome at 3 Savile Row. The building is in the heart of Mayfair, London's most fashionable district.

✦ ✦ ✦

As the four musicians climb the spiral staircase linking the top floor to the roof, each knows the band is on edge—both literally and figuratively. The "lads," as they are called, are not exactly happy to be together on this cloudy, windy day. Tension has been growing for months—some of it caused by John Lennon's girlfriend, Yoko Ono, who is a constant presence. But the record label needs product, because product is money. And the Beatles *like* money.

The rooftop session today will eventually become part of the *Abbey Road* album, which will sell an astounding thirty-one million copies. But the creative process will not be easy. The plan is to ditch the psychedelic stuff, so successful in the *Sgt. Pepper* album, and return to driving rock 'n' roll. Thus, the song "Get Back," which will lead the playlist today.

As they approach their instruments, the Beatles are joined by African American keyboard player Billy Preston, already set up for the performance. It has been almost three years since the group played before a live audience, during the final show of their 1966 American tour. The crowd at Candlestick Park in San Francisco screamed loudly enough that the band couldn't even hear their own music, a scene so frustrating that George Harrison abruptly quit the band.

"That's it, then," the youngest member of the group stated. "I'm not a Beatle anymore."

But Harrison quickly changed his mind.

Money.

George was not the only one struggling in 1966. John Lennon had gained so much weight from depression that he would later compare himself with Elvis Presley. "It was my fat Elvis period. You see the movie: He—I—is very fat, very insecure, and he's completely lost himself. . . . I was fat and depressed and I was crying out for help."*

Lennon still battles low moods, but he has slimmed down during the time away from live performances. That period saw the Beat-

---

* This quote comes from an interview with *Playboy* magazine.

les record some of their most successful albums: *Sgt. Pepper's Lonely Hearts Club Band*, *Magical Mystery Tour*, *The Beatles* (aka the *White Album*), and *Yellow Submarine*. As with every album since the release of *Please Please Me* in 1963, all the recordings went platinum, meaning sales of one million copies. Many were double and triple platinum, with the *White Album* selling an amazing eight million units.

If anything, the Beatles are more popular than ever. But as John Lennon walks to his spot on the roof with girlfriend Ono in tow, he knows his ongoing attempts to become independent have angered his bandmates. At the heart of this divisiveness is Ono herself, a nearly thirty-five-year-old conceptual artist seven years Lennon's senior.

The two met on November 9, 1966, at a preview for her art show at London's Indica Gallery. At the time, Lennon was married to the former Cynthia Powell. The couple had a three-year-old son, Julian. But soon, John Lennon was taking LSD with Yoko and recording experimental music while tripping. He then moved out of his marital home in Weybridge, just outside London, and began cohabitating with Ono. By November 1968, John and Cynthia Lennon finalized their divorce.

Three days later, Lennon and Ono released their first album together, *Unfinished Music No. 1: Two Virgins*. Wrapped in brown paper like a pornographic magazine, the album cover depicts the couple nude. The music was largely detested by critics and the public alike, with sales falling far short of Beatles standards.

It has now been ten weeks since *Two Virgins* was released, and the album is already completely gone from the charts. In New Jersey, thirty thousand copies of it were confiscated by authorities, who considered the cover obscene. But that's in the past. At twelve thirty today, as the group and Billy Preston begin tuning their instruments, John Lennon is back in the Beatles mind-set.

A bracing wind chaps the faces of the musicians as they settle in to play: John on a hollow-bodied Epiphone Casino guitar, George on a brand-new rosewood Fender Stratocaster, Paul on his trademark Hofner violin bass bearing a white-and-green sticker with the word "Bassman," Ringo on a brand-new kit of Ludwig drums. Preston sits in on a Fender-Rhodes Seventy-Three electric piano.

"The Rooftop Concert" is about to begin.

✦ ✦ ✦

The setting is elaborate. Chimney, small greenhouse, alcoves where amps are stashed to make room for the band. A crew has run cables up from the basement recording studio. A small crowd of Apple employees watches as a team of filmmakers shoots from several angles simultaneously. The band lines up just a few feet back from the rooftop's edge, their amplifiers aimed outward so people on the ground might hear them.

The show is unannounced, both to keep the concert nimble and unscripted and to prevent drawing a mob that would surely stop traffic on Savile Row. Unbeknownst to the crowd now forming below, cameras have been placed surreptitiously at street level to capture their reactions. "We set up a camera in the Apple reception area, behind a window so nobody could see it, and we filmed people coming in," George Harrison will remember.

In the basement, a pair of eight-track recording machines stand ready to capture the performance. The Beatles have been recording downstairs, so they have options as to what to play. "We decided to go through all the stuff we'd been rehearsing and record it. If we got a good take on it, then that would be the recording; if not, we'd use one of the earlier takes that we'd done downstairs in the basement. It was really good fun because it was outdoors, which was unusual for us. We hadn't played outdoors for a long time," Paul McCartney will remember.

In moments, the driving rhythm of "Get Back" echoes across Central London as McCartney leans into his microphone and begins singing. He keeps his brown hair and beard long and wears a dark suit coat and pants and a striped button-down shirt open at the neck. The left-handed bass player writes most of the band's songs with John Lennon. Harrison is often on the outside creatively.

Lennon is not only fond of mocking George's contributions, but he also refuses to play on any song the twenty-five-year-old writes. This greatly displeases Harrison, who has asked that none of his songs be used this afternoon.

"Get Back" is a Lennon-McCartney collaboration. The two have been at odds lately, both intimating they might leave the band. McCartney is on a great creative run and encourages the Beatles to record more frequently than others might like, which sometimes comes across as pushy.

During the song, after singing the words "Get back home, Loretta," McCartney cedes center stage to Lennon. Wearing Yoko's fur coat to ward off the chill, he launches into a stirring guitar solo, the January wind blowing his hair across his face. Ringo Starr, also wearing a borrowed coat—this one a bright red knee-length number belonging to wife Maureen—keeps time. Harrison, in bright green pants and a dark fur coat of his own, stands to Lennon's left. He normally plays lead guitar but is on rhythm now.

"We've had a request from Martin and Luther," John quips after the first take of "Get Back," a nostalgic reminder to his three bandmates of their days playing in German rock clubs.

Then comes the unexpected. Crowds begin to form on adjacent rooftop buildings, giving the band an audience they can actually see. This could be a problem. McCartney was the first to get excited about the prospect of filming outside, preferring not to use a venue like the Royal Albert Hall, just a few miles down the street. After so many years off the road, Starr and Harrison have stage fright. Lennon does, too, though he will not admit it. He had to be cajoled into performing by McCartney, who pleaded that doing a live show was vital to their maintaining a connection with Beatles fans.

"There was a plan to play live somewhere," Ringo will remember of the days leading up to the session. "We were wondering where we could go—oh, the Palladium or the Sahara. But we would have had to take all the stuff, so we decided let's get up on the roof. We had Mal [Evans, Beatles road manager] and Neil [Aspinall, head of Apple

Corps] set the equipment up on the roof, and we did those tracks. I remember it was cold and windy and damp, but all the people looking out from offices were really enjoying it."

Not everyone. Savile Row was a very staid street, full of banking concerns and the shops of bespoke tailors. Some businesses were upset at the sounds coming from the roof. Despite the weather, people in nearby buildings open their windows to hear the Beatles play live. The set list continues: two more takes of "Get Back" and then "Don't Let Me Down," "God Save the Queen," and "Danny Boy."

The pedestrians below cannot see the band, but they stand in the street gawking upward.

"There were a lot of city gents looking up: 'What's that noise?'" Paul McCartney will recall.

"There were people hanging off balconies and out of every office window all around. The police were knocking on the door," recording engineer Dave Harris remembered. "We really wanted to stop the traffic, we wanted to blast out the entire West End."

Yoko Ono and Maureen Starkey, Ringo's wife, are part of the small rooftop audience. Unlike the reserved Ono, the boisterous Maureen cheers and applauds loudly for each song. Many Apple staffers will not be told about the performance and will miss it completely. Others who know it is taking place will choose to leave the office, eating lunch elsewhere.

As the Beatles play, all four recognize that the band is as sharp as ever, a group of musicians totally in synch. Lennon and McCartney even exchange a look now and then, just a glance to show they know how tight the group sounds, perhaps even better than in the old days. For the time being, all thoughts of breaking up are set aside.

After forty-two minutes, it is done. The Beatles are launching into a second take of "Don't Let Me Down" when police step onto the roof. When the band's amps are turned off, an angry George switches his back on and keeps playing. Lennon's amp is also turned back on by the sound engineer, allowing the Beatles to finish the song.

"I always feel let down about the police," Ringo will recall. "Someone in the neighborhood called the police, and when they came up, I was playing away, and I thought, Oh great! I hope they drag me off. I wanted the cops to drag me off—Get off those drums!—because we were being filmed and it would have looked really great, kicking the cymbals and everything. Well, they didn't, of course; they just came bumbling in: You've got to turn that sound down. It could have been fabulous."

McCartney also hopes they'll get arrested. "We kept going to the bitter end and, as I say, it was quite enjoyable. I had my little Hofner bass—very light, very enjoyable to play. In the end the policeman, Number 503 of the Greater Westminster Council, made his way round the back: 'You have to stop!'"

When it is done, the bass player speaks into his microphone, saying "Thanks, Mo" to Ringo's wife for her enthusiastic cheering. For McCartney's part, he makes no reference to Yoko Ono, standing nearby, whom he is known to consider a cancerous presence.

It is John Lennon who ends the Rooftop Concert with a jest: "I'd like to say thank you on behalf of the group and ourselves," he says, leaning into the microphone. "And I hope we've passed the audition."

The remark elicits laughter from everyone except Yoko. Throughout the recording session, she shows no emotion at all. But every time John Lennon moves, Ono does, too, ensuring she is just a few feet away from her paramour at all times.

The band notices. They understand there is now a shadow over the Beatles.

A dark shadow.

CHAPTER TWO

JULY 1, 1969

TONGUE, SCOTLAND

AFTERNOON

John Lennon thinks he is safe. He is not.

The musician drives north on a two-lane country road along the Scottish coastline in his white Austin Maxi. The day is gray and wet. Yoko Ono sits to his left, in the passenger seat. The whitecapped waters of Loch Eriboll offer a stunning scenic vista to his right. In the cramped backseat sits Lennon's six-year-old son, Julian, along with Kyoko Cox, age five. Kyoko is Ono's daughter from her first marriage.

Lennon is not a good driver. He got his license four years ago, at the age of twenty-five, but he has barely been behind the wheel since. His eyesight is poor, and he is often so caught up in the simple act of staying in his lane that he fails to notice other drivers. And while the rest of the Beatles are back in London writing songs for the new album (which will eventually be called *Abbey Road*), Lennon and Ono are on a driving holiday.

One that is about to end badly.

✦ ✦ ✦

It has been a good year so far for the Beatles, with "Get Back" going to No. 1 on the charts. Another single, "The Ballad of John and

Yoko," released a month later, makes the Top 10—although many radio stations refuse to play it because of some of its lyrics.*

For John and Yoko, it has been a year of whirlwind travel and media attention. They were wed on March 20, John for the second time and Yoko for the third, just eight days after Paul McCartney married American photographer Linda Eastman.†

John and Yoko first wanted their nuptials to take place on an English Channel ferry, but the captain refused. They then attempted to wed in Paris, but French authorities also said no, claiming the couple needed to cohabit in France. The pair grew frustrated and finally settled on Gibraltar, a British protectorate at the bottom of the Iberian Peninsula. John and Yoko chartered a jet and flew in for their ceremony. Within one hour of saying "I do," the couple was flying back to honeymoon in Paris. But Gibraltar was not to be slighted by the quick exit: the British sovereignty quickly issuing a postage stamp in honor of their nuptials.

After five days in Paris at the Hotel Plaza Athénée, the newlyweds were chauffeured to Amsterdam. There they spent a week staging a "Bed-in for Peace." Both wore white as they conducted interviews and entertained members of the media. Signs of "Hair Peace" on their hotel room windows declared Lennon's fondness for puns.‡

Then it was on to Vienna, Austria, leaving their children with former spouses during the entirety of their getaway. Lennon and Ono are together at all times, even accompanying each other to the bathroom.

A second Bed-in was scheduled for May in New York City, but American officials refused to allow Lennon into the country because

---

* The song has Lennon singing, "They're gonna crucify me." He had earlier taken extreme criticism for stating that the Beatles were "more popular than Jesus."

† McCartney did not invite the other three Beatles to the ceremony, which was held at the Old Marylebone Town Hall in London. The wedding was meant to be a secret, but word leaked, and hundreds of fans lined up outside to get a look at the newlyweds.

‡ Lennon and Ono staged their press extravaganza in the Amsterdam Hilton hotel.

of a 1968 conviction in Great Britain for marijuana possession. Instead, the couple, and the media circus that follows them, went off to the Sheraton hotel in the Bahamas. But after one day in the tropical heat, the contingent decamped for Montreal, Canada, renting four rooms at the Queen Elizabeth Hotel.

That city was chosen for its close proximity to the New York media. Lennon sprinkled flower petals around the bedroom during their raucous eight days in Montreal. The couple also recorded a new song, called "Give Peace a Chance," while remaining in bed. Using four microphones and a simple four-track Ampex recorder, Lennon was joined by activist psychologist Timothy Leary, Beat poet Allen Ginsberg, civil rights leader and comedian Dick Gregory, comedian Tommy Smothers, and a band of Hare Krishna monks.

"Sing along," he commanded.

When asked by a reporter why he chose a Bed-in rather than talking to "the power brokers," Lennon's tone grew sharp.

"Talk about what? It doesn't happen like that. In the U.S., the government is too busy talking about how to keep me out. If I'm a joke, as they say, and not important, why don't they just let me in?"[*]

In May 1969, the Beatles decided to take two months off, and John and Yoko hit the road once again. This time with family. John normally drives a white Rolls-Royce, but he chose a customized Austin Mini Cooper for the journey north from London. When that proved too cramped, he procured the larger and more practical Leyland Austin Maxi. But instead of telegraphing their movements to the press, as they had been doing, Lennon now wants solitude. As a boy between the ages of nine and fourteen, he enjoyed family hol-

---

[*] During their frenetic travels, Lennon and Ono find time to return to London to look in on how the album is progressing. Actual recording began on February 22 and took place at Trident Studios, then at EMI on Abbey Road. The Beatles then took a break until April, when they recorded sporadically before choosing to take another pause, from May 6 to July 1. Despite Lennon's frequent absenteeism, *Abbey Road* is completed on August 20, 1969. Paul McCartney, Ringo Starr, and George Harrison will later reflect positively on the making of the album. Lennon will be quoted as disliking the record, in particular McCartney's songs, which he calls "[music] for grannies to dig."

idays in the Highlands. "John never forgot those times at Durness. They were among his happiest memories. He loved the wilderness," cousin Stanley Parkes will remember. "The croft [land] belonged to my stepfather, Robert Sutherland, and John just loved the wildness and the openness of the place."*

Now, fifteen years since his youthful trip, John Lennon is back. He has custody of Julian this week, but he has not told the boy's mother of this Scottish adventure, believing she would say no. Yoko's former husband is equally concerned about his ex's parenting skills and will grow so distressed that, two years later, he will abduct their daughter, Kyoko, preventing Yoko from seeing her for almost a decade.†

The four settle into a cottage in Durness. The windswept location is remote and private. Lennon visits relatives and rekindles old relationships. When he and Ono stop in a small tearoom, the world-famous couple is left unbothered by the locals.

Shortly after pulling away from the tearoom in their car, Lennon is startled by the sight of someone driving on the wrong side of the road, aiming right for him and his family.

The singer yanks hard on the wheel, desperate to avoid a crash.

He succeeds.

Almost.

Lennon swerves, missing the approaching car, but the Austin Maxi leaves the road, diving nose-first into a roadside ditch. The front grille caves in, the hood is bent, and so is the front axle. Everyone inside the car is injured. John and Yoko bleed profusely. Ambulances transport the four occupants to Lawson Memorial Hospital, an hour

---

* Those childhood memories of summers in Scotland will form the basis for Lennon's 1965 song "In My Life."

† Ono and second husband Tony Cox—her first spouse was Japanese composer Toshi Ichiyanagi—divorced on February 2, 1969. Ono received full custody of Kyoko. When Cox disappeared with the then seven-year-old, John and Yoko hired private detectives, but they came up empty.

away, in Golspie. The small rural facility is capably staffed on this Tuesday.

John Lennon receives seventeen stitches to his face. Yoko receives fourteen in her forehead. Kyoko needs four. The three stay in the hospital five days to heal. As for Julian, he is treated for shock but is considered well enough to be discharged to the care of John's aunt "Mater," as his mother's eldest sister, Elizabeth Jane, is called. When an irate Cynthia Lennon arrives from London to pick up their son, she detours to the hospital to upbraid her ex-husband. But John refuses to see her.

On July 4, as John and Yoko rest in narrow hospital beds, Apple Records releases "Give Peace a Chance," which shoots up the charts. Lennon will later joke about the accident, telling reporters, "If you're going to have a car crash, try to arrange for it to happen in the Highlands. The hospital there was just great." Still, their injuries are traumatizing. Yoko's back is horribly wrenched, and she is in a great deal of pain—a situation made worse by the fact that she is pregnant.*

✦ ✦ ✦

Eight days after the crash, John and Yoko are back in London. Dressed in matching black outfits, they enter the studio as the other Beatles work on the new album. "I'm okay," John assures his bandmates. Yet he does not pick up a guitar.

Instead, he calls Harrods department store and orders a double bed to be delivered to the studio. He does not inform the band, so when the delivery truck arrives, the lads think it contains a new piano. When the bed appears, the group is "gobsmacked," in the words of sound engineer Geoff Emerick.

So it is that, while the band writes and records songs, the accoutrements of recording (microphones, music stands, amps) all around them, a double bed covered in a yellow blanket and fluffy white pil-

---

* Yoko Ono will miscarry on October 13, 1969. She previously miscarried another Lennon child, in November 1968. Lennon was at her bedside on both occasions.

lows becomes Yoko Ono's temporary resting place. She wears night-gowns and a tiara that covers her stitches. The room is tight. Studio Two at EMI's Abbey Road facilities is 2,200 square feet, but the many instruments, including several pianos, clog the space. So the big bed squeezes the musicians into an even tighter spot.

Ringo Starr is confused. "I remember, she was in bed in the studio when we got to work, and it was weird. I asked John, 'What the hell is going on?' And he said, 'You know when you go home to Maureen, she'll say, "What did you do today?" And you'll say, "Well, I drummed." John said, 'We want to be there with whatever we're both doing.'"

"My memory is not so much that it was curious that she was convalescing in a bed in the corner of the studio, but that she had her entourage," sound engineer John Kurlander will recall.

On this day, Yoko kicks off her shoes and orders food. She takes pictures of the band recording while lying on her back, her feet very often in the frame. She tells friends to come visit, allowing for a steady flow of traffic in and out of the small studio as the band attempts to work. Sometimes, John joins Yoko in a romantic embrace, disregarding everyone else in the room.

Alan Parsons, one of the sound technicians, will remember that "it was a strange atmosphere: Yoko in the bed in the studio, sending someone out to run errands and pick up food . . . and she and John would occasionally snuggle in there. I don't think there was any serious hanky-panky going on, but they would be side by side, like they would be in a hotel room. . . . It wasn't our place to comment."

Paul McCartney also feels powerless. "We just had to work around her—and walk around her," he will remember later. "It was the madness of the times: you just had to put up with it. What could you do? You couldn't say, 'Get that bed out of here.' She was John's girl."

George Harrison is not so restrained. The Beatles once had a rule that the recording studio was the group's sanctum sanctorum, a special place where only the band was allowed. No girlfriends, no children, all work. Brian Epstein, their manager, who died of an accidental drug overdose in 1967, was rarely allowed inside.

This all changed during the recording of the *White Album*. Yoko Ono was a constant presence—at John's side, sitting on the floor at his feet, speaking to him in a low voice. On one occasion, she raised her voice to comment on a Lennon vocal. This set off McCartney: "Fuck me! Did somebody speak? Who the fuck was that? Did you say something, George? Your lips didn't move."

In 2016, McCartney will tell *Rolling Stone*, "We weren't sexist, but girls didn't come to the studio—they tended to leave us to it. When John got with Yoko, she wasn't in the control room or to the side," adds McCartney, who found it particularly irritating that Yoko refused to call the band by its full name, "*the* Beatles"—instead saying just "Beatles," despite his many attempts to correct her.

"It was in the middle of the four of us."

Now, as the Beatles continue recording their new album, Ono becomes more entrenched within the room. She even has a drug dealer deliver narcotics to her. Unbeknownst to the public, Lennon and Ono at the time are habitual heroin users.

"The two of them were on heroin," Paul McCartney will recall, "and this was a fairly big shocker for us, because we all thought we were far-out boys, but we kind of understood that we'd never get quite that far out."*

It is all too much. Assistant engineer Emerick witnesses a moment when Harrison has finally had enough of Yoko. "I noticed that something down in the studio had caught George Harrison's attention. After a moment or two, he began staring bug-eyed out the control room window. . . . Yoko had gotten out of bed and was slowly padding across the studio floor, finally coming to a stop at Harrison's

---

* Yoko's dealer during the making of *Abbey Road* is an American actor named Dan Richter. "It felt weird to be sitting on the bed talking to Yoko while the Beatles were working across the studio," Richter will recall of his drug deliveries. "I couldn't help thinking that those guys were making rock 'n' roll history, while I was sitting on this bed in the middle of the Abbey Road studio, handing Yoko a small white packet."

cabinet, which had a packet of McVitie's Digestive Biscuits on top. Idly, she began opening the packet and delicately removed a single biscuit. Just as the morsel reached her mouth, Harrison could contain himself no longer. 'That bitch!' he screamed." Everyone in the room hears it. Including Yoko, who simply goes back to her bed.

Despite the bizarre setting, John is unperturbed. In fact, he takes the situation to new heights. "Can we put a microphone up over here, so we can hear her [Yoko] on the headphones," he asks the engineers, who immediately comply.

For the three other Beatles, the craziness is growing intolerable.

A final confrontation is coming.

CHAPTER THREE

The end is near for the Beatles.

A London policeman stops traffic as photographer Iain Macmillan stands on a stepladder aiming his lens at the zebra-striped pedestrian crossing of Abbey Road. A white VW Beetle, not an intentional prop, is parked along one curb. Opposite, an American salesman named Paul Cole wanders into the frame without knowing he is destined to be immortalized on a Beatles album cover.

Macmillan has just fifteen minutes. The four lads cross back and forth three times. John leads the way. Paul is barefoot—he wore sandals to the studio today and took them off for the shoot. This street will give the album its name, chosen over the initial "Everest" because nobody in the band wanted to fly to the Himalayas for a photo session.

Once upon a time, the Beatles were so tight that such a task would have been natural. But as the *Abbey Road* recording sessions near their end, tension is high; discord dominates. Ringo Starr and George Harrison have both, at separate times, quit the band in a rage, only to return. John Lennon has already told the group that he wants Blind Faith's Eric Clapton to replace Harrison, should George bolt again. Lennon himself remains part of the band, but he is a man apart, refusing to play on songs he finds annoying, such as McCartney's "Maxwell's Silver Hammer" and Harrison's "I, Me, Mine."

Longtime Beatles producer George Martin understands the problem: "They'd been incarcerated with each other for nearly a decade. I was surprised that they had lasted as long as they did."

Martin agreed to produce *Abbey Road* only after Lennon assured him he would stop trying to take control. But their dispute is not just about recording, and it's not just about Yoko Ono's annoying presence in the studio. The greatest issue is John Lennon's heroin use. Even as the singer continues to downplay the effects of his habit, his bouts of rage and instability have the band on edge. It's difficult to tell when Lennon's heroin use began—perhaps one year ago but maybe as far back as 1967. The other Beatles are also bothered by Lennon's drug-infused lyrics. "Happiness Is a Warm Gun," from 1968's *White Album*, features the line "I need a fix 'cause I'm going down." And in "Everybody's Got Something to Hide Except Me and My Monkey," from the same record, Lennon alludes to the joys of dope: "The deeper you go, the higher you fly."

Paul McCartney, in particular, is furious with his writing partner. "He was getting into harder drugs than we'd been into and so his songs were taking on more references to heroin. Until that point we had made rather mild, oblique references to pot or LSD. But now John started talking about fixes and monkeys and it was harder terminology which the rest of us weren't into. We were disappointed that he was getting into heroin because we didn't really know how we could help him."

Thus, as the Beatles shoot one of the most famous album covers of all time, the band is in turmoil. Soon, Lennon will realize that he needs to end his heroin use—but that takes strong willpower.

And then there's Yoko, who is also using heroin.

She is his only ally. Lennon is a man without close friends, and now even his bandmates don't like him. Also, he blames the Beatles and their rejection of his new wife as the excuse for his taking the strongly addictive opiate.

"Heroin. It just was not too much fun. I never injected it or any-thing," he will tell *Rolling Stone* magazine one year from now. "We sniffed a little when we were in real pain. I mean we just couldn't—people were giving us such a hard time. And I've had so much shit thrown at me and especially at Yoko. People like Peter Brown in our office, he comes down and shakes my hand and doesn't even say hello to her. Now that's going on all the time. And we get in so much pain that we have to do something about it. And that's what happened to us. We took H because of what the Beatles and their pals were doing to us."

✦ ✦ ✦

Fast-forward to a month after the recording sessions for *Abbey Road* wrapped.

John Lennon is on rhythm guitar, Klaus Voormann on bass, Alan White on drums, and Eric Clapton plays lead guitar. It is September 13, 1969, and Lennon and his new bandmates are performing a live show in Toronto. The most prominent song performed by Lennon's new "Plastic Ono Band" is about his drug use. The singer will later joke that "Cold Turkey" is the story of when he got violently ill after eating Christmas leftovers. But the song is really about his quitting opioids. "I was just writing the experience I'd had of withdrawing from heroin," he will admit one decade later. "To some it was a rock 'n' roll version of *The Man with the Golden Arm* because [the movie] showed Frank Sinatra suffering from drug withdrawal."

The Toronto Rock and Roll Revival is the first time Lennon's new band performs together. Yoko, who still considers herself a conceptual performer, is at first nowhere to be seen—a temporary situation.

Three weeks ago, Lennon ordered Yoko to strap him to a chair for the day and a half needed to detox. He refused to go to a treat-ment center, knowing that if he did, the public would learn of his addiction. Even as she also went into withdrawal, Yoko oversaw the process, which included Lennon throwing up on himself. Due to the graphic nature of the drug terminology, the other Beatles rejected

"Cold Turkey" for the *Abbey Road* album, leading Lennon to release it himself.

> Praying to someone
> Free me again, I'll be a good boy
> Please make me well
> I promise you anything
> Out of this hell.

Suddenly, Yoko Ono emerges from a bag on the Toronto stage, steps up to the microphone, and begins making turkey noises.

The truth is, Lennon has not kicked his heroin habit. Just days after trying to quit, he played "Cold Turkey" for Bob Dylan, triggering a personal relapse. Lennon will actually continue to use hard drugs for many years. That situation might be responsible for his ongoing callous behavior. He is often cruel to his son, Julian, once screaming "I hate your fucking laugh" when the child giggles in his presence.

The boy will later label his father a "hypocrite" for the way he treats Julian's mother, Cynthia. "Dad could talk about peace and love out loud to the world, but he could never show it to the people who supposedly meant the most to him: his wife and son. How can you talk about peace and love and have a family in bits and pieces—no communication, adultery, divorce? You can't do it, not if you're being true and honest with yourself."

Yet there is another side to John Lennon that Julian will long remember: "Dad made me laugh a lot. He was a real comedian. He had a real sarcastic sense of humor, he could really make a fool out of people. I have to watch it a little bit, because I caught that habit from him. I was really fond of him. He was my idol."[*]

✦ ✦ ✦

It is Wednesday, August 20, 1969, and the temperature in London is a humid eighty-four degrees. This is the last day the Beatles will ever

---

[*] Julian made these remarks to the *Telegraph* in May 1998.

be in the recording studio together. The group first began making records in 1962, with "Love Me Do." Much has changed in the world since then, but the Beatles have been a musical constant throughout.

Today's first session takes place in EMI's smaller Studio Three, where the band puts the finishing touches on John's "I Want You (She's So Heavy)," which the group previously recorded back on February 22 and 23. The song is supposed to play at the end of *Abbey Road*'s first side.

The second session goes well into the night, lasting from dinner until one fifteen in the morning. The action shifts to the control room of Studio Two, where the band works to assemble the song order. There is still editing and rerecording to do, but that will be done individually over the next five days.

Ringo's "Octopus's Garden" and McCartney's "Oh! Darling" are reversed in the order. "I Want You (She's So Heavy)" remains the last song on side one. Given her presence in the studio, the song is an homage to Yoko. It is almost eight minutes long, yet the band can't find a way to end it. Lennon argues against a fade-out, feeling the song will lose its impact. Instead, he suggests that producer George Martin abruptly stop the tape at the 7:47 mark.

This sudden ending sounds very much like someone in the studio simply pulling the plug.

Fittingly, the final song on side two of *Abbey Road* is "The End."*

✦ ✦ ✦

And so, it is done. The exhausted Beatles head out into the night, going their separate ways. The goodbyes are formal and brief. It's almost like all the lads know it is over.

The seeds of a Beatles breakup have clearly been sown. "The thing

---

* Side one: "Come Together," "Something," "Maxwell's Silver Hammer," "Oh! Darling," "Octopus's Garden," "I Want You (She's So Heavy)"; side two: "Here Comes the Sun," "Because," "Medley ('You Never Give Me Your Money,' 'Sun King,' 'Mean Mr. Mustard,' 'Polythene Pam,' '"She Came in Through the Bathroom Window,' 'Golden Slumbers,' 'Carry That Weight,' 'The End')," "Her Majesty" (hidden track).

is, so much of what they held to be truth was crap," Paul McCartney will later remember, speaking of John and Yoko as one. "'War is over,' well, no, it isn't."

McCartney will add, "I had been able to accept Yoko in the studio sitting on a blanket in front of my amp. I worked hard to come to terms with that, but . . . John turned nasty. I don't really understand why. Maybe because we grew up in Liverpool where it was always good to get in the first punch in the fight."

Yet the fight will go on. There is more drama to come.

CHAPTER FOUR

Paul McCartney is breaking up the Beatles.

Or so it seems. The singer sends out a simple press release to announce his first solo album, *McCartney*. Written in the form of a question-and-answer session with himself, the statement shocks the world:

> Q: Did you miss the Beatles?
> A: No.
> Q: Are you planning a new album or single with the Beatles?
> A: No.
> Q: Do you foresee a time when Lennon-McCartney becomes an
>   active songwriting partnership again?
> A: No.

The news rockets around the globe.

"Paul: I Quit," screams one London headline.

"Paul McCartney announced today that he's split from the Beatles," writes the Associated Press, accidentally mistaking the bass player's role in the band: "Paul, 27-year-old song writer, lead guitarist and singer, blamed the break on 'personal differences, business differences, musical differences—but most of all because I have a better time with my family.'"

Fan reaction is mixed. Some are shocked; others will say they've seen it coming for some time. Many are appeased by the news of forthcoming solo albums from each band member.

But because it is McCartney who formally announces his departure first, he takes the blame for pulling the plug on the Beatles.

The truth, however, is far more complex.

✦ ✦ ✦

August 27, 1967. Thirty-two-year-old Brian Epstein lies in his London apartment, dead from an overdose of sleeping pills and alcohol. Epstein was the Beatles manager, a former Liverpool record store owner who transformed the band from an undisciplined group who often ate and drank onstage into a global sensation. He convinced the lads to dress in suits while performing and to take a bow after each number. More important, Epstein engineered the band's first recording contract, in 1962, arranging for them to work with top producer George Martin.

Epstein effectively ran the Beatles, his cut being up to 25 percent of their earnings. He was a British version of Colonel Tom Parker, overseeing every aspect of their business affairs while living with his own personal gambling problems. Epstein was also glue for the four very disparate individuals, keeping the Beatles disciplined and focused on making great music.

On the morning Epstein is discovered dead in his pajamas by his butler, the Beatles are at a pivotal moment in their careers. They have quit touring for good and have just finished recording their most creatively challenging album to date, the psychedelic *Sgt. Pepper's Lonely Hearts Club Band*, with producer Martin. John Lennon is spending more time with Yoko Ono and coming out of a long bout with depression. George Harrison is pursuing a growing fascination with Indian music. Ringo Starr is unsure whether he wants to remain with the band. And Paul McCartney is enchanted with Linda Eastman, a photographer whom he met at a London nightclub.

Because of his death, the world will never know if Brian Epstein could have continued to push the Beatles in a disciplined financial direction. His forte was business acumen. The band is incredibly creative with their music and just as imaginative with the way they spend money. However, none of them is disciplined. No Beatle has the required business know-how for handling large sums of money. Since Epstein transformed them from a rough group of Liverpool youths into history's biggest musical recording act, the band members have gotten into the habit of buying whatever they want whenever they want. In the world of show business—with the emphasis on *business*—the Beatles rely on Epstein to advise them in an honest fashion.

Without Epstein, the lads are lost. "I knew that we were in trouble [after Epstein died]," John will later recall. "I didn't really have any misconceptions about our ability to do anything other than play music. I was scared. I thought, 'We've fucking had it.'"

✦ ✦ ✦

"Your personal finances are in a mess."

The note to the Beatles is simple and direct, left in the offices of Apple Records by an unnamed accountant who has quit in frustration. In May 1968, nine months after Brian Epstein's death, the band formed a parent company called Apple Corps. In making the announcement, John Lennon described the venture as "a business concerning records, films and electronics. We want to set up a system whereby people who just want to make a film about anything don't have to go on their knees in somebody's office. Probably yours."

And while the company will go on to put out music by the Beatles and other artists, such as James Taylor, its Savile Row headquarters soon become an artists' playpen. One former staffer will remember that his main job was procuring marijuana for the lads. The company hired accountants and other financial professionals to manage the money, but lack of a guiding force like Epstein slowly leads the company, and each Beatle, toward financial insolvency.

This does not go unnoticed in the music world. Would-be managers seek an audience with the band, eager to replace Brian Epstein. Two leading candidates emerge: American businessman Allen Klein, a thirty-six-year-old New Jersey native with a reputation for making his clients money but also, in McCartney's words, for being "dodgy."

The second potential business manager is Lee Eastman, an American *and* Paul McCartney's new father-in-law upon his marriage to Linda in 1969.

In hindsight, neither will seem the perfect choice.

More than anything else, the clash between these two men will break up the Beatles.

Klein is more aggressive, a burly man with swagger. He educates himself on the history of the Beatles and then commiserates with John and Yoko, believing them to be the band's power couple. Lennon is taken with Klein and convinces George Harrison and Ringo Starr to align with him.

When it comes to situations such as this, the Beatles have long operated by a simple majority rule. But Paul McCartney dissents. Fueled by a note from fellow rocker Mick Jagger, who once had business dealings with Klein, McCartney argues that Lee Eastman is the better choice.*He does not mention the growing influence his new bride has on his thinking. In fact, Linda is no less a force than Yoko Ono. She just has a subtler method of getting her way. Her loyalty to Paul corresponds with Yoko's fealty to John. So there are really six Beatles now. John, George, and Ringo already feel Paul has

---

* Allen Klein managed the Rolling Stones from 1965 to 1970. Prior to the Beatles signing with Klein, Stones lead singer Mick Jagger advised Paul McCartney, "Don't go near him." The Stones would go on to successfully sue Klein for nonpayment of royalties and for attempting to take control of their music catalogue. One example is their $1.25 million advance from Decca Records in 1965, which was deposited into the accounts of a company owned by Klein. Unbeknownst to the Rolling Stones, Klein's contract stated that he did not need to release the money to the band until 1985.

too much power. Giving McCartney's father-in-law financial control would weigh matters further in his favor.

Paul McCartney loses: the other Beatles are suspicious of Eastman. Ringo will remember, "We met with Allen Klein and we were convinced by him. Well, I was convinced by him, and John too. My impression of him when I first met him was: brash—'I'll get it done, lads.' Lots of enthusiasm. A good guy, with a pleasant attitude about himself in a really gross New York way. So the decision was him or him—and I picked him. That was two of us—and George did the same."

George will add, "Because we were all from Liverpool, we favored people who were street people. Lee Eastman was more of a class-conscious type of person. As John was going with Klein, it was much easier if we went with him too."

The meeting with Klein occurred on May 9, 1969, just before the two-month hiatus in the middle of recording *Abbey Road*. Soon after, McCartney also stopped visiting Apple Records headquarters, no longer feeling welcome inside the company he helped create.

When the time comes for each Beatle to sign Klein's management contract, a furious McCartney refuses to place his signature on the document. Soon after, firmly established as the band's manager, and no longer needing to curry favor with Paul, Allen Klein stops taking the singer's phone calls.

✦ ✦ ✦

At first Klein does well, renegotiating a new contract between the Beatles and EMI Records. *Abbey Road* has not yet been released, but Klein succeeds in getting a higher royalty rate, raising the band's income from each album from 17.5 percent to 25 percent. Under the terms of the deal, the Beatles would record two new albums every year until 1976.

That same month—the precise date is unknown, but the contract is backdated to May 8—the group gathers in a small office at Apple Records to sign the paperwork. George Harrison, off to Cheshire to visit his mother, is not there, but he will soon sign. Ringo, John, and Paul are present, and Yoko, of course. She wears all black. In a photo taken to document the moment, Yoko clings to a denim-clad Lennon. Ringo wears a leather jacket and a white scarf. McCartney, looking fatigued, with dark circles under his eyes, is dressed in his usual waistcoat and open-collared shirt. Standing in the middle of the group in a black turtleneck, Elvis Presley pompadour, and black sideburns is a smiling Klein.

Despite the divisive past few months, and encouraged by the soon-to-be-released *Abbey Road*, Paul McCartney does a turnaround. He is suddenly invigorated, sensing a rebirth in the band.

As the new contract is being signed, Paul begins lobbying for a series of live performances. "I think we should go back to little gigs—I really think we're a great little band. We should find our basic roots, and then who knows what will happen? We may want to fold after that, or we may really think we've still got it," he tells the room.

"I think you're daft," John responds.

Just like that, the tension felt during the *Abbey Road* sessions returns. Paul McCartney has an immediate sense of foreboding about the group's future. "I must admit we'd known it was coming at some point because of his intense involvement with Yoko. John needed to give space to his and Yoko's thing. Someone like John would want to end the Beatles period and start the Yoko period; and he wouldn't like either to interfere with the other."

Lennon's memory of what happens next differs from that of others in the room. "We were discussing something in the office with Paul and [he] was saying to do something, and I kept saying, 'No, no, no' to everything he said. So it came to a point that I had to say something.

"So I said, 'The group's over, I'm leaving.'"

Others will remember Lennon stating, "I wasn't going to tell you, but I'm breaking the group up. It feels good. It feels like a divorce."

But on Allen Klein's demand, John Lennon does not announce his decision to the public. Klein feels that such a proclamation will have a negative effect on the new deal with EMI and on the sales of *Abbey Road*.

So John stays silent, even as the other Beatles personally grapple with the end of an era.

"If that had happened in 1965, or 1967 even, it would have been a mighty shock," Ringo Starr will remember. "Now it was just 'Let's get the divorce over with,' really. And John was always the most forward when it came to nailing anything."

So it is that John Lennon hammers the final nail into the Beatles' proverbial coffin.

Not even Yoko was forewarned.

✦ ✦ ✦

Their journeys to stardom were arduous.

Born Richard Starkey, Ringo Starr was abandoned by his father at the age of three. His mother fussed over her only child, working low-paying jobs to make ends meet. Richard almost died at the age of six, falling into a coma after a bout of peritonitis and spending a year in the hospital. He fell behind in his schooling during this time, and by the age of twelve, he was considered functionally illiterate. Along the way, he contracted tuberculosis and was again confined. However, he used that time learning to drum.

As a teenager, he joined a band called Rory Storm and the Hurricanes. But after sitting in for Beatles drummer Pete Best on several occasions, Richard Starkey was formally invited to replace Best. The decision was not easy, as the Hurricanes were popular in Liverpool. But, having changed his name to Ringo Starr, the drummer chose the Beatles at a most opportune time. It was 1962, and Beatlemania would hit the next year. "We wanted to be the top of Liverpool, maybe top of England. Then Denmark. Then France. And we did the whole of Europe. America was beyond our wildest dreams," Starr later told the *Times* of London.

Ringo was an outsider from the start, taking years to earn the trust of his bandmates. John Lennon famously disparaged Ringo's drumming, stating that not only was Starr not the best drummer in the *world*, but he wasn't even the best drummer in the *band*.

Lennon's decision to break up the Beatles hit Ringo Starr hard. He began drinking heavily, spending almost twenty years in and out of inebriation. His first marriage, to Mary "Maureen" Cox, fell apart. But the drummer eventually found his way, marrying former Bond girl Barbara Bach and building a solid solo career. On the day that John Lennon is shot dead, it will be Ringo Starr who immediately gets on a plane to New York to console Yoko Ono.

✦ ✦ ✦

George Harrison *is* ready for the Beatles to break up.

His departure from the studio early in the "Get Back" recordings, with Lennon's subsequent threat to replace him with Eric Clapton, underscored years of growing dissent. "It would be nice if any of us could do separate things as well. That way, it also preserves the Beatle bit of it more," he tells Lennon. Of his short-lived departure, he adds, "I'm just gonna do me for a bit."

Now George Harrison sees John's "divorce" as a chance to continue his own creative growth, singing and recording the songs he writes. In 1968, Harrison releases the soundtrack to a film titled *Wonderwall Music*, the first album released by the Apple Records label. He then continues with a solo album, *Electronic Sound*, released in 1969.*

✦ ✦ ✦

John Lennon's decision to break up the Beatles devastates Paul McCartney. "John's in love with Yoko, and he's no longer in love with the other three of us," he will tell London's *Evening Standard* in April 1970—months after the breakup occurs. In that span, McCartney loses his way. Without the Beatles—of whom he has been a

---

* These albums did not do well with critics or consumers. *Electronic Sound* peaked at No. 191 on the *Billboard* charts.

part since age fifteen, when they were the Quarrymen—he becomes uncertain about his future. Like Ringo Starr, he takes to drink. At first, it is whiskey in the evening, as he spends time with Linda; her daughter Heather, from a previous marriage; and their infant, Mary.

McCartney continues to decline. He stays drunk most of the time, not shaving or washing, unable to shake a crippling depression. "Here I am," Linda tells a friend, "married to a drunk who won't take a bath."

Done in by anxiety, McCartney can't sleep at night. Each day, he chain-smokes unfiltered Senior Service cigarettes and repeatedly re-fills his glass, not picking up his bass or writing music. He rarely leaves his bedroom.

He is twenty-seven.

Linda tires quickly of this new version of her husband. "You don't have to take this crap," she harangues him, referring to the Beatles' drama. "You're a grown man."*

By Christmas 1969, Paul McCartney is in the studio again. He records at home, completely in secret. He will call his withdrawal from the band "therapy through hell" and the new record something to get him through "one of the worst times in my life."

Three months later, McCartney calls Lennon to tell him he is officially no longer a Beatle. "Good," Lennon responds. "That makes two of us who have accepted it mentally."

One month after that, McCartney's press release announcing his new solo album also states that he is leaving the Beatles for good, making the end official.

✦ ✦ ✦

But then a strange thing happens. John Lennon's vocal departure from the band is kept secret by order of Allen Klein. The manager hopes the Beatles' rift will mend. But when McCartney makes his exit known to the public, Lennon becomes angry. *He* wants credit

---

* Linda Eastman's quotes come from Peter Carlin's *Paul McCartney: A Life.*

for the breakup. "I started the band. I disbanded it. It's as simple as that." But the world believes it is the other way around, which infuriates Lennon even more. "I think it was just straightforward jealousy," McCartney will later state in an interview.

In the end, it is Paul's 1969 refusal to sign Klein's management contract that ends the conflict. Klein and the other three Beatles will not allow McCartney to make a contractual emancipation from Apple Records. So the singer sues his former band. A court rules in McCartney's favor, formally dissolving the Beatles' partnership once and for all.

Paul McCartney will go on to a long solo career, first as leader of the band Wings, alongside Linda. He continues to successfully record after her death from breast cancer in 1998.

Meanwhile, John Lennon also forms a new band, with Yoko. "I had already begun to want to leave, but when I met Yoko is like when you meet your first woman," he will admit to *Playboy* magazine. "You leave the guys at the bar. You don't go play football anymore. You don't go play snooker or billiards. Maybe some guys do it on Friday night or something, but once I found the woman, the boys became of no interest whatsoever other than being old school friends. Those wedding bells are breaking up that old gang of mine. We got married three years later, in 1969. That was the end of the boys. And it just so happened that the boys were well known and weren't just local guys at the bar. Everybody got so upset over it. There was a lot of shit thrown at us. A lot of hateful stuff."

No matter. The clamor for a Beatles reunion never stops. There is a fervent hope that the lads will reunite. But that will never happen, as John Lennon remains unmoved.

Up until the very end.*

---

* Linda Eastman will blame the breakup on Yoko Ono and Allen Klein, stating, "They had John so spinning about Paul it was heartbreaking." In 2013, Yoko Ono tells *Interview* magazine, "It feels like I was accused of something that I didn't do, which was breaking up The Beatles. It's like you're accused of murder and you're in prison and you can't get out."

CHAPTER FIVE

OCTOBER 9, 1971

SYRACUSE, NEW YORK

EVENING

John Lennon has arrived in America.

Today is the former Beatle's thirty-first birthday, but the night belongs to Yoko Ono. The local Everson Museum here is hosting her first performance art exhibition in five years. Ono's *This Is Not Here* will run for three weeks and draw thousands of visitors, including artist Andy Warhol, actor Dennis Hopper, poet Allen Ginsberg, singer Bob Dylan, and music producer Phil Spector, who has spent time in the studio with the Beatles. Ono's art challenges viewers to use their imagination. She encourages patrons to touch her work—such as the bubble gum machine that dispenses invisible treats—to experience it for themselves.

Despite the popularity of the show, Ono will never know the fame her husband enjoys. Tonight will reaffirm this. Even as crowds view the exhibit, assistant museum director David Ross is desperately trying to arrange a top-secret midnight concert in the Everson's theater space. The other three Beatles are all invited. Ringo Starr is already known to be in Syracuse. If the plan comes together, this could be the Beatles reunion for which the world has been waiting for eighteen months.

Word leaks out. An excited crowd lines up outside the museum. The mob, worried about missing something, breaks down the doors. The bearded poet Ginsberg calms them, averting catastrophe.

To avoid any further trouble, Ono moves Lennon's surprise party to the Hotel Syracuse. Beatles manager Allen Klein is in attendance, having achieved success for the disbanded group unlike any they have known before. Evidence released during Paul McCartney's lawsuit against the Beatles showed that, in eighteen months of work, Klein's efforts brought in £9 million ($250 million in today's US dollars).

However, McCartney's attorneys voice concerns that Klein has engaged in income tax evasion.* So, despite the hopes of many ardent Beatles fans, who seem to grow more rabid the longer the group is apart, Paul McCartney does not make it tonight.

Also, after suffering in silence for two years, George Harrison is not in any mood to perform. Two months ago, Harrison organized a charitable event called the Concert for Bangladesh. It was held in Madison Square Garden, and John Lennon was invited. But Lennon insisted that Yoko Ono appear onstage during the performance and asked Harrison how she might be part of the show.

"Well, I've no objection to her listening in the audience," George said.

Needless to say, John Lennon did not show up—and Harrison will not perform tonight.

But Ringo Starr *is* here. So is Eric Clapton, along with several other musicians. After Lennon is presented with a guitar-shaped birthday cake, a forty-five-minute jam session breaks out in the hotel suite. Ringo taps out rhythm on an overturned trash can as the guitar players launch into standards like "Peggy Sue" and even the Beatles' "Yellow Submarine."

Even as the music plays, a reporter interviews John and Yoko. There is so much unexpected tension in their comments that the tape

---

* A six-count federal indictment in 1977 will charge Klein with failing to report $216,000 in personal income in 1970, 1971, and 1972. He was fined $5,000 and served two months in jail in 1980.

will become known as the Argument Interview. The reporter grows tired of the bickering and walks out. John and Yoko will repeat their differences about world issues on *The Dick Cavett Show*, but the tone will be much lighter, with Lennon making jokes in a faux-military uniform.

As for this surprise thirty-first birthday party, John and Yoko will later send warm thank-you notes to all in attendance, making no mention of their heated moments.

Most everyone in the room this evening is British—friends who made the pilgrimage to see Yoko's show and celebrate John's birthday. Soon they will go home, and a truth will be unmasked: John Lennon has no friends in his new homeland.

Just Yoko.

✦ ✦ ✦

The couple is in the United States to hunt for Yoko's missing daughter, Kyoko. The eight-year-old has disappeared after being taken away by her American father, Tony Cox.

Lennon and Ono flew to New York City last month with no return ticket back to England. The matter of custody of the young Kyoko is now with the American court system.*After taking up residence at Manhattan's St. Regis Hotel, moving in eighteen trunks of personal possessions, the couple works with Allen Klein to find Kyoko. Doctors are telling Lennon that his sperm count is too low to produce another child. Having had two miscarriages and now facing a future without her daughter, Yoko is obsessed with the situation.

John Lennon also has a child problem. He knows that by leaving England, he is effectively abandoning his son, Julian, for whom the singer pays little in the way of child support to his former wife, Cynthia. Attempts to create a bond between the eight-year-old boy and Yoko have failed, so it has been easier simply to leave his son behind.

---

* It was only in 1994, at the age of thirty-one, that Kyoko finally made contact with her mother. The two have been close ever since. Tony Cox, an artist, was never held legally accountable for the abduction, as Yoko Ono declined to pursue the matter.

Elvis and Ann-Margret in *Viva Las Vegas (Bettmann / Getty Images)*

Elvis and Priscilla Presley show newborn Lisa Marie to fans. *(PictureLux / The Hollywood Archive / Alamy Stock Photo)*

Colonel Tom Parker and Elvis
(Michael Ochs Archives / Getty Images)

Elvis's first comeback in the Las Vegas live shows, 1968 *(Album / Alamy Stock Photo)*

Elvis in 1977, near the end *(akg–images / Schmalisch)*

Graceland mourners *(Chuck Fishman / Getty Images)*

The Beatles' rooftop concert was their final performance together.
(Dom Slike / Alamy Stock Photo)

The Beatles circa 1966 *(Keystone Features / Getty Images)*

Left to right: Brian Jones, Yoko Ono, and John Lennon holding young Sean
(David Cairns / Express / Getty Images)

Beatles producer George Martin
(Photoshot / Everett Collection)

John and Yoko actively protested the Vietnam War. *(Dom Slike / Alamy Stock Photo)*

John and Paul McCartney
(akg-images / picture alliance / PictureLux / The Hollywood Archive)

John and Yoko getting
married in Gibraltar
*(Trinity Mirror /
Mirrorpix /
Alamy Stock Photo)*

John and son Julian
with John's psychedelic
Rolls-Royce
*(Keystone-France /
Gamma-Keystone /
Getty Images)*

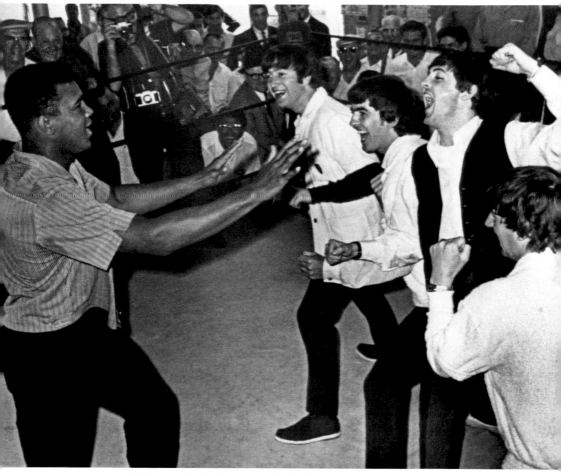

Muhammad Ali clowning with the Beatles *(GRANGER)*

Hit Factory promo picture of John and Yoko during *Double Fantasy* sessions
(Allan Tannenbaum / Getty Images)

Mourners outside the Dakota Building after Lennon's assassination
(Keystone / Getty Images)

Muhammad Ali and Joe Frazier in the "Thrilla in Manila"
(dpa picture alliance / Alamy Stock Photo)

A battered Ali after his bout with Ken Norton

(Mirrorpix / Courtesy Everett Collection)

Herbert Muhammad and Ali
(© Gunther / mptvimages.com)

Ali, his wife Belinda, and their four children *(AP Photo / Bill Ingraham)*

Ali and wife Veronica on their wedding day
(Paul Harris / Getty Images)

Ali and wife Yolanda ("Lonnie") *(AP Photo / Reed Saxon)*

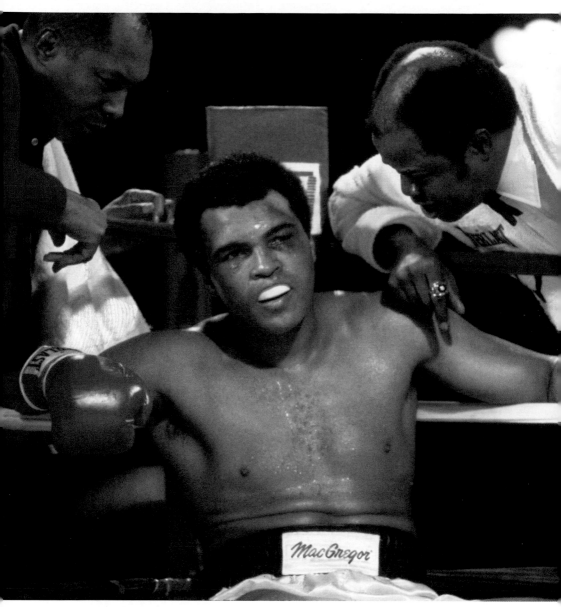

Ali's face after Larry Holmes fight *(John Iacono* / Sports Illustrated / *Getty Images)*

Ali lighting the torch at the 1996 Olympics *(Camera 4 / Imago / Icon Sportswire)*

Ali in later years with Will Smith, who starred in the movie *Ali*
(Adam Scull / PHOTOlink / Courtesy Everett Collection)

"I think I was scared of her [Yoko]," the *Irish Times* will quote Julian in 1998. "But she kept cuddling me and eventually in my little mind I somehow knew that if I wanted to keep my dad, I had to like her. It wasn't until years later that I began to understand their relationship and suddenly stopped seeing her as the weird lady."

As Klein's lawyers resume their search for Kyoko, John and Yoko get caught up in New York City's creative energy. Ono went to school nearby—at Sarah Lawrence College, in Westchester County, which Linda Eastman also attended—and spent considerable time in the city's avant-garde community before meeting Lennon.

In fact, Eastman and Ono have a lot in common. Both were raised in wealth and privilege.*Both have been married before. Both are artists, Linda having worked professionally as a photographer. Eastman's specialty is covering the world of rock 'n' roll, and her images appear regularly in music magazines. Her work led her into short relationships with famous names like Mick Jagger of the Rolling Stones, guitarist Jimi Hendrix, and singer Jim Morrison of the Doors—all before she met Paul McCartney.

Linda Eastman is confident in an aggressive, New York City manner. Yoko is equally brash but less confrontational. Fierce in their loyalty, the two women are devoted to their new husbands, destined to remain with them until death.

But with the Beatles now in the past, any chance for Linda Eastman and Yoko Ono to grow their relationship is gone. It remains a rivalry. Yet another similarity the women share is that each believes her spouse is the *better* Beatle, deserving of more credit for the band's success. However, while Linda is seen as a benign presence in Paul's life, a loving and devoted wife, Yoko is widely viewed by the public as a female Svengali, imposing her will on Lennon. Magazines

---

* Yoko Ono was raised in Japan, the daughter of a bank executive. The family moved to San Francisco and New York when she was a child but returned to Tokyo for World War II. Yoko remained in Japan when her family moved to Scarsdale, New York— coincidentally, where Eastman was born—after the war, but she joined them there in 1952, when she attended Sarah Lawrence.

even mock her Japanese heritage, such as the 1970 *Esquire* article titled "John Rennon's Most Excrusive Gloupie."*

At this point, John Lennon has pretty much ceded his life to Yoko. So, as the couple makes a new home in New York City, they not only step completely away from the Beatles but also turn their backs on London for good. "I should have been born in New York," John states soon after their arrival. "I should have been born in the Village. That's where I belong." The singer revels in the open-air poetry and impromptu musical jam sessions in bohemian Greenwich Village. Sometimes he plays for free on the streets. John and Yoko record together in their St. Regis suite, music that will later appear on a Lennon album entitled *Some Time in New York City.*†

Searching for Kyoko may be the couple's stated reason for leaving England, but it is just a pretext. The breakup of the Beatles has caused the British press to hammer Lennon constantly. The negative attention is so bad that fans stand outside Apple headquarters in London shouting that Yoko is a "nip" and a "chink" and that she should "get back to her own country."

It was Ono who suggested the permanent move to New York, her home for a large portion of her life—thus the eighteen trunks of possessions, a clear indicator that the couple is relocating for good.

✦ ✦ ✦

Almost immediately, John Lennon begins creating controversy. The man who once proclaimed that the Beatles were "more popular than Jesus" is emboldened by the antiwar movement and his long opposition to the conflict in Vietnam. Shortly before leaving England, Lennon recorded the antiwar song "Imagine," which speaks of a world without heaven, hell, or war and of the hope for a utopian society where "the world will be as one."

In New York City, Lennon grows more radical. The singer

---

* That article was written by Charles McCarry, a former CIA operative and writer of thriller fiction.

† The album was not a success, peaking at No. 48 on the US *Billboard* 200.

demonstrates an angry side with his song "Power to the People," a million-selling single he releases to coincide with a mass peace march on Washington in May 1971. Rallied by Lennon's voice, thousands of demonstrators turn out to protest the Vietnam War. Twelve thousand are arrested.

Six months later, Lennon appears at a rally in support of poet John Sinclair, sentenced to ten years in prison for marijuana possession. The performance takes place in Ann Arbor, Michigan, where John and Yoko take the stage at three a.m. In addition to music from the former Beatle and from singer Stevie Wonder, the audience of fifteen thousand also hears speeches by activists from the radical Black Panther Party and from members of the Chicago Seven, well known for their roles in protests during the 1968 Democratic Party National Convention.

Lennon's presence at this event does not go unnoticed.

He catches the eye of President Richard Nixon, whose advisers believe that Lennon's prominent antiwar voice might cost Nixon reelection. Nineteen seventy-two will be the first year that eighteen-year-olds have the right to vote in the United States. The Nixon administration fears the powerful antiwar constituency could bring it down. The race is predicted to be tight. Something as simple as famous rock stars like John Lennon spouting anti-Nixon statements might be dangerous.

Ironically, when Elvis Presley visited the White House last December, Richard Nixon tasked him with spying on John Lennon as part of the King's request for a federal Bureau of Narcotics and Dangerous Drugs badge. Knowing that Lennon smokes marijuana, a drug the King finds unpatriotic, Elvis readily agrees.*

At the direction of the White House, the FBI begins spying on Lennon, amassing a file that will grow to three hundred pieces of evidence. "The recent formation of the Youth Election Strategy (YES)

---

* The dumb spy request did not amount to anything, as Elvis Presley never saw John Lennon again.

is reported," notes an official Bureau document dated February 25, 1972. The surveillance highlights the Twentieth National Convention of the Communist Party USA, which Lennon attended.

The FBI text reads, "The New Left oriented group is being formed by British musician John Lennon . . . and former Yippie leader Jerry Rubin to raise funds for proposed demonstration activities at the Republican National Convention in San Diego during August."

It is also reported that Lennon is meeting with Rubin and activist Abbie Hoffman to plan a major concert to rally the vote against Nixon. As the singer becomes more entrenched in leftist politics, particularly in the company of individuals who have long been under investigation by the FBI, John Lennon grows wary, sensing he is being watched. During his second appearance on *The Dick Cavett Show*, a fidgety Lennon pulls out a sheaf of papers—notes, he tells Cavett—containing the many things on his mind. Yoko Ono, dressed in a black shirt and blue pantsuit, sits to his left.

When Lennon tells Cavett he is being watched by the FBI, a most unusual thing happens: the audience grows quiet, apparently doubting Lennon's accusation, and an uncomfortable Cavett changes the subject. The clandestine FBI surveillance of the singer has been done so skillfully that the American public knows nothing of the massive file being compiled on Lennon. The first time John Lennon appeared on *Cavett*, one year ago, he came across as witty. But now he sounds paranoid. His words are met by some hostility and doubt.

✦ ✦ ✦

Soon, it is not just the FBI tailing Lennon. The Central Intelligence Agency and Britain's top domestic counterintelligence and security agency, MI5, are both investigating the singer. As a nonnaturalized resident living in the United States on a visa, Lennon has a tenuous hold on remaining in the country. Any hint of illegal behavior could get him deported.

On February 4, 1972, US senator Strom Thurmond of South Carolina writes to Attorney General John Mitchell, stating that "deportation would be a good counter-measure" against John Lennon. Thurmond points to Lennon's 1968 arrest for hashish possession in London as proof the singer has broken US immigration laws.*

Richard Nixon immediately takes up Thurmond's cause. In March 1973, Lennon is ordered to be deported. Yoko Ono is spared deportation and is, instead, granted "permanent resident" status. But her husband is soon ordered to leave the country. As a prolonged court battle begins, that order is temporarily stayed.

The stress begins taking its toll. Lennon becomes bitter and sarcastic, the attitude shown on *The Dick Cavett Show* becoming a regular part of his behavior. Even as Richard Nixon is reelected and the threat of John Lennon recedes, the FBI surveillance continues.

And so does John Lennon's disenchantment.

It has been three years since the Beatles' "divorce."

Now Lennon begins looking for another separation—from his relationship with Yoko Ono.

---

* The Controlled Substances Act, which regulates the possession of narcotics, became effective May 1, 1971.

CHAPTER SIX

All you need is love.

Well, maybe not.

It is three months since John and Yoko made a home in the famous Dakota Apartments on Central Park West and Seventy-Second Street. The couple are putting down roots in New York, their earlier infatuation with the city proving authentic. But four years into their marriage, there is trouble. The hunt for Kyoko continues, but now something else is in play.

What happens next John Lennon will term "the Lost Weekend," a time of rebelliousness that will break up his marriage as he abruptly leaves Yoko. An eighteen-month epoch of debauchery and infidelity ensues. Lennon is thirty-three, a young man with an uncertain future. He is so insecure that he insists on following his wife into the bathroom, a role reversal from a few years ago. So, as Lennon records a new album named *Mind Games*, the couple decides to split. They are fighting constantly. John and Yoko take a break, not sure if divorce is the next step.

Yoko Ono will later argue that this divide in their marriage was *her* idea—a vacation, not a break. "I needed a rest. I needed space.

Can you imagine every day of getting this vibration from people of hate? I started to notice that he became a little restless on top of that, so I thought it's better to give him a rest and me a rest."*

The hatred directed at Yono for being the woman accused of breaking up the Beatles is punishing. She will say that John was growing irritated with married life. So, incredibly, she approaches a young woman currently serving as the couple's assistant, May Pang, a twenty-two-year-old New Yorker born to Chinese parents. Ono proposes that Pang become Lennon's consort. Yoko considers her "a very intelligent, attractive woman and extremely efficient."

One summer morning—the exact date is lost—Yoko Ono startles May Pang.

"Yoko came to me at 9:30 in the morning—I hadn't even had my first cup of coffee—and said: 'May, I've got to talk to you. John and I are not getting along.'" The assistant already knows of the tension, having been around the couple long enough to observe their failing relationship.

"He's going to start going out with other people," Yoko says. "I know you don't have a boyfriend, and I know you are not after John, but you need a boyfriend, and you would be good for him."

A stunned Pang responds, "I don't think so."

"You don't want him to go out with somebody who is going to be nasty to him, do you?" says Yoko.

"Of course not."

"You will be perfect," Ono responds and walks out of the room without another word.

Shortly afterward, John Lennon moves into May Pang's New York City apartment.†

✦ ✦ ✦

---

* The quote from Yoko Ono comes from the *Telegraph*, March 26, 2012.

† May Pang's account of the arrangement comes from several interviews published in 2011 and 2012.

John Lennon has long gotten his way, starting with his first band, a group called the Quarrymen. From his mid-teens into his thirties, the singer did as he pleased. In his first marriage, he conducted a series of affairs. In his professional life, he wrote scores of songs on his own. But John Lennon has never been independent. There has always been a Paul McCartney or a Yoko Ono to rein him in when he became outlandish.

Not anymore. Beginning in the summer of 1973, John and Yoko are done. Lennon and May Pang are now a couple. The singer leaves for Los Angeles in October to promote *Mind Games*. The breakup with Ono is now public. Being a Beatle has long meant that every relationship a band member indulged in has been followed by the press. It was this way with McCartney and his girlfriend Jane Asher, soon after replaced by Linda Eastman. Now the media are running wild with the May Pang story. The couple's ten-year age difference is not an issue. As the couple makes the rounds in LA, Lennon's Lost Weekend becomes a time of drugs, sex, and rock 'n' roll. Their every move is scrutinized by the tabloids, with Yoko keeping tabs back home in New York, later claiming that John called her every night to check in.

The situation in Los Angeles quickly deteriorates. Nine months into his separation from Yoko, Lennon is spotted at the Troubadour, a nightclub on Santa Monica Boulevard. He is there to see soul singer Ann Peebles. Yet the former Beatle becomes so drunk that he wanders through the audience with a sanitary napkin attached to his forehead, ignoring the singer he came to see.

As Lennon departs, a waitress heckles him for leaving a poor tip.

"Do you know who I am?" he demands.

"Yeah," says the waitress. "You're some asshole with a Kotex on your head."

✦ ✦ ✦

John Lennon's physical appearance is far different from his Beatles days: hair cut short, face clean shaven, body trim and athletic. He still wears his trademark round spectacles. May Pang has the natural beauty of a model, although she has been told she is "too ethnic" for most photographic jobs. She and Lennon settle into a California lifestyle that includes destructive behavior by Lennon.

"Suddenly, I was out on me own," Lennon will remember. "I'd be waking up, drunk, in strange places or reading about myself in the paper, doing extraordinary things—half of which I'd done and half of which I hadn't done."

Drugs and alcohol are a constant, mostly cocaine and marijuana. "The guys were all drinking—and John was being one of the guys," Pang will later tell an interviewer. "Everyone was as blitzed as he. One of the bass players got into a car wreck. We got kicked out of A&M [studios] when someone threw a bottle of liquor down the console."

Lennon makes friends with singer Harry Nilsson. The two carouse almost nightly. "I was with Harry Nilsson, who didn't get as much coverage as me, the bum. He encouraged me. I usually have someone there who says 'Okay, Lennon. Shut up.'"*

✦ ✦ ✦

On the evening of March 12, 1974, Lennon and Nilsson are drinking on Sunset Strip. The Smothers Brothers, old friends of Lennon's, are headlining at the Troubadour. Actress Pam Grier, another celebrity, is in the house to watch the show. Without warning, Lennon begins heckling Tommy and Dick Smothers from the audience, hurling insults as they try to perform. Their manager walks over to quiet Lennon, only to get punched by the singer. Lennon then pushes a waitress. Troubadour security steps in to remove him and Nilsson, causing a scuffle that leads to Lennon losing his glasses. When finally ejected from the club, a furious Lennon kicks the parking valet.

"The heckling got so bad that our show was going downhill rap-

---

* Harry Nilsson, a successful singer in his own right, will be remembered for an odd, ghoulish coincidence: the Mamas and the Papas singer Cass Elliot and Who drummer Keith Moon will both die accidentally in his London apartment at 9 Curzon Place, flat number 12. Singer Alice Cooper also caroused with the hard-living Nilsson, who died of a heart attack in 1994 at the age of fifty-two.

idly," Tommy Smothers will remember. "No one cared, because it was just a happening anyway, but there was a scuffle going on, and we stopped the show."

"I got drunk and shouted," Lennon will explain. He sends flowers to the Smothers Brothers in the morning, and a letter of apology to Pam Grier. The actress was sitting at his table, along with Nilsson and actor Peter Lawford, during his disruptive behavior.

Regarding the waitress he assaulted, her name is unknown, Lennon is unapologetic: "There was some girl who claimed that I hit her, but I didn't hit her at all, you know. She just wanted some money and I had to pay her off, because I thought it would harm my immigration. So I was drunk. When it's Errol Flynn, the showbiz writers say: Those were the days, when men were men. When I do it, I'm a bum. So it was a mistake, but hell, I'm human."*

✦ ✦ ✦

Against the odds, Lennon's creative output survives the drugs and alcohol. He records a new album covering 1950s and early '60s rock standards with producer Phil Spector and helps Harry Nilsson make a record of his own. In addition, he and May Pang rent a beach house in Santa Monica. Lennon invites Nilsson to join them, hoping it will ensure that both get to the studio on time after a night on the town. Soon, they will be joined by Ringo Starr and Keith Moon of the Who. Pang prods Lennon to continue this reconnection with his past—which leads to the sudden appearance of one Paul McCartney.

Lennon is at Burbank Studios when Paul and Linda McCartney drop in. "I jammed with Paul," John will fondly remember. "There were fifty other people playing, all just watching me and Paul."

The two former Beatles make plans to meet soon in New Orleans, where McCartney will be working on a new album with Wings.

---

* This quote can be found in volume 2 of *The Beatles Diary: After the Break-Up, 1970–2001*, by Keith Badman.

Lennon is eager to join him and excitedly discusses the upcoming journey with May Pang.

✦ ✦ ✦

It is now one year since the split from Yoko. John and May Pang are back in New York City. The couple buys a penthouse apartment on Fifty-Second Street in Manhattan. Lennon quits drinking and heroin to focus on his music, recording the album *Walls and Bridges*—Pang can be heard whispering his name on the song "#9 Dream." The album single "Whatever Gets You thru the Night" becomes Lennon's first solo No. 1 hit in the United States. Fellow British singing sensation Elton John is featured on piano and backup vocals.

It is not just John Lennon who benefits from his time with May Pang. Her creative work in the studio will earn her a gold record and open up other job opportunities in the music industry. Later, she will produce albums by David Bowie, Ringo Starr, and Elton John.

Though Lennon calls their time together "the Lost Weekend," it becomes one of the most enjoyable periods of his life. "I may have been the happiest I've ever been," he will later tell an interviewer, showing no hint of regret. "I loved this woman, I made some beautiful music and I got so fucked up with booze and shit and whatever."

✦ ✦ ✦

Thanksgiving Day 1974. Elton John performs live at Madison Square Garden. An extremely nervous John Lennon paces backstage, soon to join Elton in front of the sold-out crowd. This will be the first time Lennon has played before a large audience since the Rooftop Concert in London. He wears a gardenia on the front of his long black jacket. Yoko Ono has sent flowers backstage, with a note wishing him good luck. She is in the audience, a woman with a mission. For months, Ono has been asking Lennon to come by the Dakota so she can share a new method of curing his cigarette addiction.

She is obviously seeking a reunion.

Elton John's guitarist Davey Johnstone tunes Lennon's instrument.

"I think I wanna throw up," Lennon says to him. "I feel so nervous."

"I'll see you up there. It's gonna be great," Johnstone responds.

And it is. With long hair flowing, Lennon settles in near Elton John, and the pair play three songs. The crowd is delirious. A camera captures Yoko Ono calmly appraising the performance.[*]

✦ ✦ ✦

The Lennon-Ono reunion does not take place for three months. In February 1975, she finally convinces him to come by the Dakota for the smoking cessation hypnotherapy.

May Pang is not immediately alarmed, but when Lennon does not return home that night, she calls the Dakota in the morning. Yoko tells her that John is "unavailable"; he cannot come to the phone. Tomorrow is the day Lennon is supposed to fly to New Orleans to work with Paul McCartney. He doesn't make the flight. His jam session with Paul months ago, back in Los Angeles, will mark the last time the legendary songwriters ever play together.[†]

Two days later, Lennon returns to see Pang. She will remember that he appeared lost and disoriented. He informs his paramour that he is going back to his wife. Amazingly, John Lennon and May Pang will continue to see each other and have intimate relations for several more years, ending the relationship only shortly before his death.

✦ ✦ ✦

Despite his continuing involvement with May Pang, the Lennon-Ono marriage is on again. "It slowly started to dawn on me that John

---

[*] Elton John and John Lennon performed "Whatever Gets You thru the Night," "Lucy in the Sky with Diamonds," and "I Saw Her Standing There."

[†] According to author Richard White, Paul McCartney knew of Lennon's long-held desire to spend time in New Orleans. Thus, McCartney invited him down while he was recording *Venus and Mars* with Wings. Lennon was about to pack for the trip when Ono invited him to the Dakota.

was not the trouble at all. John was a fine person. It was *society* that had become too much. We laugh about it now, but we started dating again. I wanted to be sure. I'm thankful for John's intelligence," Pang will tell *Playboy* magazine.

And so it is that John Lennon is once again under the influence— not of substances but of Yoko.

In the summer of 1975, she informs him that she is pregnant.

CHAPTER SEVEN

APRIL 24, 1976

NEW YORK, NEW YORK

11:30 PM

John Lennon and Paul McCartney are watching *Saturday Night Live*.

Their strained relationship appears to be on the mend. The two men are in Lennon's Dakota apartment along with Linda Eastman and Yoko Ono. *SNL* is broadcasting a little more than a mile away, at Rockefeller Center. Suddenly, a long-haired young man wearing a dark blue jacket over an open-collared shirt appears on-screen seated behind a desk.

"Hi, I'm Lorne Michaels, the producer of *Saturday Night*. Right now, we're being seen by approximately twenty-two million viewers, but please allow me, if I may, to address myself to four very special people. John, Paul, George, and Ringo: the Beatles."

Lennon and McCartney lean in, listening closely.

"The Beatles are the best thing that ever happened to music," Michaels continues. "It goes even deeper than that. You're not just a musical group. You're a part of us. We grew up with you. It's for this reason that I'm inviting you to come on our show.

"Well, if it's money you want, there's no problem here. The National Broadcasting Company has authorized me to offer you a certified check for three thousand dollars." Michaels holds up a check. "Here it is. As you can see, verifiably, a check made out to you, the Beatles, for three thousand dollars."

The studio audience loves the gag and laughs loudly. But with NBC headquarters so close, Lennon and McCartney actually discuss getting into a cab and collecting the money. "We should go down, just you and me," McCartney says. "We'll just show up. There's only two of us; we'll take half the money."

After the fact, McCartney assessed the situation in a later interview: "For a second we were like, shall we do it? I don't know what stopped us. It would've been work and we were having a night off so we elected to not go to work."

"We nearly got into a cab, but we were actually too tired," Lennon will remember.

Incredibly, the Lorne Michaels bit was a coincidence. He didn't know the two Beatles were watching, and Lennon and McCartney had no idea their names would be mentioned on the show that night.

✦ ✦ ✦

As the months pass, John Lennon steps farther away from the music world. Many continue to blame Yoko. Some say she has put a "spell" on him. When Lennon hears this, he reacts angrily. "Nobody ever said anything about Paul having a spell on me or my having one on Paul. They never thought that was abnormal in those days, two guys together, or four guys together. Why didn't they ever say, 'How come those guys don't split up? I mean, what's going on backstage? What is this Paul and John business? How can they be together so long?' We spent more time together in the early days than John and Yoko: the four of us sleeping in the same room, practically in the same bed, in the same truck, living together night and day, eating, shitting and pissing together! All right? Doing everything together! Nobody said a damn thing about being under a spell."*

---

* This quote came from a *Playboy* interview published in January 1981.

Spell or no spell, John Lennon is now retreating from public view. The singer places himself in his home—and in the hands of Yoko, whom he now calls "Mama."

"It is a teacher-pupil relationship," Lennon will later state. "That's what people don't understand. She's the teacher and I'm the pupil. I'm the famous one, the one who's supposed to know everything, but she's my teacher."

John Lennon now devotes himself to baby Sean, rarely leaving the apartment and forsaking old attachments—including that with Paul McCartney, who remains eager to collaborate with him. "That was a period when Paul just kept turning up at our door with a guitar. I would let him in, but finally I said to him, 'Please call before you come over. It's not 1956, and turning up at the door isn't the same anymore. You know, just give me a ring.' He was upset by that, but I didn't mean it badly. I just meant that I was taking care of a baby all day, and some guy turns up at the door."

"Some guy." McCartney gets the message. He will never return to the Dakota. On occasion, Lennon and McCartney will speak on the phone, but the *Saturday Night Live* weekend is the last time they will see each other.

✦ ✦ ✦

Four years pass—a long spell to be away from the music world for any artist, let alone the famous John Lennon. He travels not at all, never attends shows, and nearing forty, he has no interest in making records. He spends his days as a househusband, doting on Sean and performing tasks like baking bread and cleaning the house. Lennon no longer listens to rock 'n' roll; he prefers Japanese folk music.

Life in their Dakota home, which the singer and Yoko Ono purchased for its location and high level of security, is peaceful. A great number of celebrities live in the Gothic-style structure. Next-door neighbor Roberta Flack, a bestselling singer herself, often hears the Japanese music.

"Rock 'n' roll was not fun anymore," Lennon will tell an interviewer who asks why he stepped away. "I chose not to take the standard options in my business . . . going to Vegas and singing your great hits, if you're lucky, or going to hell, which is where Elvis went."

John and Yoko renovate the kitchen of their seventh-floor apartment to make it look more like a loft. The other rooms are simple, uncluttered, and plain. Young Sean often plays with the children of Warner LeRoy, who owns the Tavern on the Green restaurant, across the street in Central Park. Once Sean learns to ride a bicycle, John walks over to the park to watch him. Father and son often hold hands. There is no security present.*

Meanwhile, Lennon stays in contact with his other son, Julian, for whom Paul McCartney wrote "Hey Jude" to console the child after his parents' divorce. They speak on the phone. John has purchased Julian a guitar and shown him chords. Yet Julian still lives in England. "It's not the best relationship between father and son," Lennon admits. "But it is there. He's seventeen now. Julian and I will have a relationship in the future."

However, Lennon seems to be haunted by the Julian situation.

"Ninety percent of the people on this planet, especially in the West, were born out of a bottle of whiskey on a Saturday night," Lennon will say. "I don't love Julian any less as a child. He's still my son, whether he came from a bottle of whiskey or because they didn't have pills in those days. He's here, he belongs to me, and he always will."

There is a twelve-year age gap between Julian and Sean, who is now five years old. Their father loves them both. But it is clear Sean is the priority.

"We worked hard for that child," Lennon will tell an interviewer. "We went through all hell trying to have a baby, through many miscarriages and other problems. He is what they call a love child in

---

* The Dakota was built between 1880 and 1884 by architect Henry Janeway Hardenbergh for Edward Cabot Clark, owner of the Singer Manufacturing Company. The structure takes its name from its Upper West Side location, which at the time was considered to be as remote and unpopulated as the Dakotas region of the United States.

truth. Doctors told us we could never have a child. We almost gave up. 'Well, that's it, then, we can't have one.' We were told something was wrong with my sperm, that I abused myself so much in my youth that there was no chance. Yoko was 43, and so they said, no way. She has had too many miscarriages."

John Lennon's domesticity frees Yoko Ono. She spends her days managing the couple's considerable financial assets. She buys other apartments within the Dakota, to be used as storage, offices, and a place for guests. In the very exclusive world of the famous apartment building, where every potential owner must be interviewed by an extremely selective board before being allowed to buy, this is unpopular. Their neighbors—as fans did with the breakup of the Beatles—prefer to dislike Yoko. To them, John is the nice guy who brings sushi to the building's annual potluck.

Ono purchases six country estates and a herd of dairy cows for the Lennon investment portfolio. Lennon's entire fortune is estimated to be $150 million. "When I was cleaning the cat shit and feeding Sean, she was sitting in rooms full of smoke with men in three-piece suits that they couldn't button," John will tell *Playboy* magazine.*

✦ ✦ ✦

Sean grows. John Lennon bakes.

Then, in April 1980, Paul McCartney releases a new single. "Coming Up," which he recorded in a Scottish barn, bursts with a new, radical sound. Paul's high-pitched vocals are a departure. John Lennon is immediately hooked by the record. He has long disparaged Paul's music, but now McCartney and Harrison are both selling more records as solo artists than Lennon. The competitive side of John returns. After five years away, the singer wants back in the game.

Lennon has long considered himself the most creatively "mature" of the Beatles. Yet McCartney has surpassed him—and he admits it. "I thought that 'Coming Up' was great and I like the freak version

---

*Yoko's investment in the dairy cow herd was profitable. One Holstein sold for $250,000.

that he made in his barn," Lennon will later state. "If I'd have been with him, I would've said 'that's the one' too."

So John Lennon decides to make music once again.

The project will be called *Double Fantasy*—and it will hit big.

Yet even before he finishes making the record, danger is approaching.

John Lennon has seven months to live.

CHAPTER EIGHT

AUGUST 7, 1980
THE HIT FACTORY
NEW YORK, NEW YORK
2 P.M.

John Lennon is getting the band back together.

But it's not the Beatles. Here on the corner of Tenth Avenue and Forty-Eighth Street in Manhattan, Lennon assembles musicians for his first album in five years. The four-man group rehearsed late at the Dakota apartment last night and now gather in this sixth-floor studio at New York's famous Hit Factory. John wears an all-black Western outfit with an embroidered shirt and a cowboy hat. A picture of Sean Lennon hangs in the control room, to remind the singer "not to lose contact with what I'd got . . . looking at me all the time."

Producer Jack Douglas, who has worked with Aerosmith and Cheap Trick, chose this location over studios in Los Angeles upon Yoko Ono's instructions. Ono felt California had negative connotations because of John's Lost Weekend months with May Pang more than five years ago.

Also on Yoko's behalf, Douglas required every musician here today to provide their birth dates. Ono then took this information to her astrologist to be analyzed. Engineer Lee DeCarlo knows of a few musicians who did not get hired because of their star signs.

It was in May that John Lennon got the inspiration for *Double Fantasy*, as this album will be known. On the advice of her astrology consultants, Yoko suggested he sail from Rhode Island to Bermuda on a seven-hundred-mile trip. After reaching the island, Lennon began composing. Using an Ovation guitar and two Panasonic boom boxes, he recorded a few demos of songs he would eventually put on the new album. While at a disco, he heard the B-52's new record "Rock Lobster," which reminded him of Yoko's prior recordings. Excited that there might be a new market for his wife's sound, Lennon plans to include her on *Double Fantasy*.

Back in New York, it is John Lennon, not Yoko Ono, whom every musician in this room is eager to work with. His long absence from recording does not matter, for his new songs are strong.

"Jack brought John's demo tape to my beach house in Montauk," Stan Vincent, Jack Douglas's business partner, will remember. "That's the first time we heard it. If Jack liked this tape and thought we could make a record, John would come out of retirement . . . to do this album. If Jack didn't think it had merit, then the record would not be made. So we put the tape in and we both flipped out. Our jaws dropped open. It was the most amazing stuff. All the material was there: 'Beautiful Boy,' 'Woman,' 'Nobody Told Me.'"

The Hit Factory was chosen over New York's other top recording studio, the Power Station, because Yoko does not like the Station's owner. Also, because of privacy. The remote West Side location of the Hit Factory ensures that paparazzi and fans will not suspect the famous John Lennon is making a record here. The sixth-floor elevator requires a key to access the studio, meaning that no uninvited guests can intrude.

But *personal* security is not discussed. No one fears an outraged fan might charge into the studio to do physical harm. Each day, Lennon and Ono are driven in a private limousine, but without bodyguards. The idea of an armed security detail never comes up.

In general, John Lennon keeps a low profile. He has a private phone number and is quiet about where he goes. Yoko often arranges his business meetings using elaborate measures—as producer Jack Douglas found out: "I got these instructions: John wants to talk to me about making this record. Don't say anything to anyone. Just go to 34th Street, get on a seaplane and come out. I got flown to [Lennon's] big house out in Glen Cove. The seaplane landed right onto the beach. Yoko handed me an envelope marked 'For Jack's ears only.' Inside of it was a cassette of all of John's demos. . . . Then Yoko said, 'John's gonna call you now.'"

Despite these theatrics, John and Yoko are so unbothered by potential risk that they agree to pose outside the Hit Factory for pictures. Once those shots are published, anyone can discover where Lennon is recording.

The reality of public figures getting assassinated is, of course, well documented: John F. Kennedy, Bobby Kennedy, Martin Luther King Jr., Malcolm X. Alabama governor George Wallace was paralyzed after an assassination attempt in 1972. Later, in 1981, President Ronald Reagan will nearly die after being shot shortly after taking office.

But those are politicians and activists, not rock stars.

Thus, Lennon and Ono do not consider that *they* might become targets. Killing entertainers is unheard of.

But New York City is a dangerous place. In 1980, there will be almost 1,900 murders within its five boroughs. In spite of this, John and Yoko feel secure, and that is not unusual.

Despite the same high level of fame as Lennon, Paul McCartney also does not have personal security of any kind. He feels it would be like living "as a recluse." Later, after Mark David Chapman attacks Lennon, McCartney will change his mind—as will George, Ringo, and many top stars throughout the movie and record world. "It was," Paul will remember, "not just for the guys [the Beatles]. Everyone in entertainment suddenly thought, whoa—we'd better get security."*

✦ ✦ ✦

---

* Elvis Presley was an exception to this. At all times, he was surrounded by at least two bodyguards.

John Lennon works fast in the studio.

The recording of *Double Fantasy* is completed on October 19, just ten weeks after the first session. Rumors about the new project fill rock magazines like *Rolling Stone*, which Lennon reads throughout the production to see how much of the recording remains a secret.

Shortly after *Double Fantasy*'s release one month later, an enthused Lennon calls producer Jack Douglas. The record is receiving great acclaim, and after a slow start, sales are rising. Lennon is feeling very well—he quit heroin for good last year, with the help of an immersive tank of saline solution in which he would float for thirty minutes at a time. The experience simulates getting high, but without the negative health issues. By his own admission, the end of Lennon's heroin addiction reignites his musical creativity.

Jack Douglas sees the transformation firsthand: "John was totally satisfied with himself mentally and physically. He was starting to make a break. It had to do with his 40th birthday. He told me: 'I'm happy to be 40 years old. I'm in the best shape I've ever been in my life and I feel the best I ever felt.'"

Now there are plans for a world tour behind *Double Fantasy*. John envisions a stage shaped like a giant crab, with cameras extending from the claws. Images of the crowd recorded by the claw cam would then be projected onto a giant screen. Lennon plans on one show per city. Rehearsals are to start in March 1981. The tour itself will begin in April.

"We talked about where we were gonna shop in Tokyo and how we were gonna go to a store called Milk Boy. We talked about where we were gonna eat in Paris. He was particularly excited about going back to play in England," recalls rock photographer Bob Gruen, who served as John and Yoko's personal shooter from the time they moved to New York in 1971.

But even as he makes plans to tour, Lennon is amazed at how things have changed from when he did live shows with the Beatles. Whereas the Beatles performed for forty minutes, singers like Paul

Simon sometimes play for two hours onstage. If the tour is to work, John Lennon knows he will have to work hard.

✦ ✦ ✦

Three weeks after the release of *Double Fantasy*, John and Yoko book a studio at the Record Plant, on Forty-Fourth Street in Manhattan. It is here where Lennon recorded "Imagine" back in 1971. The plan now is to record a follow-up album to *Fantasy*.

But that record will never be completed.

✦ ✦ ✦

It is December 8, 1980. John Lennon awakens, slips on a black kimono, and goes to a window to watch the sun rise over Central Park. The time is seven thirty a.m. Today is already spoken for: a photo shoot followed by a lengthy radio interview, then another recording session with Yoko. The lead song is a duet called "Walking on Thin Ice." The new album will be entitled *Lennon Bermuda*. It is mostly upbeat music, reflecting the dance craze at the time.

"Walking on Thin Ice" deals with life and mortality.

> *Walking on thin ice*
> *I'm paying the price*
> *For throwing the dice in the air*

At four thirty p.m., John and Yoko depart the Dakota, heading for the recording studio. Lennon wears a black leather jacket over a blue sweater and a red T-shirt. On the way to the car, he stops to sign an autograph for a young man.

The recording session goes well. Jack Douglas is once again in charge. Halfway through, producer David Geffen pokes his head into the studio to tell John that *Double Fantasy* has just been certified a gold record. This buoys Lennon. He's eager to begin recording again tomorrow. A nine a.m. start is scheduled.

The time is now 10:35 p.m. Clutching a rough copy of "Walking on Thin Ice" and a cassette player, Lennon steps back into the limousine with Yoko. The car travels north up Eighth Avenue, bends around Columbus Circle, and follows Central Park West to Seventy-Second Street and the Dakota entrance.

But there is a problem. The couple sees a line of cars impeding access to the Dakota driveway. So they decide to walk the short distance to their home unaccompanied.

It is a cold night. The streets are devoid of most pedestrians.

But not all.

Standing watch outside the Dakota's entrance is the same man who obtained Lennon's signature six hours ago. His name will soon become infamous. He pats the gun in his jacket pocket.

It is the end for John Lennon. He will never see his forty-first birthday.

EPILOGUE

There was no funeral for **John Lennon**. The day after his murder, the singer's body was transported to Ferncliff Cemetery in Westchester County, New York. There, Lennon was cremated. Yoko Ono quietly scattered his ashes in Central Park, within view of the Dakota. On December 14, 1980, shortly after his death, millions of fans gathered in cities around the world to celebrate Lennon's life. The largest of these memorials took place in New York City. Tens of thousands assembled in Central Park, near Seventy-Second Street. Lennon's music played loudly over the crowd, but there were no speeches. Many mourners clutched daffodils and irises as a remembrance of the "flower power" movement of the 1960s. Precisely at two p.m., per Ono's request, ten minutes of silence was observed. The *New York Times* reported that, other than the clicking of cameras and the overhead noise of news helicopters, the quiet was complete.

No members of the Beatles were in attendance.

In March 1981, the City of New York designated this 2.5 acres of Central Park across from the Dakota as "Strawberry Fields," in honor of John Lennon.

At the time of this writing, John Lennon would have been eighty-two years old.

✦ ✦ ✦

On January 6, 1981, **Mark David Chapman** was charged with second-degree murder. His lawyers suggested to Chapman that he plead insanity, but instead, he pled guilty to Lennon's murder. He was sentenced to twenty years to life, with the possibility of parole. Since 2000, he has been passed over for release eleven times. Chapman is incarcerated at the Wende Correctional Facility outside Buffalo, New York. He is sixty-seven.

✦ ✦ ✦

Yoko Ono is now eighty-nine. She still lives at the Dakota Apartments in New York City. Though she continued making music after the death of her husband, she has now mostly withdrawn from public life.

✦ ✦ ✦

Sean Lennon is now forty-seven years old. In addition to working with his mother to manage the Lennon estate, he has been a musician since 1987. He has a longtime girlfriend but is not married.

✦ ✦ ✦

Julian Lennon was not initially included in his father's will. However, he was granted a large settlement in 1996, said to be $20 million. Now fifty-eight, he is a musician and documentary film producer. He has never married or had children. Julian remains close with Paul McCartney and Ringo Starr, the two living members of the Beatles.*

✦ ✦ ✦

On November 29, 2001, **George Harrison** died of throat cancer at the age of fifty-eight. His widow, Olivia, lives outside London. His son, Dhani, is forty-three and a musician.

✦ ✦ ✦

---

*The annual income of John Lennon's estate is valued at an estimated $14 million.

At age seventy-nine, **Paul McCartney** continues to make music and tour. He is married to Nancy Shevell, his third wife. He has residences in London, Manhattan, Tucson, Beverly Hills, and a farm in Scotland.

✦ ✦ ✦

At age eighty-one, **Ringo Starr** is still a practicing musician. He performs with Ringo Starr & His All-Starr Band. He is married to his second wife, Barbara Bach, and has residences in Los Angeles and Monte Carlo.

PART III

✦

The Greatest

CHAPTER ONE

OCTOBER 1, 1975
QUEZON CITY, PHILIPPINES
11:51 A.M.

Muhammad Ali feels like he's dying.

The heavyweight champion of the world sits on a small stool, looking across the ring at his battered adversary, Smokin' Joe Frazier. Both fighters have been through a brutal fourteen rounds, forty-two minutes of combat. The savagery is so intense that blood has spattered spectators in the front row—among them, Philippine president Ferdinand Marcos and his wife, Imelda. The so-called Thrilla in Manila has become a "death match."*

The Araneta Coliseum, where the fight is taking place, is on fire—the temperature in the building is well above one hundred degrees. Midday heat, humidity, a broken air-conditioning system, a tin roof, and hot TV lights combine to make it a sauna. Even spectators have a hard time breathing in this inferno. The seats are filled, as are the aisles and rafters. In all, about twenty-seven thousand people

---

* Marcos will tell promoter Don King that he brought the match to Manila to draw attention to Filipinos who fought and died in World War II. In fact, the president declared martial law three years earlier, and the fight was meant to be a distraction from the corruption, poverty, and threats of revolution brought on by his "New Society."

surround the ring, but the fighters have little awareness of them. Their pain is too distracting.

This is the third fight between Ali and Frazier. Joe won the first, at Madison Square Garden in 1971, keeping his heavyweight crown away from Ali. Billed as the "Fight of the Century," it was the most-watched sporting event in history at the time. On January 28, 1974, also in New York City, Ali won the second contest, recapturing the title. Now the most brutal of the three bouts has just one round remaining.

Slouched against the corner post and the ropes, Muhammad Ali sprawls on his stool. He can barely breathe from the cigarette smoke and heat. His body aches. Joe Frazier has hit him approximately 440 times today. Ali has had trouble staying alert between rounds. He has visible lumps on his forehead from Frazier's punches—and from a secret weapon Joe has never displayed before. At the insistence of trainer Eddie Futch, the southpaw Frazier has learned to throw a strong right-hand punch. Previously, Frazier was most well known for his vicious left.

"You can't do that! You ain't got no right hand," Ali yelled at Frazier when, in the sixth round, he first felt the sting of the other's right.

"Somebody told you all wrong, pretty boy," Frazier replied, whereupon the contender immediately blasted Ali with another blow.

"I hit him with punches that would bring down the walls of a city," Frazier will later state.

In addition to the lumps on his forehead, Ali's eyes are swollen, his midsection throbs with pain, and the bones in his hands are nearly broken from hitting Frazier so many times with lightweight (eight-ounce) gloves. In fact, for months after the fight, Ali will not be able to shake hands.

Frazier's wounds are easier to see. His face is also swollen, particularly his eyes, which are almost shut. Even before stepping into the ring this morning, Joe Frazier successfully concealed a cataract in his left eye brought on by pieces of metal flying off a speed bag during training. This condition allowed Ali to land numerous punches Frazier could not see.

✦ ✦ ✦

It is precisely 11:51 a.m. in the Philippines. Ali and Frazier have three minutes more of suffering, and according to the three judges' scoring cards, the fight is close. Yet the thirty-three-year-old Ali has had enough—he does not want to answer the bell for the fifteenth round. Surrounded by four men attending to him, including trainer Angelo Dundee and boxing physician Ferdie Pacheco, the champ sits in his corner sweating heavily.

Fight referee Carlos "Sonny" Padilla has kept the match moving tonight, not allowing either man to hold or clinch excessively. Padillo, a Filipino, now stands in the ring. Dressed in a light-blue short-sleeve shirt and black pants, he looks back and forth at the Ali and Frazier corners, watching to see if someone will signal an end to the fight.

Ali is conflicted. His personal and financial situation is in disarray, and being heavyweight champion of the world ensures a steady income as challengers step forward. He tells friends he is terrified of ending up like Joe Louis, the former heavyweight champion of the world, who lost all his money and spent his final days as a greeter in a Las Vegas casino.*

Muhammad Ali owns a farm in Michigan, pays alimony to his first wife, and is soon to divorce his second. That woman, Khalilah Ali, has waited at home with the fighter's four children while the champ traveled here with his mistress, Veronica Porché. Soon, Porché will become Ali's third spouse. In fact, when, in the days leading up to the match, the fighter was heard referring to Porché as his "wife," Khalilah Ali flew immediately to Manila to confront her husband. Coinci-

---

* Joe Louis was heavyweight champion of the world from 1937 to 1949, successfully defending his crown twenty-five consecutive times—a record for all weight classes. In addition to being married four times, Louis began using cocaine, which led to heart problems and financial difficulty. In need of money late in life, to supplement his casino work, he has also appeared on quiz shows.

dentally, Joe Frazier's wife and four daughters are on Khalilah's San Francisco flight into Manila, traveling to watch the fight. "They reported that she [Khalilah] looked mean enough to bite the bumper off a Buick," Joe Frazier will remember.

Yet Muhammad Ali totally ignores the situation. In his hotel suite, Khalilah confronts him about his many infidelities—loudly enough that her shouts can be heard down the hallway. At five foot ten and possessing a black belt in karate, the twenty-five-year-old Khalilah is a physical force. But the champ ends the battle by putting his soon-to-be ex-wife on the next plane home.

Ali will gross at least $6 million from tonight's fight ($34 million today), but the money is split many ways—including among the sycophants who obey his every wish. The champ has long had cash-flow problems. Joe Frazier even loaned his rival money to help him. At an advanced stage in his career, Ali knows there is no big cash beyond boxing. If he quits now, his chances of securing another lucrative fight are narrow.*

But Muhammad Ali wants to end the pain. The previous round, fourteen, was a brutal exposition. Although bleeding from his face, his eyes almost swollen shut, Joe Frazier continued to stalk Ali, methodically punching his kidneys and stomach. In turn, the six-foot-three champ launched blow after blow to Frazier's head. Some ring analysts estimate that Ali hit Frazier in the face thirty-three times in the fourteenth round alone.

Despite this assault, Ali believes he is done.

"Cut 'em off," the fighter demands of Angelo Dundee, referring to his gloves. The veteran trainer wipes the sweat from Ali's torso with a towel. He's heard Muhammad try to quit before—most notably, in the sixth round of his first epic fight with Sonny Liston, eleven

---

* Ali was stripped of his title in response to his 1967 refusal to fight in the Vietnam War. During his three years away from boxing, he ran low on money. Feeling it best for the sport to have Ali in the ring, Joe Frazier lobbied for the ban to be lifted and gave his fellow boxer a small loan to help him through the ordeal.

years ago. Then, as now, Dundee ignores his fighter and prepares to push him back out into the ring.

However, Dr. Pacheco, looking at the battered Ali, does not like what he sees. Pacheco believes he is witnessing "the tip-top of a slow murder."

The doctor speculates that one of the boxers, if not both, may die if a fifteenth round takes place.*

✦ ✦ ✦

The same conversation is happening in Frazier's corner.

"Joe, I'm going to stop it," trainer Eddie Futch tells Frazier.

"No, no, Eddie. You can't do that to me."

"You couldn't see in the last two rounds," says Futch. "What makes you think ya gonna see in the fifteenth?"

"I want him, boss," Frazier argues. He starts to stand. He would rather die than lose, as he will later admit. From this moment on, Frazier and Futch will become estranged.

"Sit down, son," Futch orders. He places one hand on his fighter's shoulder. "It's all over. No one will forget what you did here today."

✦ ✦ ✦

"I think it's going to be over," TV announcer Don Dunphy yells into his microphone.

Eddie Futch gestures to referee Sonny Padilla. Futch knows Frazier would rather risk permanent loss of vision than lose this fight to Ali. It takes Padilla less than five seconds to wave his arms, signaling that Joe Frazier will not answer the bell for the fifteenth round.

"It *is* over," Dunphy tells the worldwide audience of millions.

Ali's corner erupts in jubilation—but not the fighter himself. Angelo Dundee assists him to his feet, but the champ quickly collapses

---

* Pacheco will blame Ali's later physical ailments on the third Ali-Frazier fight: "Do you think after the beating he took that day in Manila he went home happy and had chocolate ice cream? He goddamn near died. It's the reason he's a shambling, neurological wreck." The doctor was quoted by ESPN.

to the floor of the ring. The television cameras cannot see Ali because he is surrounded by his entourage, but it is clear he is down. After a short time, the cameras do capture the champ kneeling on the canvas. A few feet away, Dunphy begins interviewing Ali's manager, Herbert Muhammad.

Joe Frazier walks over to congratulate Ali, who, after kneeling for a full minute, finally stands. A microphone is shoved in the champ's face, ending Frazier's attempt. Someone puts a stool beneath him, and Ali, unable to remain on his feet, sits down to continue the interview.

"Did you have any doubt about winning at any time?" Dunphy asks.

"Round ten," Ali answers, forgetting his demand to have his gloves cut off just minutes ago. Then the champ turns the discussion to Frazier. In the past, he has called his opponent, the son of South Carolina sharecroppers, dumb and ignorant. He has also called Frazier an Uncle Tom and, in a racist rhyme—"a killa and a thrilla and a chilla, when I get that gorilla in Manila"—compared him to an ape.

In the days leading up to the fight, Ali even carried around a small rubber gorilla, telling reporters it was Joe Frazier.

Now Ali heaps praise on Frazier: "He is the greatest fighter of all time," Ali says into the microphone. He then adds a clarification: "Next to me."

Still sitting with his head bowed, a spent Ali concludes the interview. "I want everyone to know that I'm the greatest fighter of all time. And the greatest city of all time is Louisville, Kentucky."

✦ ✦ ✦

The sun is shining brightly at noon outside the arena. Satisfied spectators pour into the daylight as Ali is assisted to his dressing room in the bowels of the arena. He collapses onto a couch and does not get up for an hour.*

---

* The early-morning fight time was to accommodate American and European TV audiences.

The champ is too beat to move, saying to his entourage, "I'm sore all over. My arms, my face, my sides all ache. I'm so, so tired. There is a great possibility that I will retire. You might have seen the last of me. I want to sit back and count my money, live in my house and my farm, work for my people and concentrate on my family."

Finally, Muhammad Ali shuffles into the press room, where he opens up: "I'm tired of being the whole ball game," *Sports Illustrated* will report his saying. "Let the other guys do the fightin'. You might never see Ali in the ring again."

There is no hospital visit. No medical exam. Apparently, Ali believes hospital visits show weakness.

Yet the champ remains broken.

The next morning, Ali's voice is a whisper as he talks to reporter Mark Kram in his suite at the Hilton Manila. The veteran fight writer has covered all the champ's battles with Frazier.

"I heard something once," Ali tells Kram. "When someone asked a marathon runner what goes through his mind the last mile or two, he said that you ask yourself, why am I doing this? You get so tired. It takes it out of you mentally. It changes you. It makes you go a little insane. I was thinking this at the end. What am I doing in here against this beast of a man? It's so painful. I must be crazy. I always bring out the best in the men I fight, but Joe Frazier, I'll tell the world right now, brings out the best in *me*.

"I'm gonna tell you, that's one hell of a man. And God bless him."

Muhammad Ali does not catch the first flight out of Manila. There is trouble at home—wife and mistress at war—no place to regain his strength. The Philippine people love him. Why leave? So Ali remains at the Hilton Manila, sleeping through the days with the curtains drawn. Not even a television is allowed in the room. When pressed, physician Pacheco makes small mentions to the media about his famous client's condition: "He is badly beaten up. It took 24 hours for his brain to recuperate and for his thought processes to announce it was the closest to death he knew of."

The champ cannot eat solid food; he shies from direct sunlight.

Childlike in his movements, he is unsure on his feet. When Muhammad Ali finally emerges back into public life on October 13, nearly two weeks after the fight, he is still noticeably feeble. He walks alongside Philippine First Lady Imelda Marcos. Like a caregiver, she guides him on their stroll through the elaborate Malacañang Palace, home to her and her husband. As a dinner crowd watches, she leads the battered champ up a long red-carpeted staircase to a buffet. A jazz band plays softly. There is applause at the sight of this great man.

Ali walks with tentative footsteps. The man who defeated Joe Frazier twelve days ago is unable to help himself. There is no laughter in his famously playful face, none of the witty banter the world has come to expect. The champ speaks only to Imelda, placing his lips to her ear in a whisper no one else can hear.

Mrs. Marcos fills a plate for him, and the two sit at the head table with President Marcos, the fighter's bruised right eye almost closed. Cautiously, he lifts food to his mouth, but he has trouble holding his fork. Ali's lips are pink, as if he has fallen on them face-first. Journalist Kram will describe them as "scraped."

Chewing is obviously a problem. Ali's battered jaw moves up and down painfully. The light from the gaudy candelabras in the room makes him shut his eyes.

"It was like death," Ali will later admit. "Closest thing to dyin' that I know of."

✦ ✦ ✦

In downtown Manila, Joe Frazier is *actually* close to death.

"Who is it? I can't see! I can't see! Turn the lights on!" he yells at the sound of a guest entering his Manila villa.

But the lights *are* on.

Frazier's face is mottled and swollen. There will long be debates over whether Eddie Futch was right to stop the fight, but it is two weeks later, and Joe Frazier is still suffering grievously. He is under a doctor's care; family and friends are very concerned.

Yet, in eight months, Joe Frazier will be fighting once more. Taking medicine to diminish the cataract in his eye, he boxes former world champion George Foreman. Frazier is knocked out in the fifth round. He retires—but then comes back to fight one more time, a ten-round draw with Floyd Cummings. After that, he hangs up the gloves for good. His animosity toward Muhammad Ali and their third fight will linger until his death.

"Truth is, I'd like to rumble with that sucker again—beat him up piece by piece and mail him back to Jesus," Frazier will write in his 1996 autobiography. "People ask me if I feel bad for him, now that things aren't going so well for him. Nope. I don't. Fact is, I don't give a damn. They want me to love him, but I'll open up the graveyard and bury his ass when the Lord chooses to take him."

✦ ✦ ✦

While Joe Frazier will soon be done with the fight game, Muhammad Ali will box for many years to come—not because he wants to, but because he is no longer in control of his life.

The world's most charismatic athlete finally returns to Michigan in late April with Veronica. His wife, Khalilah, is fed up with his infidelities, but as a devout Muslim, she concedes that her husband is allowed to have up to four wives. At first, the couple reconciles. But Veronica again becomes a distraction. Khalilah chooses to divorce Ali in late 1975, keeping her half of their "His and Hers" Rolls-Royce collection as she moves with their children to a four-bedroom apartment in Chicago. There, she works as a publicity agent and photographer at *Bilalian News*, the official Nation of Islam newspaper.

Meanwhile, mistress Veronica Porché and Ali remain together at his farm estate in Michigan.

They met at the champ's fight against George Foreman in 1974, just eleven months before the Manila bout.* The couple will have

---

* The fight with Foreman on October 30, 1974, was called the "Rumble in the Jungle" because it was held in Zaire, Africa. Ali knocked Foreman out in the eighth round. Veronica modeled at the event, working as a "poster girl," a model whose job was to help promote the fight.

two children together; their daughter Laila is destined to become a top female boxer.

But in Ali's universe, his personal life does not take precedence. It is his allegiance to the Nation of Islam and to his manager, Herbert Muhammad, that is top priority.

And there are many things happening in those areas that the heavyweight champion of the world does not know.

Many things.

CHAPTER TWO

OCTOBER 1, 1975

MANILA, PHILIPPINES

NIGHT

Herbert Muhammad is taking care of business.

As an exhausted Muhammad Ali sleeps in his Hilton hotel suite, his forty-six-year-old manager feels good. Just a few hours after the "Thrilla," Herbert knows he will be receiving perhaps as much as $4 million of the total purse for his fighter's efforts. This will add to the manager's already fabulous wealth.*

It has been a long day. Herbert Muhammad sat ringside in the sweltering heat, protected by personal security. Always nervous when a fight does not go Ali's way, the manager almost left the arena on several occasions—not out of concern for the champ's well-being but because it looked like Ali might lose.

That would have put a severe crimp in Herbert Muhammad's personal finances. At this point, Ali has earned more than $20 million since he turned pro in 1960. And the Nation of Islam is praying he will have many more big earning years ahead.

---

* Ali's total purse, $9 million, would be worth $47 million in today's money. Ali was guaranteed $4.5 million against 43 percent of gross profits. Joe Frazier received $5 million for the fight—$2 million guaranteed against 22 percent of the gross—a total of $25 million in 2022 dollars.

Per his custom, Herbert, as he is known by everyone, is staying at a different hotel from the champ. He now dines alone in his suite, his tropical tan suit baggy on his rotund frame. At home he prefers to wear black.

Herbert is not the typical manager or agent, spewing bluster and glad-handing his lone client. He believes it is his life's work to educate Ali about the Muslim way of life. For Herbert, this means prayer, silence, and an aversion to the spotlight. He constantly scolds the champ for his womanizing—to no avail.

Herbert is the opposite of his charismatic client. One longtime friend calls him the "invisible man." Others say he is just "dull." At home in Chicago, he drives a Cadillac, from which he does most of his daily business by phone; that is the only flash in his life.

"Most of the world thinks Angelo Dundee is Ali's manager," Herbert says in a rare interview. "When I go to a town, I have to call up Angelo to get me into places. But that's fine with me. I only care if Ali and the *bank* know me."

This low-key style of doing business is intentional. Herbert's preference for solitude is well known, and so is his fondness for money. He runs many enterprises: banks, bakeries, barbershops. In addition, he has real estate holdings in Michigan, Alabama, and Georgia and a lavish apartment overlooking New York's Central Park.

His father, Elijah Muhammad, became a member of the Nation of Islam in 1931, taking over when the sect's leader, Wallace Fard Muhammad, mysteriously disappeared in 1934. As the group grew in wealth and power, Elijah became a virtual dictator.

Earlier this year, Elijah Muhammad passed away at the age of seventy-seven from congestive heart failure, allowing Herbert's brother Warith (né Wallace) to take over the entire organization. The reclusive Herbert preferred to focus on his role as Muhammad Ali's manager. The champ is the Nation of Islam's most visible figure and a generator of a massive cash flow.

Herbert Muhammad is married, with five sons. Out the door every morning at seven, he walks slowly, choosing each step carefully.

He hates having his picture taken. The manager does not smoke or drink but loves to eat. He reads extensively. He is punctual, formal. Friends marvel at how strictly he diets when it is time to slim down, showing his iron will. No less than Don King, one of the most flamboyant and successful boxing promoters of all time—and a man who served time after being convicted of murder—admits to *fearing* Herbert Muhammad. King compares the manager to a greedy lion in the wild, eager to prey on every other animal.*

It was a year ago that Don King learned the hard way that Herbert Muhammad is a master negotiator. King was working for a company known as Video Techniques, which specialized in closed-circuit television. The forty-three-year-old King was looking to expand into fight promotion. He knew that Herbert offered a 10 percent finder's fee to any promoter who could fund a title fight. Don King also learned that Muhammad Ali and the world heavyweight champ at the time, George Foreman, were each being offered $2.5 million for a title bout. King approached Herbert, saying he could get double that amount.

And he did.

The fight would be fully funded by the African nation of Zaire. Ali would call it the "Rumble in the Jungle" and would go on to defeat Foreman. The victory once again made him the heavyweight champion of the world.†

King found Herbert after the fight. "I figured I'd get $500,000 from both Ali and Foreman," he said later, referring to the 10 percent commission. "But Herbert told me, 'That's too much money for you,' and gave me $150,000. Still, I thought, $150,000 and $500,000,

---

* Unlike his father, who was often accused of meting out his own private version of justice, Herbert is not a violent man. However, if he senses betrayal in any way, whether in the boxing world or in the Nation of Islam, he will ostracize the other person almost immediately.

† At the time, Zaire—now known as the Democratic Republic of the Congo—was run by a brutal dictator known as Mobutu Sese Seko. Although the country was one of the poorest in the world, the people living in destitution, Mobutu managed to pay $5 million each to Foreman and Ali, plus another one million for promotional expenses—all to bring attention to himself. To attract a prime-time American audience, the Rumble in the Jungle took place at 4 a.m. in Kinshasa, the capital.

that adds up to $650,000, so I told Herbert okay. But then I went to George Foreman [to collect] and he wanted to knock me out.

"It was a good lesson," he added. "Everything had to be in writing."*

✦ ✦ ✦

The Muhammad Ali industry began in 1964, when a young fighter then named Cassius Clay first captured the heavyweight crown with a technical knockout of Sonny Liston. At the time, Clay's managers were a group of businessmen in Louisville, Kentucky, the fighter's hometown. But a Muslim named Malcolm X, a powerful presence among African Americans, was quietly grooming the young fighter, who first showed his potential by winning an Olympic gold medal four years prior in Rome.

In 1975, the Nation of Islam boasted almost seventy thousand members and more than one hundred mosques in America. The church had a net worth of $75 million. It was not only a religious organization but a social one, too. Male NOI members would often patrol the streets of tough neighborhoods dressed in suits and bow ties. The men were disciplined, well groomed, and polite to neighborhood residents. However, they would impose violence on anyone deemed a threat to the community—or a traitor to the NOI.

Over the years, its leader, Elijah Muhammad, became a very powerful person. His rivals had a habit of disappearing. For this reason, he lived in a heavily guarded Chicago compound. Born Elijah Poole in Georgia, he was arrested in 1942 for failure to register for the wartime draft and eventually served four years in a federal prison on eight counts of sedition for ordering his followers not to serve, either. He preached that Blacks were the original human beings and that whites were an "evil" race intent on suppressing his people. Elijah believed that power must be taken from whites—by force, if necessary.

The young, charismatic Cassius Clay appealed to fans of all races

---

* Foreman also gave King $150,000.

and appeared to believe the exact opposite of Elijah Muhammad's racially divisive preaching. Therefore, the world was shocked when, the morning after beating Sonny Liston, Clay confirmed that he was joining the Black Muslim movement and changing his name to Cassius X. (He would later change it again to Muhammad Ali.)

Jabir Herbert Muhammad, as Elijah Muhammad's son is formally known, soon became Ali's personal manager.* The fighter's contract with his Louisville backers expired in 1966, whereupon Herbert began supervising Ali with his father's blessing. The new manager had no prior boxing experience. Before Ali, Herbert ran a bakery and dry cleaner in Chicago. The only thing he knew about boxing was that each round was three minutes long.

Along with keeping the champ focused on the Nation of Islam, Herbert controls Ali's entire financial portfolio. This created a rivalry between Malcolm and the Nation of Islam. "Nobody leaves the Muslims without trouble," Malcolm once warned the fighter.

Those words would prove prophetic. In 1965, Malcolm X was assassinated.†

An FBI report dated June 14, 1966, states, "Clay's whole life is influenced and directed by Elijah Muhammad. [The informant] said there is no other person known to him who exerts as great an influence on Clay. He said he would blindly do whatever Elijah Muhammad would ask."

✦ ✦ ✦

Herbert Muhammad became skilled at negotiating the best possible fees for his client—even as Ali did the hard physical work of absorbing punches.

---

* The history of Muhammad Ali's professional fighting career is written about in the book *Killing the Mob*. It is widely believed Sonny Liston threw the two fights against Cassius Clay/Muhammad Ali.

† Malcolm X was shot in the chest with a sawed-off shotgun on February 21, 1965, just before he was to deliver a speech in New York City. Two days earlier, Malcolm had told an interviewer that the Nation of Islam was trying to kill him.

As today's "Thrilla" demonstrates, the two men have made each other rich. The plan going forward is for the champ to gross $50 million in earnings before eventually retiring. Herbert believes Ali can bring in more than $15 million in the coming year alone.*

So, as his client suffers here in Manila, Herbert is busy finding new fights. The simple math of boxing two to three times annually—no matter what the physical cost to the fighter—ensures that the money will flow in. Following this formula has allowed Ali to make back (and then some) the cash he lost in legal fees during his three-year ban from boxing for avoiding the draft. "Standard Oil doesn't try to sell a small amount of oil," Herbert likes to remind the champ.

Standard Oil didn't urinate blood, either. Muhammad Ali's body is now rebelling against his chosen profession; he cannot even get out of bed. Yet Herbert will not let the champ rest for long. By this time next year, Muhammad Ali will fight an incredible five more times.

---

* That would be $261 million in 2022 dollars.

CHAPTER THREE

Jean-Pierre Coopman is afraid.

The brown-haired, prominently sideburned "Lion of Flanders" is four inches shorter than his opponent, Muhammad Ali. The champ's reach is five inches longer. The Belgian's professional boxing record is 24–3, with fifteen knockouts. He weighs twenty pounds less than Ali.

And tonight, he is also less *sober*. His badly broken nose curving to the left and his face pink from the champagne he drank before stepping into the ring, the Lion knows that this will be his only chance to become the heavyweight champion of the world.

However, no one is here, on this tropical Caribbean night, to watch Jean-Pierre Coopman—except maybe his wife and mother, who are openly fearful for his safety.

Everyone else is here to see Ali.

Herbert Muhammad sits ringside, surrounded by money. Everywhere he looks, people are symbolically putting cash in his pocket. Roberto Clemente Coliseum is packed with 10,000 members of Ali's ever-growing fan base, poor and rich alike. Ringside seats go for $200 apiece. Another 11,500 fans watch on closed-circuit television in a stadium next door. Don King Productions has also arranged for forty million people to watch the bout on CBS television in the United States.

As referee Ismael Quiñones Falú waits for the bout to begin, the Lion of Flanders is smiling—this despite his deep fear of the beating he might endure.

Five weeks ago, during a prefight lunch at a place called Mamma Leone's in New York City, Ali was friendly to the affable Belgian. To Coopman, this was a relief. But as the bell rings, Ali shows no sign of a smile. The champ's face is a mask of grim determination.

It is four months since the Thrilla in Manila. Having finally recovered from that bout, Ali demanded that Herbert Muhammad find him an *easy* opponent, one he could dispatch without much pain.

Herbert did as he was asked.

This is not a big-money fight: Ali is getting just $1 million, with Coopman receiving a grand. (When he is not boxing, Coopman makes the Flemish equivalent of $4.50 per hour sculpting religious statues.) The manager also contrived to earn money in the days leading up to the fight by charging fans $5 apiece for the privilege of watching Ali spar at the El San Juan hotel. No matter whether the revenue source is closed-circuit TV, the million paid by CBS for broadcast rights, or other capitalization, it is all money in the bank for Muhammad Ali—and for Herbert. Already, the manager has lined up the next fight—in San José, Costa Rica, with a boxer named Jimmy Young. Ali will be paid $1.5 million. Then it is on to Tokyo, to fight a martial arts champion for $6 million. After that, a legitimate match against a true contender, Ken Norton, who, three years ago, broke Ali's jaw.

The champ wants payback.

"I need money," Ali admits to the press before tonight's fight. "I got a million for this fight, but look what's left. Taxes cut it to $600,000 here, and my expenses and taxes at home knock it down to $350,000. Then out comes my manager's end. I can't go on forever, but I'm gonna raise some hell while I can."

Tonight, the only real challenge Ali faces is avoiding a surprise knockout punch. That would surely put a halt to Herbert's "Standard Oil" strategy.

Yet even Jean-Pierre Coopman doesn't see that happening. He quietly admits to reporters, "I don't think I have much of a chance."

✦ ✦ ✦

Predictably, Ali is taking criticism for the decision to fight a much lesser opponent.

"Why do they always want me to fight for my life?" he responds to the media. "Floyd Patterson once fought Pete Rademacher, an amateur in his first pro fight, but that was all right. Floyd Patterson was a good boy, but I'm a bad n*****. George Foreman fought José Roman—who's he? Ain't nobody banned it. Ain't nobody wanted to stop it. Joe Frazier fought Terry Daniels, a college student, and he fought Ron Stander, a beer-bellied boy from Omaha, and nobody stopped it. But everybody wants me to fight for my life. I got Ken Norton and George Foreman ahead of me. Let me have a little rest in between."

Ali goes on to say that Coopman is just a "white hope."

✦ ✦ ✦

The first round goes fairly well for Coopman, who, despite his nickname, enters the ring wearing an orange robe with an eagle on the left shoulder. The Lion of Flanders is known in the boxing world as an "absorber"—meaning he can take a punch. Sometimes, the Belgian winks at opponents after enduring a particularly hard blow, just to show his toughness.

Muhammad Ali also has a long history of showing off in the ring. It all started when he was twelve years old. When someone stole his red Schwinn bicycle, the young Cassius Clay told a Louisville police officer that he wanted to beat up the thief. The cop replied, "Well, you better start learning to fight before you start challenging people."

That policeman was Joe E. Martin, who also ran a boxing club at a nearby gym. Within two years, Clay had won his first fight by a split decision. Two years after that, he won the Golden Gloves novice tournament. By 1959, Clay had become the national Golden Gloves champ. The following year, Rome and the Olympics beckoned, after which the young fighter turned professional.

Now, after more than twenty years in the ring, the champ does not want to simply throw punches. When possible, he likes to entertain the crowd, as he does tonight in San Juan.

Much to Herbert Muhammad's displeasure.

Herbert wants Ali to quickly knock Coopman out, pocket his take, and fly home. And although it is obvious the fighter can do that anytime he likes, he prefers to clown around.

Rahman Ali, the champ's younger brother, working the corner of the ring tonight, screams at him to "be tough" as the boxer fights flat-footed in the first and second rounds, snapping playful punches at Coopman's head. Rahman yells at Ali so many times that the champ finally tells him to shut up.

Drew Bundini Brown, another cornerman, also grows tired of the charade. "The Chief," he yells, referring to God, "is watching in his living room."

Still, the Lion of Flanders absorbs blow after blow. All the while, Herbert Muhammad grows angrier and more vocal. Fearing a lucky knockout might destroy his carefully laid plans, he mutters, "It looks like this cat's got a hard head."

Finally, Herbert has had enough. He gets up out of his seat, walks to Ali's corner, and in a voice clearly heard above the noise of the arena, gives very specific orders to the champ's handlers: "Tell him to stop all this foolin' around, or I'm walkin' out of the building." In the words of *Sports Illustrated*, "If Herbert had walked, it would not have been an ordinary manager taking his leave. It would have been the son of the late Elijah Muhammad, founder of the Muslims. It would have been the Number Two man in the Muslim empire turning his back on a subject. Such a gesture would have grave implications. Ali got the message."

Jean-Pierre Coopman gets knocked out in the fifth.

Muhammad Ali personally helps the challenger out of the ring when Coopman is unable to stand. Again, he is clowning for the crowd. He is sending a signal that this fight was simply an excuse for people to be entertained by "the Greatest."

✦ ✦ ✦

Reaction to the fight is muted. However, dangerous contenders like George Foreman and Ken Norton watch closely. The talk among fight people is that Muhammad Ali, now thirty-four years old, is not the force he used to be. The punishment Ali absorbed from Joe Frazier lingers. It is apparent to some that age and physical impairment have weakened the champ.

And then there is Ali's chaotic personal life. He is now living in Michigan with Veronica, who has no income and is pregnant with their first daughter. The champ's four children with his second wife, Khalilah, are in Chicago. Ali is now fully supporting them, as well as his first wife, Sonji Roi, a model, who also lives in Chicago. Published reports say the champ's monthly expenses are more than $60,000.* Also, a variety of hangers-on and relatives routinely ask for money. The champ almost always gives it. In San Juan, Muhammad Ali has covered the expenses for more than fifty people.

✦ ✦ ✦

Within hours of defeating Coopman, Ali leaves Puerto Rico, knowing his next ring combat is just two months away. The challenger is young, Jimmy Young, a twenty-seven-year-old journeyman fighter from Philadelphia. Once again, Ali will box in the tropics—but this time the bout will be more challenging, as Young is experienced. Ali knows he must train, and he doesn't much like it.

The champ is weary—but there is no rest.

---

* $316,000 in today's money.

CHAPTER FOUR

APRIL 30, 1976
LANDOVER, MARYLAND
8 P.M.

Jimmy Young wants to "take it from the champion."

The twenty-seven-year-old challenger looks across the ring at a bloated Muhammad Ali. The champ weighed in at 230 pounds for tonight's fight, the heaviest he's been for all fifty-three of his bouts. Young stands at six foot one and is a lean 210 pounds.

Ali's condition stems from boredom with training. Although his $1.6 million purse for tonight includes an additional $200,000 for "training expenses," he has done little conditioning. In fact, in the weeks leading up to this fight, he traveled to London, where women eager to see the champ broke down rope barriers protecting him during an appearance at Selfridges department store.* Also, he has accepted an invitation from the Turkish prime minister to visit Istanbul later in the year, a trip scheduled just three days after his September 28 bout with Ken Norton.

The champ knows he has done little to prepare for tonight's fight. "I'm in terrible shape," he admits. "I've been eating too much pie, too much ice cream."

---

* Ali was in London promoting his book *The Greatest*.

His challenger is in prime condition. The son of a welder, Jimmy Young has been training hard at Joe Frazier's gym on Broad Street in North Philadelphia. Young, ranked ninth in the world, well knows the boxing wisdom that says a challenger must land twice as many punches as the man wearing the title belt. Thus the axiom "Take it from the champion."

Young aims to do just that.

He's the only one in the arena who thinks he can.

"This Young is a joke, like Coopman," promoter Bob Arum says before the fight. Then, referring to the champ's next bout, in Munich, Germany, scheduled for just three weeks from now, he says, "Ali will fight [Richard] Dunn, too."

Herbert Muhammad has been busy—he has already lined up the fights against Dunn, Japanese wrestler Antonio Inoki, and Ken Norton.

ABC sports announcer Howard Cosell is calling the shots ringside this evening—a live broadcast throughout the United States and overseas.* The fight was supposed to have taken place in Costa Rica, but it was moved to Maryland when Capital Centre owner Abe Pollin guaranteed Herbert bigger money. Boxer Ken Norton, sitting near Cosell, is ready to provide commentary.

Ali is in white trunks, Young in black. When the bell rings to start the first round, the contender approaches cautiously. He is not a knockout fighter, so he will avoid that strategy. Instead, the Philadelphian will frustrate Ali with a defensive stance.

The first and second rounds are slow. Nobody fights Ali like this. Usually, opponents attack. Ali counts on this. He is hard to knock out, able to absorb a tremendous number of punches. He lets opponents get inside his jab before responding with precise three and

---

* Howard Cosell had a long history with Muhammad Ali, dating back to the Sonny Liston bout in 1964. When Ali announced his name change and conversion to Islam, reporters refused to call the champ by his new name—all but Cosell. The former "Howard Cohen" also backed Ali when the fighter refused to be drafted for the Vietnam War. The two became friends, each using the other to increase his fame. Cosell was often called a "n*****-loving Jew" by his enemies because of this friendship. Howard Cosell died in 1995 at the age of seventy-seven.

four combinations. The champ prefers to circle back and to the left, making his opponents come to him.

But Young waits on Ali, letting the champ stalk *him*. In this way, Young controls the tempo of the fight.

By the fifth round, the stunned crowd senses they might be watching history being made. The arena is no longer in a pro-Ali frenzy. The champ is visibly tired, lumbering. He lunges, something no one can remember ever seeing Ali do before. Most punches miss. Meanwhile, Young bides his time.

Suddenly, Young launches a right hook. It shatters Ali's eardrum.

"I don't remember which round," Ali will say after the fight. "I hurt it in the Philippines once before and he reopened it. I was hurt twice. He hit me with two right hands. I saw stars and my knees started to buckle."

In his ringside seat, Herbert Muhammad is visibly concerned.

Ken Norton, also watching from ringside, grows anxious. He is due for a big payday with his next Ali bout. But a Jimmy Young victory means that will never happen. "Don't blow the money, Ali. Don't blow the money, damn it!" Norton yells at the champ.

The crowd boos Ali's lackluster performance.

"I don't blame 'em," Herbert says. "I'd boo, too. I hope Young hits him on the side of his head and wakes him up."

Furious at his fighter for his awkwardness, Herbert yells to Dundee, "Angelo, tell him to stop that stuff! He's embarrassin' everybody when he does that!"

Young's punches pike up. Incredibly, after all his years as a fighter, Muhammad Ali is not slipping many blows. When Young hits him, the punches land solid against the champ's face and body. Ali begins leaning back, trying to pull away from Young—which leaves him off balance.

By the start of the sixth round, Ali is behind 76–35 in number of blows landed.

"The kid slips punches well," Howard Cosell says of Ali's challenger, mystified at the direction the fight is taking.

The crowd senses doom. Herbert Muhammad is *irate*. Ali's cornermen, Angelo Dundee and Dr. Ferdie Pacheco, grow stony silent. The champ himself is worried and begins throwing more punches. In his seventeen previous title defenses, Ali has never had to go to the body—always aiming for the knockout blow to the head. But with Young hanging back, covering up his head with both gloves when Ali gets close, it is clear the champ must switch tack.

With forty-three seconds left in the seventh round, Jimmy Young finally makes a mistake. As Ali hits the challenger's torso, Young sticks his head beneath the rope and out of the ring. The judges notice the escape attempt. This is not "taking it from the champion." This is *running* from the champion. The Philadelphian will continue to use this ploy several more times. The judges begin to turn against Young. Despite the younger man's clearly landing a solid right in the ninth, the judges give the round to Ali.

But most of the crowd dissents. Young is clearly the better fighter tonight. "Ali has not really gotten a sharp blow into Young," Cosell opines.

As a desperate champion corners Young and lands blows that simply glance off him, Cosell does play-by-play: "Ali trying to over-power him. Ali can't get through."

Ken Norton thinks Ali looks pitiful and says so.

"Have you ever seen Ali miss so often?" Cosell asks him.

"No, I haven't," Norton says. "Ali's trying to overpower him, but there's nothing in his punches."

In the twelfth round, Jimmy Young once again sticks his head outside the ropes. Referee Johnny McAvoy has had enough of this. He calls a standing knockdown, once again tilting the scorecard in Ali's favor.

Young wins the fourteenth round with a pair of right jabs to the champ's chin. As Ali staggers backward, the Philadelphian hits again with a right, snapping the champ's head backward.

"You're losing!" Ali's brother, Rahman, seated next to Herbert Muhammad, yells to the fighter.

Fury washes over Herbert's face. "Who told you to say that?" he snaps at Rahman. "Judges hear that, people hear that, they start believin' it. Now keep quiet."

Howard Cosell also believes Ali is in trouble. "The only thing that can cost Jimmy Young is the frequency of defensive tactics," he tells Norton. "I think you made an effective point [about] taking the title away from the man."

The last round is almost over. "We're down to seconds now," Cosell tells the audience.

"The fight will have gone the limit." Jimmy Young has never fought more than ten rounds.

Tonight, he will land 41 percent of his punches to just 19 percent for Ali.

But, stunningly, the decision will *not* go to Jimmy Young. He listens in disbelief as two out of three judges score the fight for Ali. The disbelieving crowd erupts in loud booing.*

Muhammad Ali is quickly swarmed by a thick scrum of supporters. They usher him out of the ring and back to his dressing room.

Ken Norton has the final word: "The Ali you saw tonight is not the guy I have to fight. I wish it was, but it won't be. He'll be ready for me. You can count on it."

✦ ✦ ✦

"I made a mistake by contracting myself to fight too much this year," Ali tells the press after the fight. "The training is getting so boring. Do you realize that I have to go back in training two days from now? I really don't want to train."

But he has to. The European heavyweight champion, a British

---

* Jimmy Young will go on to defeat George Foreman in March 1977 but then will lose another shot at the title with a split-decision loss to Ken Norton eight months later. Young will retire from the ring in 1990, widely considered the best fighter never to win a world championship title.

fighter named Richard Dunn, is waiting in Munich. In twenty-four days, Ali and Dunn will slug it out on German soil.

✦ ✦ ✦

After leaving Maryland, a deflated Muhammad Ali travels to his training camp in remote Deer Lake, Pennsylvania. The nearest city, Allentown, is thirty-five miles away. A simple white sign two miles past the Deer Lake Motel reads, "Ali's Camp," directing visitors up a steep road into a forest hideaway.

The training camp is sparse. It has a mosque, eight cabins built from trees from the property, and little else. The names of famous boxing personalities are painted on stones as inspiration: Joe Louis, Sonny Liston, Angelo Dundee. There are no luxuries and few distractions on-site. Breakfast each day is filet mignon and a gallon of orange juice.

But Muhammad Ali cannot live like a Spartan. Over the three weeks of training, he will seek "diversions."

The champ has built a house for himself at Deer Lake and a separate cabin for his family. This, he says, allows him to focus completely on proper sleep. But Ali is not joined by his children or girlfriend this time. So he orders his entourage to provide a steady stream of women with whom to spend the evenings. Ali encouraged these procurements even before his recent divorce. "He knew it was wrong," his second wife, Khalilah Ali, will say of the champ's many affairs. "As long as he was having fun, he didn't care."

Ali's trainers know he must get back into shape and avoid distractions or he will get destroyed in Germany. Most of the time, Ali trains hard. Sometimes, he rises at one in the morning for a fourteen-mile run. Soon, he drops ten pounds. He spars aggressively and has set aside a bunkhouse solely for use by his sparring partners. The champ demands that they hold nothing back when stepping into the sparring ring, but these fighters know not to go too far—knocking down the champ will get them sent home.

The regimen at Deer Lake does not last long. Just two weeks after fighting Jimmy Young, Muhammad Ali is on a plane for Munich to fight "Frankenstein." His entourage requires forty rooms at the Hotel Bayerischer Hof, for which Ali will foot the bill. He is also arranging for two thousand US soldiers stationed there to be given free tickets to the fight.

"Frankenstein" is an odd nickname for Richard Dunn. He stands at six foot four—only one inch taller than Ali—and has light red hair and blue eyes. The former British paratrooper is also lighter than Ali by fourteen pounds, weighing in at 206.

Dunn and his trainers have watched footage of the Young fight closely. They are confident.

"I'm no prophet, but the only prediction I'll make about the flight is that I'll be the winner," Dunn boasts upon his own arrival in Munich.

✦ ✦ ✦

Herbert almost cancels the fight. The German promoters are short on cash and fail to realize their original promise of a $1.65 million purse for Ali. High ticket prices and the lackluster Ali performance in the Young fight have driven down demand. The twelve-thousand-seat Olympiahalle is far from sold out. But Herbert makes a last-minute deal with German tax authorities—they will lower Ali's obligation by $65,000, the exact amount the promoters can't come up with.

So the fight goes on.

It is 3:15 in the morning when the bell sounds for the first round—the very late start again due to the bout's being televised live in the United States. As if to remind viewers that the Young fight was a fluke, a much leaner Muhammad Ali immediately starts pummeling Dunn. Apparently, the British boxer learned little from the Young fight. He goes straight at Ali—and takes blow after blow to his prominent chin. After three rounds, Dunn is hurt but still standing. "I'm glad we took this fight seriously," Ali tells Dundee in his corner.

The fourth round spells doom for Dunn.

Ali knocks him down four times, but each time he is knocked to the canvas, the British fighter gets back up. "I've got to live with myself for the rest of my life," Dunn said earlier in the week. An incredulous Ali is shocked when a wobbly Dunn tags him with a blow to the chin.

The bell rings.

Ali goes straight to his corner. He sits upright against the ropes as his trainers wipe away sweat with a towel and offer him a sip of energy drink. Then, even before the one-minute break is over, Ali is standing, eager to end it all. He points his red glove at the blue canvas, warning Dunn that if he chooses to come out for the fifth round, he will go down.

Richard Dunn's two cornermen do their best to revive their fighter. Thinning hair pressed to his skull, the English boxer is groggy but determined. He does not react as Ali taunts him. Instead, when the bell rings, Dunn rises from his corner stool and marches straight to Ali, punching the champ square in the jaw.

The fifth round becomes a brawl. Dunn repeatedly attacks. He backs Ali onto the ropes and pummels him with blows to the torso and head. But there is no longer any strength behind Dunn's punches. They land softly, inflicting no pain. Ali covers up and leans back against the ropes, looking for his moment.

With less than one minute left in the round, the champ lands a solid right that drops the challenger. Dunn stays down until the referee's count of eight. He uses the ropes to pull himself to his feet. Once again, Dunn comes out swinging, unwilling to admit defeat. Ali wades in and lands another hard right to the head, knocking down the challenger once again.

But Richard Dunn staggers to his feet. Now he is unsteady, unable to balance. Referee Herbert Tomser waves his arms in the air, signaling that the bout is over. Dunn has been knocked down six times in the last two rounds.

Muhammad Ali makes a big windmill motion with his right arm, the only display of flamboyant behavior this evening.

However, the champ's bravado foreshadows his diminishing power: Richard Dunn is the last boxer he will ever knock out.

✦ ✦ ✦

The trip back to America awaits. Ali will fly commercial along with his forty-plus-person entourage, enduring the usual public frenzy in the Munich Airport once he is recognized. Now, in the hours after the fight, the champ sits down with America's top boxing writers in his suite at the Hotel Bayerischer Hof. The enormous five-star hotel fronts the leafy Promenadeplatz, a small park in Munich's Old Town. Outside, the temperature is a cool fifty-four degrees.

Ali was jubilant after the fight, but he is now more reserved. He admits that he wants out of boxing but that "they really won't let me quit." Ali does not specify who *they* are. "I'm nowhere what I was a while ago," he adds, referring to his diminishing skills. "I have just enough to carry me through the year and destroy Norton."

That's Muhammad Ali's plan: defeat "that Japanese rassler" next month in Tokyo, beat Ken Norton in September, then retire as heavyweight champion of the world. "I don't want to leave defeated," he adds. "I'm going to get out of this business ahead of the game."

Then he backtracks: "Some oilman will come and give me ten million dollars to fight the Great White Hope," the champ notes. "Or it'll be ten million to fight George Foreman in the desert somewhere. I really want to quit. But if someone offers you ten million, it ain't easy."

✦ ✦ ✦

And things are about to get even more difficult. In just thirty-one days, Muhammad Ali will travel to Japan for another moneymaking exhibition.

But this one will go terribly wrong.

And Ali will never be the same.

CHAPTER FIVE

JUNE 14, 1976
BURBANK, CALIFORNIA
6 P.M.

Muhammad Ali is on *The Tonight Show.*

"We're in a new field now," he tells guest host McLean Stevenson, who is subbing for Johnny Carson. The forty-eight-year-old actor, best known for his role on the television show *M*A*S*H*, is a huge fan of Ali, this evening's only guest. *Tonight Show* announcer Ed McMahon sits next to the boxer on the set, laughing loudly at each of the champ's jokes.

"We're going to Japan to take on Antonio Inoki, the world heavyweight karate wrestling champion. This is a whole new thing," Ali explains. "People have always wondered how would a boxer do with a wrestler. I've always wanted to fight a wrestler. I've seen them grabbing each other. Throwing each other down and twisting each other's arms. And I said, 'Boy, I could whoop him.' All you gotta do is hit him really fast and really hard and move off of him.

"And now I'm going to get a chance to do it. This will be something."

Ali goes on to explain the rules: "We're going fifteen rounds.... He's allowed to use his bare fists. He's allowed to use karate. No punching in the eyes and no hitting below the belt." Seeking to entertain, Stevenson calls Ali's six-foot-four, 240-pound opponent "Hokey Inoki." He cites reports that, to prepare for this fight, the wrestler is allowing sparring partners to kick him in the face.

The thirty-three-year-old Inoki is a national hero in Japan. Famous for his toughness, he has reportedly lost three teeth in preparing to fight Ali.*

This time it is Ali himself who is responsible for the exhibition. In April 1975, the champ had a conversation with Ichiro Yada, president of the Japanese Amateur Wrestling Association, who was in the United States on business. Ali boasted that he could beat any "Oriental fighter." The challenge made headlines in Japan and caught the eye of Antonio Inoki.

It took nearly a year of negotiations, but the terms of the Tokyo bout were finally agreed on. Herbert Muhammad arranged for Ali to receive a $6 million purse. In addition to funding this, Inoki's management company will cover all travel expenses for the champ and his entourage.

In Ali's mind, this was never meant to be a serious fight. The bout is theater. Despite the "rules" the champ shared with tonight's television audience, the fight is heavily scripted—or so Ali believes. In the last round, he will throw a punch that will accidentally hit and knock out the referee. As a "compassionate" Ali bends down to help the official, Inoki will deliver a kick to Ali's head. The revived referee will then count out the champ. In this way, Inoki will not lose honor in his home country, and Ali will be seen as a gentleman for helping the referee.

Everybody wins.

But as the champ evaluates his upcoming trip, the *Tonight Show* audience is surprised to see his usual bluster disappear. "I'm a little nervous, I must admit," Ali tells Stevenson. "If this man grabs my arm or gets in behind me and gets one of those body snatchers or those backbreakers on me, I'm in trouble. But I'm counting on my

---

* Even more than four decades later, Inoki's profile remains famous in Japan. He has his own line of vitamin water and also condoms that somehow promote "Inoki-ism."

speed and reflexes, because if I hit him right and he don't fall, then he can do what he wanna do."

✦ ✦ ✦

Muhammad Ali's commercial plane from Los Angeles touches down in Tokyo on June 16. The champ's flair for promotion is once again on display. The arrivals hall is packed with media and fans. As Ali's entourage surrounds the champ, opening a path to their waiting limousines, he loudly shouts, "There will be no Pearl Harbor! Muhammad Ali has returned!

There will be no Pearl Harbor!"

The champ is just having fun. A normal fight sometimes requires these theatrics to help sell tickets when the arena is not sold out or when pay-per-view television sales are lagging. But the bout with Inoki ten days from now is already a phenomenal financial success. All 14,500 seats at the Nippon Budokan are sold out. Ringside seats cost more than $1,000 dollars ($4,500 in 2022 currency). The fight will be seen on television in 134 countries; more than one billion spectators will watch. This includes the thirty-two thousand boxing enthusiasts viewing it live on a big screen at Shea Stadium in New York City.*

Ali's hype continues. After getting his entourage settled in on the forty-fourth floor of the plush Keio Plaza Hotel (where the bill for the four suites plus the thirty one standard rooms will come to $2,166 per day—$12,000 in modern currency), the champ resumes training. He wakes every morning at three o'clock to run the streets of Tokyo before the city's heavy traffic lessens the air quality. After a nap, he spars each day at noon, alternating between boxers and martial artists.

On June 18, Ali and Inoki sit for the usual prefight press conference. The champ's name in Japanese is pronounced "Ah-ree," which

---

* The undercard—or warm-up acts—in New York will include the "Showdown at Shea," a fight between boxer Chuck Wepner and wrestler Andre the Giant. Wepner, who went fifteen rounds against Ali in 1975, was a huge underdog against the seven-foot-four, 540-pound wrestler. As an aside, actor Sylvester Stallone will later claim that he based the character of Rocky Balboa on Wepner in his March 1975 battle with Muhammad Ali.

sounds very much like the Japanese word meaning "ant." When Ali states that his nickname for Inoki is "the Pelican," the Japanese press quickly dubs the fight "the Ant versus the Pelican."

Inoki does not back down from his new nickname. "When your fist connects with my chin, take care that your fist is not damaged," he tells the champ. As a gift, Inoki presents Ali with a crutch, to be used in his post-fight recovery.

It will be needed.

✦ ✦ ✦

The next day, Ali holds a solo press conference to assure the world that the fight is not fixed. "This match is serious," the champ pronounces. "It's not your average rassling match. The worst thing I could do would be to involve myself in a public scandal, or fraud, taking six million and deceiving the people of the world. That's the worst thing I could do as a religious man. A fixed or rehearsed fight? Never. I'm not gonna go out in nothing like that."

Then, as he does many times before a fight, Ali insults his opponent, pretending to forget Inoki's name. Although the champ doesn't know it, this serves to enrage the wrestler. "Not remembering my name is a very serious insult in Japan," Inoki tells the press. "I had no serious intention of harming him, but now, because my fans have so much faith in me, it may be necessary to do something along those lines."

On June 20, six days before the fight, Ali and his entourage visit a public exhibition at Inoki's gym during a training session. The champ is stunned by the ferocity of the holds and kicks. Inoki routinely lands a roundhouse kick to his sparring partner's chest. Despite his vow that the bout isn't fixed, Ali wants reassurance that the bout with Inoki will indeed be a "staged" exhibition. "What I've promised to do is an exhibition fight. [Inoki] will not be hitting me with full force," the Japanese media will later report him saying.

Quietly, Ali asks Inoki's interpreter what time rehearsals will be. The startled man replies, "No, no. This isn't an exhibition. It's a real fight!"

Ali's apprehension only grows when sports columnist Red Smith, writing for the *New York Times*, pens a long column showing that wrestlers have a decided advantage—but only if the grapplers fight without boxing gloves.

"Let the rassler go in barehanded," Smith notes, mentioning historical fights against wrestlers by heavyweight champions Jack Dempsey and Archie Moore that did not go well. "If the performance is on the level, the boxer will stand no chance. All the rassler need do is hit the floor, where he is safe, and go for the legs."

Red Smith is a prophet, as Inoki will fight bare-fisted.

Publicist Bob Goodman will remember the confrontation. "Inoki was a scary guy. He was always calm and spoke in a casual way about breaking Ali's arm or pulling out a bone or muscle. Ali would always banter with [Inoki], but I think he was concerned because of the unknown pieces."

The heavyweight champion is definitely concerned. Yet it is too late to back out. The money and his reputation are on the line.

However, Herbert Muhammad will change the rules.

✦ ✦ ✦

Negotiations begin immediately. Soon, it is agreed that Ali will be allowed to fight in any way that works best for him, but Inoki is forbidden from kicking the champ unless one knee is on the ground. No drop kicks. No throws. He cannot tackle Ali and try to pin him. And he cannot use a karate-style "chop" to immobilize the boxer.

The public is not told of the new rules. Herbert Muhammad stipulates that if word of them gets out, the fight will be canceled. It is left for Inoki to find a unique method of battling Muhammad Ali.

Which he does.

✦ ✦ ✦

The bell sounds for the first round.

Antonio Inoki sprints across the sixteen-foot-wide boxing ring. A startled Muhammad Ali steps forward in a fighting stance and waits for the wrestler.

The champ wears baggy white boxing trunks and lightweight (four-ounce) gloves. Inoki is clad in a tight black wrestling brief. Shoes are optional tonight, but the wrestler wears black footwear. Inoki is taller and heavier than the champ.

Neither man is allowed to butt, gouge, elbow, punch to the throat, or slap.

But the rules say nothing about lying down.

Inoki immediately hits the canvas. He slides at the champ feet first, attempting to trip Ali. The boxer quickly dances aside but cannot escape entirely. Inoki, lying flat on his back like a crab, kicks him. When the champ circles him, looking for some way to throw a punch, Inoki rotates his body and keeps kicking—always keeping one leg on the ground.

Ali jumps up onto the ropes to escape.

Fans inside the stadium erupt into a chorus of confused cheers. It is common knowledge that the bout is a *yaochō*—a fix. They don't care. All the people want is a good fight.

As the rounds continue, the blows to Ali's legs mount. The frustrated boxer cannot get close enough to hit his opponent.

"One punch!" the champ screams. "I want one punch."

And still, Inoki remains in his crablike fighting style.

"Coward, Inoki!" Ali screams at his opponent. "Inoki, no fight!"

The wrestler keeps kicking. Ali is no longer just confused; he is in pain. The champ begins to bleed. Welts form up and down his legs. One kick strikes Ali's groin. In the fourth round, Inoki traps the champ in a corner, showering him with kick after kick.

In the sixth, Ali grabs hold of Inoki's boot and tries to halt the kicks. The wrestler turns this to his advantage, pulling the champ down to the canvas and sitting on him before once again rolling off to fight from his back.

For fifteen long rounds, the fight continues. Inoki rarely gets off his back, and Ali throws just six punches all day. Inoki kicks Ali so many times, he breaks his own foot.

The bout ends in a "draw."

As the decision is announced, the Budokan crowd showers the ring with trash—which is also how many observers of the time describe the whole exhibition.

Even promoter Bob Arum cannot find good things to say about the fight. "It was terrible," he will remember. "It was embarrassing."

Muhammad Ali immediately returns to his Tokyo hotel, where his legs are packed in ice. The swelling makes it difficult for him to walk. Fearing blood clots, Dr. Ferdie Pacheco implores the champ to go to the emergency room.

But there will be no hospital. Not yet. Herbert Muhammad has arranged paid public appearances for the champ in South Korea, on the way home. Doctors are telling Ali not to leave Tokyo, but he ignores them. He will follow Herbert's instructions.

✦ ✦ ✦

It is on July 1, one week after facing Inoki, that Muhammad Ali finally checks himself into St. John's medical center in Santa Monica. He is in California to discuss making a movie, but the pain in his legs has become too much to ignore.

Diagnosis: in the words of attending physician Dr. Robert Kositchek, the champ has two blood clots around the knees and "severe muscle damage, vein damage and accumulation of both fluid and blood in the entire left leg."

Muhammad Ali is ordered to stay off his legs, but Herbert Muhammad knows that will not be possible for very long.

In just two months, the champ is set to fight Ken Norton, who broke Ali's jaw back in 1971.

Therefore, Muhammad Ali must train.

Now it is a matter of survival.

CHAPTER SIX

SEPTEMBER 28, 1976
NEW YORK CITY
9:30 P.M.

Muhammad Ali is the bionic man.

"That's right," the champion told reporters this morning. The allusion is to a character on a popular television show called *The Six Million Dollar Man*, starring Lee Majors. The premise of the program is that a badly injured Majors is scientifically rebuilt.

"I am the true Six Million Dollar Man in money, genius, personality, charisma," Ali boasts. "The whole world's coming to see this fight."

The champ is referring to the championship bout with Ken Norton. It will be shown live on ABC in the United States and on pay TV worldwide. Ali's portion of the purse is, ironically, $6 million.* He will also be paid 50 percent of the total revenue.

The scene outside Yankee Stadium on this wet autumn night is chaotic. Angry off-duty police officers are picketing for higher wages. Their on-duty brethren working crowd control join the protest— doing nothing to stop pickpockets or unruly fans.

---

* That's $31 million in today's money.

Sports Illustrated magazine puts it this way: "Their eyes were turned away as one saw a man hit over the head and then frisked rapidly [by the assailant] while he was on the ground; as one watched an arm reach into a limousine and pull out a necklace; as one looked on while three photographers were robbed of all their equipment; as [fight] tickets were stolen right out of hands and women were pawed. It was not a pretty sight." Advance news of the police protest has spurred some teenagers to scale stadium walls in order to gain entrance to the fight. They do so unopposed.

Muhammad Ali sees the pandemonium. All entrances to the stadium are blocked as he tries to find a way in. Finally, he is successful. His dressing room is crowded with cornermen, hangers-on, and members of the Nation of Islam. The champ is preparing to defend his title for the fifth time in less than a year. After that, he has plans. He will fly from New York to Istanbul for a brief visit, then on to Los Angeles. On October 6, he will begin filming a movie based on his life. He will play himself.

But first, Ken Norton looms. Ali steps into his white shorts with the black stripe running down the thigh. High white socks and shoes come next. The thirty thousand spectators can be heard quite clearly from the locker room. Yankee Stadium's fabled baseball diamond is now a carpet of chairs arranged around a temporary ring.

At age thirty-four, Ali weighs a hard 222 pounds to Norton's 215. The champ has trained diligently for this fight. It shows in his trim waist and sinewy shoulders. He has sparred more than one hundred rounds during his preparation and has increased his daily regimen of running and calisthenics.

Even Angelo Dundee, normally hard to impress, likes the champ's fitness today. "Ali's in the best physical condition of his life," the trainer says to the media. "He's trained for this fight like Rocky Marciano. I think he'll stop this guy in the ninth, tenth or eleventh round."

Ali doesn't think it will take that long. He pledges to knock the challenger out by the fifth round, telling reporters earlier that "Norton got knocked out in the second round by George Foreman, and I'm Foreman's daddy."

✦ ✦ ✦

In a nearby dressing room, Ken Norton performs the same prefight ritual as Ali, but the mood is calmer. A half-dozen friends guard the door, allowing Norton to avoid energy-draining visitors. After spending the day resting in his hotel, he now slips into his dark trunks and shoes while talking strategy with trainer Bill Slayton. A representative of the New York Athletic Commission steps into the locker room to oversee the taping of Norton's fists. First, long strips of soft gauze are used, and then eight feet of adhesive tape. No water or any foreign substance can be applied. The official waits until Norton's gloves have been slipped onto his hands and laced. Then he leaves to oversee the same process with Ali.

Slayton, who replaced Eddie Futch when the veteran trainer left to work with Joe Frazier, remains with Norton as they await the signal to step out into the night. For the long walk to the ring, the boxer will be escorted by a phalanx of New York City police officers.

"I know this will be a big scene in Yankee Stadium," Norton says. "But a big crowd like this will be more beneficial to me. Looking around at a big crowd will make me feel the electricity more, will get adrenaline flowing. The crowd will be for Ali, but I won't hear it." The thirty-three-year-old Norton stands six foot three. He is a former marine, known in the fight world for his sculpted musculature. This has already led to roles in films that required him to take off his shirt. He admits to covering up his face during fights, to avoid punches that might damage his movie star looks.

Sensing history, Norton more than doubled down on Ali's preparation, with 225 sparring rounds for tonight. He studied film of the champ's fights and read books on sports psychology. A handwritten sign proclaiming "I Will Beat Ali!" has been taped to the door of his training room at Grossinger's Resort in upstate New York.

It is a reminder of his first encounter with Ali.

✦ ✦ ✦

Back in March 1973, at the San Diego Sports Arena, Norton was a lightly regarded and little-known opponent. His only fame was having once been Joe Frazier's sparring partner.

Ali came into the fight having won ten straight bouts after losing the title bout to Joe Frazier in 1971. Norton was just one more opponent in his march to reclaiming the heavyweight crown. Ali sprained his ankle in training but refused to postpone the fight, claiming that "it's not going to be that tough" to beat Norton.

That all changed when Ken Norton broke the champ's jaw. Ali will claim it happened in the second round. Norton will say it was a right hook in the fifteenth. But no matter. Boxing fans witnessed Ali take a thorough beating. The judges awarded the fight to Norton.

Howard Cosell, who gave the challenger no chance to win, approached for an interview afterward. "Kenny, you made me look silly."

"That's okay, Howard," the fighter answered. "You always look silly."

That night, in the San Diego hospital where Ali's jaw was being wired shut, Norton paid a visit. "The Greatest" told the victor he never wanted to meet him in the ring again.

But six months later, they fight once more. This time it was Ali who got the decision. Now, three years after that second bout, Ken Norton and Muhammad Ali will battle one last time.

✦ ✦ ✦

The oddsmakers favor the champ 8–5.

Yet, as midnight approaches in the Bronx, Ken Norton is dismantling him. The challenger wins round after round. Everyone in Yankee Stadium can see Ali's decline. This is not the man who fought

Joe Frazier one year ago. The champ's timing is off. His legs are still tender from the Inoki fight, and he looks sluggish. Norton's unorthodox jab, which comes from below instead of over the top, finds Ali's jaw again and again. The crowd chants, "Ali! Ali! Ali!"—which only serves to motivate Norton.

In a very unusual display, the challenger does not sit down between rounds. He also does not take a sip of water. Ken Norton knows he is badly outclassing Muhammad Ali.

"He seemed a pathetic figure, merely a master of illusion, groping with his loss of reflexes; his feet knew precisely where to be, but his hands and mind seemed to be hooked up in some diabolical plot against him"—is how *Sports Illustrated* will describe the champ.

Veteran boxing fans in Yankee Stadium know a contender has to be twice as effective as a champion in order to get the victory. And for this reason, the judges score the fight as close going into the final round.

But Ken Norton and his trainer, Bill Slayton, think they have it. As the challenger prepares to fight the fifteenth round, Slayton reminds him that Ali needs a knockout to win.

He tells Norton to play it safe.

✦ ✦ ✦

Boxing history will record this as the moment Ken Norton lost the fight. Despite outboxing Ali throughout the night, the judges will base their final decision on the champ's aggressiveness in the fifteenth round. But Norton doesn't see it that way.

"I beat you! I beat you!" he shouts at the champ at the end of that final round, following Ali back to his corner.

Yet the judges say otherwise.

The unanimous decision goes to Muhammad Ali.

"If Norton had started in the first minute of [the fifteenth] round," judge Harold Lederman later concedes, "and started with that right hand, he would have been champion."

Not everyone agrees.

"Norton got a raw deal," says Joe Frazier, here to watch the fight in person. "I thought he won all the rounds."

As the decision is read, Ken Norton weeps. "When you fight Ali, you're behind at the start. It's obvious you have to knock him out to win. When it's that obvious, you have to think the judges stole it. They made asses out of themselves."

Ali's doctor, Ferdie Pacheco, takes a pragmatic approach: "I thought Ali stepped into the last downhill phase of his career. . . . But he's a champion. He still had enough to take the fifteenth round and keep the title. Norton didn't. Norton was like a guy who goes to medical school and flunks out in the eighth year."

As always, Muhammad Ali has the last word: "Do you think I paid the judges? They never give me anything. I'm not a good American boy. I'm an arrogant n*****. They're white men. They wouldn't give it to me if I didn't win it."

✦ ✦ ✦

The next morning, Muhammad Ali travels to Madison Square Garden to pick up his $6 million check. There, waiting for him, is Teddy Brenner, longtime fight matchmaker for MSG's boxing group, Madison Square Garden Boxing, Inc., which helped organize the Yankee Stadium bout. The fifty-nine-year-old Brenner, an astute boxing authority, kept his own scorecard during the fight, as per his professional habit, scoring it 10–5 for Norton.

"What are you going to do now?" Brenner asks the champ.

"What do you think I should do?"

Ali heard the boos as the decision was announced last night and read the papers this morning criticizing that decision. During a post-bout press conference, the champ stated that he would enjoy a rematch—but only if Norton first defeated George Foreman.

Teddy Brenner looks at the champ. "I don't think you should fight anymore."

"You don't think I can?" Ali responds. There is none of his usual swagger. He speaks softly, almost in a whisper.

"I didn't say that. But if you want to fight, why fight the same guys again and again?"

"I'll think about it," Ali responds, taking his wages and leaving for Istanbul.

✦ ✦ ✦

Ali's plane lands in Turkey at 4:45 a.m. He visits the famous Blue Mosque at noon for prayers. By midday, his mind is made up. "Mark my words, and play what I say right now fully," Ali tells the media. "I declare I am quitting fighting as of now, and from now on I will join in the struggle for the Islamic cause.

"I do not want to lose a fight, and if I keep boxing, I may lose. I may gain much money, but the love of the Muslims and the hearts of my people are more valuable than personal gain. So, I am going to stop while everyone is happy and I am still winning."

Few believe him.

"It's obvious why he retired," says Ken Norton at a Midtown Manhattan news conference. "He knows he didn't win the fight, and he's very embarrassed over that wrong decision."

Muhammad Ali doesn't remain embarrassed—or retired—very long. On May 16, 1977, the champ returns to Capital Centre arena in Landover, Maryland, to battle the lightly regarded Uruguayan contender Alfredo Evangelista. Ali's take is $2.7 million.

The fight goes the full fifteen rounds.

The judges score a unanimous decision for the champ.

✦ ✦ ✦

Herbert Muhammad has no intention of allowing his fighter to quit the ring. In fact, there is yet another title fight already set up.

But first, there is something Muhammad Ali has to do.

CHAPTER SEVEN

JUNE 19, 1977
BEVERLY HILLS, CALIFORNIA
I P.M.

Muhammad Ali is getting married for the third time.

Two hundred forty invited guests fill the lobby of the Beverly Wilshire Hotel, waiting for the doors of Le Grand Trianon ballroom to open. There are chandeliers, marble walls—and tight security. The famous faces from the sports and entertainment worlds are many: Sugar Ray Robinson, Bill Cosby, Dick Gregory, LeVar Burton, and Los Angeles mayor Tom Bradley. Actor Warren Beatty, who lives at the hotel, works his way through the crowd, trying to get to the elevator. British actor Christopher Lee is there because the champ loves his horror films.

"Ali's usual retinue of hangers-on, bag carriers, gofers, and assorted friends was noticeably missing," the *Washington Post* will report. "His longtime personal bodyguard Pat Patterson, a former policeman for the Chicago Police Department, was one of the few Ali regulars on hand."*

The most special guest of all is former heavyweight champion

---

* Ali's autobiographical film, *The Greatest*, was released on May 19, just one month before the wedding. Starring Ali, Ernest Borgnine, and Robert Duvall, it received warm critical reviews but was only a modest financial success.

Joe Louis, now sixty-three years old. Herbert Muhammad did not make the trip from Chicago. The manager has become even more controlling of the champ's public image, even demanding that he be allowed to personally approve and initial each manuscript page of Ali's latest ghostwritten autobiography. But weddings are not a source of revenue.

When the guests are finally allowed inside, they enter a ballroom filled with trees, birds, and flowers. The aisle Muhammad Ali and Veronica Porché will walk down is lined with white sprays of baby's breath, a small white flowering plant from a genus native to Africa.

At one end of the room, three tall, arched windows let in natural sunlight on this warm spring afternoon. A raised platform stands against one wall, the metal canopy atop it decorated with white carnations and more baby's breath. Alabaster cherub statues stand on either side of the canopy, supporting cages filled with white doves. The champ had hoped to set these loose after the ceremony but changed his mind out of fear for the birds' safety.

Los Angeles Superior Court judge Billy Mills will officiate at today's civil ceremony. He now walks to the platform where the vows will be exchanged. Like almost everyone else in the room, Mills does not know that Ali and Porché were secretly married in a Muslim ceremony three years ago in Zaire. That arrangement will be kept confidential for many years to come, as Ali was still married to second wife, Khalilah, at the time. The public relations consequences of the Zaire wedding could be disastrous.

Now Ali and Veronica make it official—or try to. The ceremony is supposed to start at two p.m., but news of the nuptials has leaked out. Dozens of uninvited people are trying to crash the ceremony. Some, dressed in formal wedding attire, attempt to talk their way past Los Angeles police. Le Grand Trianon's maximal occupancy is 263. As the room fills to near capacity, the service is delayed as invitations are checked for authenticity.

Security quickly becomes a problem. It is Jeremiah Shabazz, an Ali assistant from the Nation of Islam, who finally brings order. "Unless you were invited, you can't get in," he tells the group as they assemble in the lobby. "You cannot just walk in with the champ."

Muhammad Ali is thirty-five years old, and his bride, the daughter of a retired Los Angeles builder, is twenty-one. The champ enters and walks to the front of the room with his wedding party, joining Judge Mills on the platform. Observers note that Ali looks unusually subdued. He wears a white tuxedo with white tie and tails, a white ruffled shirt, white gloves, and white shoes. His best man is Howard Bingham, the self-described "world's greatest" photographer, also dressed in white tails. The two have known each other since the earliest days of Ali's career and will remain lifelong friends.

Veronica now enters as vocalist Sam Fletcher sings Stevie Wonder's "You Are the Sunshine of My Life." A long train follows her bright white gown. She is three months pregnant with the couple's second daughter. Their first child, Hana, is just under fifteen months old. The baby sits placidly with her grandparents. Muhammad Ali's four children from his second marriage are not in attendance. The *Los Angeles Times*, in its reporting on the wedding, points out that Khalilah Ali received a $2 million alimony settlement, but, apparently, some bitterness remains.*

The five-minute service ends with a kiss. The pair leaves the ballroom to the strains of "Isn't She Lovely," also by Stevie Wonder. The bride beams.

As the couple poses for photos and then cuts a five-tier wedding cake, Ali maintains his silence. He almost appears to be scowling. When pressed to explain his behavior, the champ simply states, "This is sacred to me."

In the morning, the Alis will fly to Hawaii for a honeymoon. But while Veronica enjoys the white sands of Waikiki, the champ is quickly bored and does not join her on the beach. Predicting that this would happen, the new Mrs. Ali had the forethought to bring Howard Bingham along, to keep her husband company. The two

---

* That would be $9.3 million in today's money.

men spend most of the trip in Ali's suite. When the champ ventures out for some shopping—buying two Pierre Cardin belts at a Bugatti leather shop—he is swarmed by autograph seekers, all of whom he patiently accommodates.

Coincidentally, the champ's second wife, Khalilah, is also in Honolulu, to make her acting debut in the television drama *Hawaii Five-0*. Incredibly, she is staying in the same hotel as the newlyweds! Veronica and Ali are in the Diamond Head Tower of the Hyatt Regency, with Khalilah in the opposing Ewa Tower.

The honeymoon lasts just two days. The champ and his new bride fly back to Los Angeles on Wednesday.

✦ ✦ ✦

One month later, in a very unusual move, the couple flies to the British city of Tyneside, to see an audacious local boxing coach who has written to Ali requesting fund-raising help. Not only does the champ show up in person with his wife and young daughter, but he pays a visit to the local mosque, where the imam blesses his marriage.

The trip to England ends the social part of Muhammad Ali's schedule. Now it is back to business.

✦ ✦ ✦

The date is September 29, 1977. Ali fights a hard-hitting contender named Earnie Shavers in Madison Square Garden. Herbert Muhammad is not in attendance, preferring to watch the bout from his New York City apartment, just blocks away. Ali is being paid $3 million to the $300,000 the "Black Destroyer" will receive. But tonight's money does not matter much to the thirty-three-year-old Shavers: he senses the heavyweight championship will soon be his. In the second round, the Destroyer hits Ali with a ferocious punch. The champ staggers back, wobbling, but does not go down. He will later say that only Joe Frazier hit him harder.

The Alabama-bred Shavers grows in confidence, but Ali does not falter during the fight. It is a back-and-forth brawl, with both boxers landing serious blows. Shavers knocks Ali down in the fourteenth round, but the referee rules it a slip.

As the fifteenth round is about to begin, the judges score it close. As always, Ali, the champion, is given more latitude than the challenger. Both men show damage.

Shavers has never fought more than twelve rounds before. He is exhausted and drenched in sweat. Ali is even more drained, slumping on his stool in the corner, tormented by pain in his kidneys.

After the fight, Shavers will say he actually felt sorry for Ali heading into the fifteenth round. "Fighting Ali was hard for me to do, because he was such a good man. He was my idol. I loved him personally, and you hate to see a champ defeated."

What Shavers did not understand was that the champ was anything but defeated. In fact, Ali is acting. Yes, he is hurt, but not as badly as he wants the "Acorn"—as he calls Shavers, for his bald head—to believe. Later, Ali says that he talked to himself during the bout: "Just three more minutes. Fight hard until you die. Do it now."

The challenger does not go for the knockout blow in the fifteenth—but the champion does. The round begins slowly, both fighters too tired to land a hard punch. But with just one minute left in the fight, Ali summons his remaining energy and lands a vicious combination of lightning-fast blows that stagger Shavers. The challenger takes a dozen punches to the head. He bends over, trying to cover up, but a suddenly confident Ali continues to rain down blows. For a moment, it appears Shavers will go down. Longtime observers will say this is Ali at his best—a true champion finding the strength to come back when all appears lost.

The final bell rings. Both men return to their corners. Ali's rally has won the day. He retains his world heavyweight championship by unanimous decision.

The champ quickly returns to his dressing room. Ferdie Pacheco examines him. The doctor is very concerned, especially about the kidney damage. He tells Ali he must retire.

The champion refuses. "As long as I get my three million, that's all that counts. I'm in it for the business now," he tells reporters in the Garden's Felt Forum interview room one hour after the fight in the main arena ends.

Pacheco is so disturbed that he will never work in Ali's corner again.

Trainer Angelo Dundee, however, is ecstatic about the fight, as he tells the champ: "I don't know how you do it, you son of a bitch. But I love you for it."

✦ ✦ ✦

So the beat goes on in a literal sense for Muhammad Ali. He knows his body is in decline. Thus, he will wait before he fights again.

The champ goes home to Michigan, where a pregnant Veronica and a toddler are waiting. He will rest and recuperate, but he will not count his money. Herbert does that. And there is more money yet to be made.

Another title fight is set for February, just five months away.

CHAPTER EIGHT

FEBRUARY 15, 1978
LAS VEGAS
7 P.M.

Muhammad Ali is no longer the heavyweight champion of the world.

The forlorn thirty-six-year-old fighter sits in his dressing room here at the Las Vegas Hilton, beaten by an unknown twenty-four-year-old opponent named Leon Spinks. The heavyweight bout has shocked the world—Spinks had only seven previous professional fights, yet he thoroughly beat up Ali.

The champ once again tried to win the bout with a flurry of punches in the last round, the fifteenth. But Spinks secured the victory long before then, flashing a stunning display of toughness. The challenger was raised in the poverty of St. Louis, his father fond of telling people his son would never amount to anything. Those words were Spinks's motivation.

Ali entered the fight with his own need for motivation. "No one was excited about [the fight]," reports the *Las Vegas Sun*. "Ali viewed it as drudgery, just another day at the office. A prime Ali would knock Leon out in two rounds. But he wasn't up for it. He was mentally vacant. He'd been through a very tough fight with Earnie Shavers and he wanted an easy opponent."

Leon Spinks did not comply.

As Ali trapped him against the ropes in the tenth round, the challenger had a childhood flashback. Twelve years younger and almost 30 pounds lighter than the 224-pound Ali, Spinks decided to prove his dad wrong.

Serving in the US Marine Corps was not enough.

Winning an Olympic gold medal at the Montreal Olympics in 1976 was not enough.

Only beating his childhood idol for the championship will erase those painful words uttered by the man who fathered him.

So Leon Spinks came back. He is a technical fighter, elbows tucked tight against his rib cage. His fists lashed out, pounding Ali's body. Absorbing relentless jabs and hooks to the torso, the champ covered up to protect what felt like a broken rib. When he backpedaled to escape, the challenger chased him around the ring.

Walking back to his corner after the tenth, an ecstatic Spinks slapped Ali on the rump. The champ turned but said nothing.

Ali plopped onto his stool.

"You've got him!" said an obsequious Drew Bundini Brown, the champ's longtime handler. "You've got him!"

"Shut up," said Ali.

✦ ✦ ✦

In the fifteenth round, Ali needed a knockout to win. As the boxers sallied forth from their corners, Brent Musburger, commentating for CBS Sports, wondered if the champ was finished. Ali punched first, a right to the side of the head that staggered Spinks. The champ followed up with two more quick shots and then a four-punch combination. But Spinks quickly fired back. Ali had never been knocked out in his professional career, but he was now clearly in trouble.

The crowd was on its feet, sensing an upset. Both fighters were exhausted, taking turns sagging against the ropes. The judges were watching closely to see who was more aggressive in the final round. Punches were thrown—very few missed. Spinks was bleeding from a cut above his right eye. Ali's blows connected with the challenger's temple. But Spinks absorbed the shots and then punished the champ with flurries of his own. A final right to the head at the end of the round staggered Ali, and he almost went down just as the bell rang. Shaking his head to ward off the pain, the champ trudged to his corner.

Moments later, there was quiet and tension in this small arena as the fighters and their entourages gathered in the center of the ring to hear the judges' verdict. Ring announcer Chuck Hull began announcing the split decision. All it took were the words "The *new* . . ." for the audience to erupt, drowning out the rest of the sentence proclaiming Spinks heavyweight champion of the world.

Those in the crowd knew they had just witnessed one of the most stunning upsets in boxing history.

✦ ✦ ✦

After the fight, promoter Bob Arum is not disappointed. "I finally got Herbert Muhammad where I want him," he exclaims.

As long as Muhammad Ali was champion of the world, Herbert dictated the terms: who the challengers were, where the fights took place, and how much the payday would be. But Ali is no longer champ. He is not even first in line to take back the crown—that position belongs to Ken Norton. So the aging ex-champ must *earn* a rematch by fighting quality bouts against known contenders. Herbert Muhammad will not be able to name his price any longer.

Arum and his company, Top Rank Inc., will now promote the new champion's fights.

They will also dictate if, and when, Ali gets a title shot. Arum is confident he is in control.

He is not.

✦ ✦ ✦

Muhammad Ali knows he can beat Leon Spinks. So he has to find a way to go up against him again. The pathway will not be easy. And it is made more difficult by his personal life.

Ali is now spending most of his time in Chicago, at a large brick mansion on South Woodlawn Avenue. He has maintained this residence for a decade, originally purchasing it to be closer to Elijah Muhammad, who lived just a few blocks away. The champ moved his family back there in 1973. The fighter now has six children, two ex-wives, and a new spouse.

As always, money is a problem for Ali. A huge tax bill is due. Fearful of enduring the same legal issues with the federal government that bedeviled Joe Louis, Ali has hired a tax attorney recommended by Herbert. The former champ is told to place $2.5 million in escrow to cover taxes for his last three fights. He does so. However, when it comes time to transfer the money to the government, the escrow account is empty. The new attorney tells Ali the money has vanished. The fighter knows he is owed a $1 million bonus from Herbert for past performances, but the manager says that money is gone as well, used to pay off even more tax obligations.*

Muhammad Ali is furious.

For the first time since Herbert began to manage Ali, in 1966, the fighter begins to distrust him. He decides to look elsewhere for financial guidance. Herbert will still be the manager, but Ali wants an expert to look out for his money. He meets with a banker in downtown Chicago to discuss the situation. Ali's kidneys are so devastated from the Spinks fight that he actually urinates in the elevator taking him up to the banker's office.

As precarious as the former champ's finances might be, the Nation of Islam is in worse straits. Ali does not give the Nation cash directly; Herbert Muhammad does—and it is rumored that some of the money comes from Ali's bank account. According to reporting by the *New York Times*, the Nation of Islam is selling off many

---

* On March 1, 1978, Muhammad Ali fired attorney Spiros Anthony. The following month, he filed a $2 million suit, claiming Anthony had "breached his duties as a trustee," using the money, among other things, to purchase expensive antiques for his own use. In an out-of-court settlement, Anthony agreed to repay Ali $390,000 of the missing money at a rate of $20,000 a month. The attorney is believed to have fled the United States on an unrelated issue in July 1978. So, once again, Ali has been fleeced.

businesses to cover its taxes. The *Times* also notes that Ali is "a major source of prestige and income to the Muslims."

✦ ✦ ✦

The once-powerful Nation of Islam has drastically deteriorated.

The problems began when Warith Muhammad ascended to the top leadership position after his father, Elijah Muhammad, died three years ago. Elijah had an astounding twenty-three children combined, from his one wife and numerous extramarital affairs. Warith is not the oldest heir, but he is the most aggressive. Both Ali and Herbert swear allegiance to him.

However, Herbert Muhammad *does* seek more power in the Nation of Islam. So he decides to build his own mosque in Chicago. But, of course, he needs Ali's cash to do that.

To this day, the boxer is listed as one of the founders of Masjid al-Faatir.

✦ ✦ ✦

Muhammad Ali knows he needs to make more money. He envisions himself in Hollywood after his boxing days are over, but for now, Herbert, even though his commission is being cut, still wants him to fight.

So Herbert actively discourages Ali's ambitions other than boxing. Actor Warren Beatty, a force in Hollywood, wanted the champ to play a role in a film called *Heaven Can Wait*. The character is a boxer who comes back to earth after being reincarnated. Beatty actually flew to Chicago to pitch the story to Ali. But when Herbert showed the script to his brother Warith, the two decided the character's behavior and reincarnation were both in conflict with Muslim beliefs—so Ali could not take the part. Warren Beatty eventually played the role himself, rewriting the character as a professional football player.

And then there are the continuing giveaways and bad investments. Ali constantly hands over money to people who ask. He also makes bad investments, like the restaurant Champ Burger, and Mr. Champ's Soda—both of which fail. He gives $40,000 to a friend named Harold Smith to form a company called Muhammad Ali Professional Sports—years later, Smith is convicted of embezzlement. Then there is the expense sheet—$64,000 a month in car payments, insurance, and rent that Ali pays for family and friends. A weekly routine for the champ is to travel to the Chicago Western Union office to wire cash to people around the country.

In addition, Ali lives well. He drives around Chicago in a green Rolls-Royce. One cold winter day, the fighter spots a woman walking with her shoeless child. He stops the Rolls and asks why the child is barefoot. When the woman responds that she cannot afford shoes, Ali drives them home. The woman, a prostitute and drug addict, has no food, and the heat in her home is turned off. Her stove and refrigerator are broken. Ali gives the woman $1,500 (the equivalent of $10,000 today) on the spot to buy food and new appliances. To make sure she doesn't spend it on drugs, he has a friend check up on her.

It becomes clear that Muhammad Ali, a generous man, no longer has the resources to finance his life. However, Herbert has a plan.

✦ ✦ ✦

In a shocking turn of events, the manager convinces Top Rank Inc. to schedule an Ali-Spinks rematch *before* a Spinks-Norton fight. Professional boxing rules dictate that the titleholder first fight the highest-ranked contender, and Ken Norton is that man. Almost immediately, critics accuse Spinks of ducking the hard-hitting Norton in favor of an aging opponent he has already beaten. But in actuality, Spinks is so enamored of Muhammad Ali—and the $5 million payday he has been promised—that he is willing to give up his heavyweight crown to placate his boyhood idol.

Thus, Leon Spinks is stripped of his new crown by the World Boxing Council.

Like Ali, Spinks is a big spender. He is very loose with his money, burning through cash buying cars and jewelry—but not new teeth, as seen in the wide gaps in his mouth. The new champ likes to tell people he spends because he was born poor and is making up for lost time.

The rematch with Muhammad Ali will be Spinks's first big payday. For him, money trumps official recognition, as the purse climbs to an estimated $10 million, supposedly to be split between the two fighters.

"Boxing owes Muhammad a rematch," Top Rank vice president Butch Lewis states. "Ali gave a quick rematch to Sonny Liston when he won the title, and I'm sure Leon wants to give him one." Lewis goes on to say that "all parties are agreed to a rematch as soon as we can put it together."

The second Ali-Spinks fight, Lewis concludes, will take place in "a small African country." Bophuthatswana is mentioned, then the island of Mauritius.

But logistics in Africa prove to be impossible.

Finally, it is settled: the rematch will be held at the Superdome in New Orleans, before a crowd of sixty-three thousand, one of the biggest crowds in boxing history.

Herbert Muhammad is happy. The floundering Nation of Islam is happy.

Muhammad Ali remains in pain.

CHAPTER NINE

Muhammad Ali swears, yet again, that this will be his last fight. The Superdome is sweltering as Ali dances around the ring in "the Battle of New Orleans." Jab, bear-hug Spinks for a short rest, push him away, and float back to the left—all night long, never letting the new champion get close enough to pound the body. Half the televisions in America are tuned to what some are calling a "pop culture phenomenon."

Ali entered the arena to "When the Saints Go Marching In." Spinks, the former marine, entered to "The Marines' Hymn." White shorts for Ali, cardinal and gold for Spinks. A *Playboy* model performed a striptease in the ring before the battle.

It's New Orleans.

This is not a perfect fight. In the words of trainer Angelo Dundee, who now firmly believes Ali should retire, Ali is "beautifully sloppy. Gorgeous sloppy. Wonderful sloppy."

Sports Illustrated will write that tonight is "a demonstration by an old master educating an inexperienced youngster in the fine points of the craft."

Leon Spinks looks confused. The new champ's corner is in chaos.

His trainer, George Benton, actually quits in the fifth round, fed up by his undisciplined fighter. "It's like there is a mystical force guiding his life, making him not like other men," Benton said of Ali before the bout, adding that Spinks could lose only if he didn't fight smart—which is what is happening. But even before the respected trainer walks out of the Superdome, no one is in charge on Spinks's side of the ring. There is little professional expertise. A group of hangers-on crowds the corner, shouting strategy tips.

"Wiggle!" the fighter's brother, Michael, also a top boxer, calls out. "Wiggle!"

No one knows what that means.

Spinks did train hard for the fight, running miles, jumping rope, and hitting the speed bag. But he drank even harder, finishing each night in dive bars far from New Orleans's tourist sites. After one argument with Michael about not taking care of his family, the boxer wept openly and then disappeared from his hotel. Such is Spinks's distraction that he arrived at the ring this evening without his protective cup and had to borrow one from a boxer on the undercard.

Ali, for his part, has worked hard to get his body fit for this bout. He first trained at Fighter's Heaven, as his Deer Lake, Pennsylvania, retreat has been nicknamed. Locals saw the former champ, dressed in matching warm-up tops and bottoms, out on the roads at sunrise for his early-morning run. In the days leading up to the fight, he flew to Louisiana, where he rented a house on massive Lake Pontchartrain to be away from the temptations and women of New Orleans. In the days leading up to the fight, he has done more than eight thousand sit-ups.

Now Ali puts that conditioning to use. Round after round, he jabs at Spinks, tapping him on the jaw.

Angelo Dundee is unusually vocal, taunting the young champion from Ali's corner with cries of "Goodbye, Leon!" The trainer is emotional watching this battle, thinking this might be the end of a great partnership. It's not just Ali's diminished skills that trouble Dundee. He has seen the tremor in Ali's hands, and long periods of silence have replaced the once-jocular personality. He knows of the strange salt, iron, and potassium deficiencies that require eleven pills a day to correct. The days of Ali fortifying himself with a sirloin steak, a gallon of orange juice, and a hooker are long gone.

"The last fight," Muhammad Ali pronounced during training.

The fighter often shakes so badly that Veronica has to feed him his breakfast of trout, unbuttered whole wheat toast, and scrambled eggs. "It's time for a new life. I'm going to put on a three-piece suit, carry a briefcase, and fly around the world working for human rights and dignity. . . . I've been doing it for twenty-five years, and you can only do so much wear and tear to the body. It changes a man. It has changed me. I can see it. I can feel it."

Everything about the New Orleans fight is familiar to Muhammad Ali: a smoke-filled arena jammed to the rafters with fans swaying back and forth chanting "Ali"; the aromas of sweat and blood inside the ring; the sudden jolt of pain when a jab snaps his head back; fancily dressed men and women in the ringside seats—among them, Herbert Muhammad—watching two men beat each other for entertainment.

John Travolta, Sylvester Stallone, and Liza Minnelli are in the house. ABC's Howard Cosell is overwhelmed by the energy in the massive arena, telling the television audience that "in twenty-five years of sports, I've never heard such a crowd."

But behind the scenes, there *is* something different.

Herbert Muhammad and Ali recently have come to a new agreement—because professional boxing has changed. Promoters now can deal with fighters directly, potentially cutting Herbert out of the equation. Understanding this, Ali has slashed Herbert's cut down to 15 percent.

This shift in their twelve-year relationship occurred when the $5 million Ali thought he was making tonight was mysteriously reduced to $2.5 million. The fight was originally supposed to be held in an independent tribal homeland within South Africa, with a total budget of $14 million. But that nation's racially charged policy of apartheid caused a public outcry. The NAACP said the fighters would be "selling their souls" if they fought there. Thus, the fight has been moved. Gone now are the deep-pocketed investors from South Africa's Southern Sun hotel chain, which would have funded the larger purse.

Neither Ali nor Leon Spinks was initially aware of their change in fortune.

Angered by yet another financial setback, the former champ tells Herbert that if he wants to continue as his manager, he will have to get him better terms. They may be Muslim brothers, but cold, hard cash is coming between them.

✦ ✦ ✦

As the Battle of New Orleans continues, Ali avoids going blow for blow with Spinks. He also rejects his own "rope-a-dope" move, a tactic that would only exhaust him. He used it to good effect against George Foreman and Earnie Shavers, but Spinks is too young and fit to be worn out by it—this despite the drinking and cocaine use that marred his training regimen.

Using his jab and a few effective combinations, Ali soundly defeats Leon Spinks—thus becoming the first man in history to win the world heavyweight title three times.

"I am from the House of Shock," he crows, alluding to the reaction from fans who thought he would never be champ again.[*]

A few months later, Muhammad Ali announces he is going to retire.

This time he sounds like he means it.

Kind of.

---

[*] The three judges scored the fight unanimously for Muhammad Ali: 11–4, 10–4–1, 10–4–1. It was a rout from which Leon Spinks would never fully recover.

CHAPTER TEN

It is good to be the champ.

The "Fabulous Forum," home to the Los Angeles Lakers basketball team, is packed. It is almost a year since Muhammad Ali defeated Leon Spinks. The arena is crowded with celebrities: Richard Pryor, Lou Rawls, Chevy Chase, Jon Voight, Jane Fonda, Kris Kristofferson, Kenny Rogers, and a host of other famous names, all here to pay homage to the champ. Thousands of fans fill the seventeen-thousand-seat arena to capacity. Aging boxer Sugar Ray Robinson, whom Ali admires tremendously, is also in the house for this retirement extravaganza.

But so far, there is no sign of Ali. Announcer Johnny Gilbert, emcee of many Hollywood game shows, coaches the crowd as they restlessly await the champ's arrival. Gilbert warms up the audience with instructions to chant "Ali!" as the fighter enters the arena.

Fifteen minutes later, the Forum goes dark. The crowd roars with expectation. A single spotlight picks up Ali as he walks in with wife Veronica. The champ, surrounded by security, presses through the crowd on the floor. Six years ago, almost to the day, Ali beat Ken Norton here in their second fight.

Now there is no conflict, just relaxed affection. Ali wears a dark suit and a striped tie. Veronica is dressed in white, her hair swept to the side. On cue, the crowd bursts into "Ali!" The sight of the champ, his face now round and body noticeably heavier, produces a frenzy of adulation.

The boxer and his wife take their seats for an evening of testimonials. Ali is pensive and unsmiling, not knowing what to expect from this all-star retirement party. It has been two months since he sent a formal letter to the World Boxing Association stating that he would not defend his title. Instead, the boxer's missive stated that he would be hanging up his gloves and would like a formal retirement party—which his associates will produce.

A Jehovah's Witness convention had already booked the arena for July 5, the date Ali wanted. So the gala was pushed back two months. The delay turned out to be providential, allowing celebrities time to clear their schedules and rehearse.

With singer Lou Rawls as master of ceremonies, the champ is treated to a thirty-minute comedy set from comedian Richard Pryor. Then Lola Falana sings a song specially written for tonight.

Then comedian Billy Crystal enters to deliver a twelve-minute monologue called "15 Rounds," in which he impersonates Howard Cosell and Ali while taking the crowd through a history of the boxer's career. At first, the risky performance does not go well. The champ remains grim as Crystal mimics his voice and theatrics. Fans take note of Ali's disapproval on a monitor. There are few laughs as the comic stands alone on the stage, which is decorated to look like a boxing ring. Crystal continues his routine to almost total silence.

But a minute and a half in, Veronica whispers to her husband. Ali cracks a smile. Then he laughs out loud. After tonight, the fighter will refer to Crystal as his "Jewish little brother." By the end of the performance, the champ and fans are mesmerized by the comedian's routine, laughing loudly at every punch line. A visibly relieved Crystal leaves the stage in triumph.

Finally, it is Muhammad Ali's turn. A lectern is brought forward, and he steps up onto the stage to speak. The champ has never been one to use notes and does not do so tonight. He first thanks handler Drew Bundini Brown for being an effective cheerleader. Ali then tells the audience about the one man most of them do not know: Herbert Muhammad.

"I said, 'I want you to manage me,'" the fighter tells the audience. "And he's been expert." Ali then calls his manager up onto the stage. "Herbert Muhammad, come out. Where you at?" For the first time in memory, the very private Herbert shares the limelight with his client, stepping onstage in a tuxedo and a large bow tie.

Ali drapes an arm around the smaller, rounder man. "This insignificant butterball," he tells the crowd. "He's wise."

Ali moves on, thanking Los Angeles mayor Tom Bradley for honoring him with a special Muhammad Ali Day. The boxer gets emotional, bringing Sugar Ray Robinson to the stage; he is Ali's idol and, according to the champ, might even be the greater boxer.

After that, Ali begins to vamp. He performs boxing footwork while throwing jabs—much to the crowd's delight. Throughout the performance, Ali keeps Herbert Muhammad onstage with him. The manager laughs at the fighter's impromptu act. Finally, the champ ends by saying, "Thank you, everybody, for everything." He leaves the stage, Herbert Muhammad by his side.

It seems to be a fitting ending for the greatest era in boxing history.

Seems to be.

✦ ✦ ✦

Muhammad Ali is looking for ways to stay relevant. The last months of 1979 are spent traveling the world with Veronica on a retirement tour. She has a favorite cockatoo that goes everywhere with her, requiring Ali to continue his lavish spending—including buying the bird its own first-class airline seat.

President Jimmy Carter has appointed the champ goodwill ambassador on some of the travels.

But then, things take a turn. On November 4, Iranian terrorists kidnap employees of the US embassy in Tehran. In exchange for their safe return, the mullahs demand that the shah of Iran, currently in exile in New York City, be returned to his home country to face trial.

Six days later, Ali publicly requests that the captive Americans be freed. In exchange, he says, *he* will take their place as a prisoner of the Ayatollah Khomeini. There is widespread support for the ambitious idea from US congressional leaders, including Speaker of the House Tip O'Neill. The Iranians are not thrilled with the proposal, yet Ali remains hopeful. "If someone like myself could see the hostages and see that they are all right," he tells the Associated Press, "it might cool off things."

In the end, Iran denies Ali's request. The hostages will spend 444 days in captivity.

Ali's next visit is to New Delhi, India. The champ steps back into the ring for some halfhearted boxing exhibitions with Indian fighters. He barely throws a punch, preferring to dance around the mat and speak playfully to children sitting ringside. Ali is now 255 pounds—30 pounds over his optimal fighting weight. The tremors in his hands have gotten worse, his speech is slowing, and he has become an insomniac—all early signs of a nervous system disorder known as Parkinson's disease. The most newsworthy moment of the visit comes when the champ is introduced to Indian prime minister Indira Gandhi. Eschewing diplomatic formalities, Ali wraps her in a hug and kisses her cheek.

While in New Delhi, the boxer receives a summons to the White House. On February 8, 1980, he arrives with Veronica to meet President Carter. The Soviet Union has just invaded Afghanistan, a Muslim nation. Carter is arranging an international boycott of the 1980 Moscow Olympics in protest. The president asks Ali to travel to the African nations Tanzania, Nigeria, and Senegal to speak about the boycott. He will travel by government jet, with an official escort of senior diplomatic officials.

But as the journey unfolds, the champ begins to disagree with the Carter administration's policy. Twenty-two African nations boycotted the last Olympic Games, in Montreal, in a show of opposition against the policy of apartheid. The United States did not support them. In addition, many African countries owe their burgeoning economies to the Soviet Union's monetary assistance.

"Maybe I'm being used to do something that ain't right," Ali says in Tanzania, where that nation's leader refuses to meet with him. "You're making me look at things different. If I find out I'm wrong, I'm going back to America and cancel the whole trip."

As the trip moves on to Kenya, Ali ranges farther from his mission. "I am not here as the Uncle Tom pushing America's ideas on my people," he says to the press.

Africans see it otherwise. "We may or may not agree with the boycott," one Liberian journalist notes. "Ali is popular here, or rather *was* very popular, but it is an insult for Carter to send a black American here just because he is black."

In the end, the champ's journey is a *partial* success. Tanzania and Nigeria choose to compete in Moscow, but Kenya and Liberia will boycott.

Time magazine calls Carter's use of Ali "the most bizarre diplomatic mission in U.S. history."

Amid the fallout, the champ is embarrassed. This is not the reaction he had hoped for in his new phase of life. He hints that a change is coming.

✦ ✦ ✦

On February 14, 1980, Ali tells the Associated Press that he is "75 percent certain he will fight again." Friends try to dissuade him. They are worried about his health.

Ali disagrees. "I made a mistake. I'm not ready to stop fighting. The world will forgive me," the champ responds.

The truth is, almost no one in the fighter's life wants him to box again: Veronica is against it. Ali's mother, Odessa, tells him she will not watch. And his father, Cassius Sr., blames the "damn Muslims" for asking his son to step into the ring for another big payday.

That's true. Herbert Muhammad is very much in favor of a fight. Upon hearing that Ali is thinking of a comeback, promoter Don King calls with an offer—and it's a big one.

The money is hard to ignore. On April 28, it is announced that Muhammad Ali will fight world heavyweight champion Larry Holmes. The undefeated "Easton Assassin" is a former Ali sparring partner who has knocked out twenty-seven of his thirty-five opponents. Holmes stands six foot three and weighs a solid 211 pounds. A victory would make this the fourth time Ali won the title. His share of the purse: $8 million—$27.5 million in today's dollars. Amazingly, Holmes, the champion, is being offered *half* that amount.

"If someone asked you to come out of retirement for eight million dollars," Ali asks good friend and adviser Tim Shanahan, "wouldn't you do it?"

Shanahan does not really want Ali to fight again. He has seen the physical decay in him. But the logic of so much money makes sense.

"Yep," he replies.

✦ ✦ ✦

At this point, Ali weighs 256 pounds. The champ dyes his hair. *New York Magazine* ridicules the fighter, saying he now "floats like a butter churn"—stiff, slow movements also being an early indicator of Parkinson's.

To make certain he can pass the prefight physical, Ali flies to the Mayo Clinic in Minnesota for a battery of tests. Despite the warning signs, he is given a clean bill of health. He is pleased.

"The doctors at Mayo examined my hands, my skull, my kidneys, everything. I've got thirteen copies of a letter from the Mayo doctors to hand out to the world. There's nothing to stop me [from fighting again] now. This report is not from some boxing commission, but from the best doctors in the world. . . . Holmes is in trouble."

CHAPTER ELEVEN

Muhammad Ali cannot feel the cool desert breeze as he slumps on a stool in his corner.

So far, Ali has fought nine rounds against the heavyweight champion Larry Holmes in the "Last Hurrah," as this battle in a Las Vegas parking lot is being billed. Blood trickles from Ali's nostril. His left eye is red and swollen. Here, in the makeshift ring outside Caesars Palace, he has landed just ten punches all night.

The more than twenty-four thousand fans in attendance wait to see if Ali will come out for the tenth round. An estimated two billion more worldwide watch the fight on television. The former champ weighs a slim 217 pounds, but the drastic weight drop from 255 has sapped his strength.

Across the ring, in Holmes's corner, the current champ's handlers know this. "He went too far," physical therapist Keith Kleven will later say of Ali. "When you lose so much so fast, after such a dramatic change in diet and physical activity, there is a drastic change in the function of the body's enzymes. Instead of losing fat, you begin to deplete muscle substance. Strength and stamina are lost."

Ali's once-formidable right jab is now nothing more than a hard shove. He has the stamina to dance, but mostly he fights flat-footed. The boxer actually knew the fight was over in the first round. *Oh, God, I still have fourteen rounds to go*, he told himself.

"I had nothing. Nothing. I knew it was hopeless," Ali will later admit. "I knew I couldn't win, and I knew I'd never quit. I looked across at Holmes and knew he would win but that he was going to have to kill me to get me out of the ring."

The ninth round was brutal. Holmes hit Ali so hard with a right uppercut that the challenger was driven back against the ropes, barely able to stand. Ali staggered away. Holmes gave chase, viciously pounding his stumbling opponent. Ali did not go down, but a sharp blow to the kidneys doubled him over in pain.

Now trainer Angelo Dundee is about to do the unthinkable. He wants to call the fight. In his entire twenty-year professional career, Muhammad Ali has never failed to answer the bell.

"Do you want to do it?" Dundee asks the fighter. Across the ring, a menacing Larry Holmes stands for the tenth round. His face is untouched. Muhammad Ali was once his employer, and Holmes has a great deal of respect for him, but he will do everything in his power to knock Ali out in the tenth round.

The bell sounds.

"The Greatest" steps forward to meet his fate.

✦ ✦ ✦

One night ago, Ali spoke with Ted Koppel on the television show *Nightline*.

"How'd you lose all that weight?" Koppel began his questioning.

Ali was not in the studio with the host, instead appearing from Room 301 at Caesars Palace. The fighter wore a dark shirt and showed no sign of levity, his face unsmiling and his words coming out in a slow rasp. He had been passing the time between training sessions watching tape of Holmes fighting a boxer named Mike Weaver. Should Ali defeat the champion, he plans to fight Weaver next.

"Well, I got determined. I didn't rush it. It took me six months, watching my sweets, watching my food, not drinking sodas and ice cream and candy and all the junk foods, and been determined and [I] promise you [I will] KNOCK HOLMES OUT. Regardless of all the talk about old man, too old, inactive, I promise you."

Koppel smiled at Ali's sudden enthusiasm. "Before you psyche yourself up for that again, let me ask *why* you do it. Eight million isn't a bad reason for doing anything, but why do you come back at age thirty-eight and put yourself through all that torture?"

"Well, I'll tell you, it wasn't no torture," Ali replied. "Why are we going to the moon? Because it's there. Why are we going to Mars? Because it's there. . . . History will probably never produce a man who can fight [for the title] four times. It's something I gotta do."

"Can you leave it behind? You've got so many people who depend on you."

Ali admitted that he would one day no longer be able to box, then launched into a long monologue about his loyalty to Nation of Islam leader Warith Muhammad.

"Did you consult with him about this fight?" Koppel asked.

"He's a spiritual man," Ali answered. "Boxing's my living. He knows I'm a boxer. . . . I might retire after the fight and come back every two years until 1985."

Koppel offered a bemused look, humoring the former champ. Ali sounded drunk, slurring his words and often forgetting his train of thought. He asked Koppel to repeat questions. The cadence of the former champ's speech was labored.

"All of us here wish you well," Koppel said warmly, ending the interview.

✦ ✦ ✦

Larry Holmes was not on television the night before the title bout. He rested in Suite 4520 at Caesars, calm and focused after training harder than for any fight of his career. He ran five miles every morning to build endurance. Holmes's pace was not the slow trot favored by Ali but a brisk seven minutes per mile. Since arriving in Las Vegas three weeks ago, the champion had continued these workouts.

Holmes's sparring sessions were equally rigorous. He boxed 210 rounds in training, averaging 75 punches per frame. Rather than send partners home if they knocked him down, Holmes offered $10,000 to anyone who could.

This fixation on toughness almost cost the champ his shot at Ali. Four weeks before this fight, Holmes landed a hard right against sparring partner Leroy Diggs. Holmes felt a sharp pain and believed his hand was broken, having fractured it several years earlier against a boxer named Roy Williams. He continued with the fight, though, switching to his left and winning a ten-round unanimous decision. He credits that victory with launching his climb to the top of the heavyweight ranks.

But with time running out before the Ali match, Holmes not only needed the damaged fist to heal but also had to keep the injury quiet. An immediate visit to the emergency room near his training camp offered hope: the bone was severely bruised but not broken.

So the fighter never stopped training, pushing through the intense pain. When his training shifted from Pennsylvania to Las Vegas, physical therapist Kleven fashioned a foam splint to be worn under Holmes's glove during sparring sessions. The fighter also wore the splint at night, removing it each morning before reporters showed up to watch the champ train.

In his suite, Holmes found inspiration in his family and the new home he was building: "FIRST: MY WIFE, MY CHILDREN, MY FAMILY. MY HOUSE. P.S. MY POOL," he wrote on a sign taped to a wall.

By the time the Ali fight began, Larry Holmes was ready to use his right hand to do damage.

"I'm not mad at him," Holmes said of Ali. "In fact, I find him amusing. He makes me laugh. I'm a nice guy outside of the ring. But no one should mistake my kindness for weakness. In the ring I am a different person."

✦ ✦ ✦

Ali also trained ferociously, but trainer Angelo Dundee sensed that something was wrong.

"I begged him, 'Show me something. Just show me a little.' It wasn't there. He didn't have anything to show."

Dundee would be proven right.

But the rest of Ali's camp was impressed by the fighter's flat stomach and cocky manner. They felt that all signs pointed to the former champ's winning a fourth title.

"It's no contest," handler Gene Kilroy told Ali. "You'll eat him alive."

✦ ✦ ✦

Muhammad Ali entered the arena at 8:07 p.m. to chants of "Ali!" Larry Holmes arrived seven minutes later. The champ was thoughtful, not betraying emotion. Ali and Bundini Brown taunted him, the challenger screaming "I want you" at Holmes. Holmes pretended to lunge out of his corner, only to have Brown restrain him in a piece of carefully rehearsed shtick.

But once the bell rang, the night belonged to Larry Holmes. The *New York Times* would describe the fight as one-sided: "The champion showed almost everything in his repertory in the opening round. There were overhand rights and rights to the body and left jabs and hooks to the head and body."

Ali took the punishment but could not dish it out—at least, not physically. The only blows he landed were verbal.

"I'm your master," he taunted Holmes. "I'm your teacher." The champ responded with a quick combination that rocked Ali.

"The Greatest" does not win a single round.

Amazingly, the fans still rally around him. Rather than cheering Larry Holmes for a brilliant display of boxing talent, they take pity on a slow and confused Ali. Holmes batters his opponent, taking no pity. After the fight, Holmes will say, "He's one hell of an athlete, one hell of a man. Even trying to win a fourth title is one hell of an achievement."

✦ ✦ ✦

The tenth round is more of the same—Larry Holmes punching a now-defenseless Muhammad Ali, who barely makes it back to his corner after the bell.

In twenty years of high-level boxing, Ali has never been knocked out. But as two billion people watch on television, the former world champion remains seated when referee Richard Green asks if he can continue.

Ali cannot. It is over.

CHAPTER TWELVE

JANUARY 19, 1981
LOS ANGELES, CALIFORNIA
4 P.M.

Muhammad Ali may be delusional.

The champ drives down Wilshire Boulevard in his Rolls-Royce. He has a lot on his mind, now believing that his loss to Larry Holmes was based not on age or lack of fitness but on a thyroid medication that robbed him of his strength. The side effects are weakness and an inability to cope with hot weather—both of which were present in Las Vegas. This makes the champ eager to fight again.

But it's complicated.

Since the Holmes bout, Ali has played himself in a boxing movie called *Body and Soul* and answered questions from the FBI about Harold Smith, who embezzled $21 million from the company Muhammad Ali Professional Sports. In addition, the fighter is at odds with his wife, Veronica. She was adamant that he not fight Larry Holmes, concerned about his diminishing cognitive skills and slurred speech. Veronica thought the Holmes fight would only make Ali's condition worse. She asked her husband to put family before money and not to fight.

Ali refused, infatuated with the $8 million payday. Now Veronica's fears have been proven correct. The former champ is often sullen and moody. The shaking in his hands is getting worse. His third marriage is in trouble.

Despite all this, the siren call of the boxing ring still sounds for Ali. So, as he drives through the Los Angeles neighborhood known as the Miracle Mile on this unseasonably cool sixty-degree winter day, his biggest concern is *not* his failing marriage, diminished body, or even the FBI. The greatest issue confronting Muhammad Ali is that he has essentially been banned from the ring. Larry Holmes beat Ali so badly that no state will license him.

Nevada requested that he surrender his boxing credentials last month, which he did. However, the former champ then agreed to box a British contender named John L. Gardner, in Honolulu—but Hawaii won't let him fight, either. No one will.

Yet there must be someplace.

✦ ✦ ✦

Now at the wheel of his two-tone brown Rolls, Muhammad Ali comes upon an LAPD roadblock. Before Ali left his nearby home, good friend Howard Bingham called to alert him of a potential suicide jumper from a downtown building. The champ drove the wrong way up a one-way street to be of assistance. Now, a crowd looks upward to where a Black man in a hooded sweatshirt stands on the ninth-floor ledge of an office building. The man yells that he is "crazy" and "no good." It seems certain he will jump.

Some in the crowd even relish the prospect, yelling, "Go, go!" and "Jump!"

Ali gets out of his car and approaches the police. He learns that negotiators have been talking to the distraught Vietnam veteran without success. A psychologist and chaplain have also failed to persuade the troubled man to come down.

The champ offers his services.

Police lead him inside the building. Spectators are amazed when the famous boxer leans his head out a window near the jumper.

"You're my brother," Ali tells him. "I love you, and I couldn't lie to you. You've got to listen. I want you to come home with me. Meet some friends of mine."

Ali then walks out onto the fire escape and beckons to the vet to come in off the ledge.

The man falls into the fighter's embrace and begins to weep.

✦ ✦ ✦

Nearly a year later, it is Ali who needs a safe place.

The date is December 11, 1981, and the former champ is preparing to step into the ring. He has finally found a country that will let him fight: the Bahamas.

It has been fourteen months since Larry Holmes pummeled Ali. The new fight will be against a lesser opponent. The "Drama in Bahama" pits the former world champion against Trevor Berbick, a twenty-seven-year-old Jamaican. Unlike Ali, Berbick did go the distance against Holmes, but lost. He is looking to make a comeback.

Ignoring reports that Ali suffers from a brain injury, Kendal Nottage, Bahamas' minister of youth, sports, and culture, approved the fight. "I was shown a number of medical reports, and they were satisfactory to me," he stated—but there are rumors that the deal came to pass only when "financial stimulus" was provided to Bahamian officials.

Yet, indeed, after a series of tests at the UCLA Medical Center, Ali was given a clean bill of health and was said to have "the vessels of a young man." Dr. Harry Demopoulos of New York University performed a follow-up visit with Ali here in the Bahamas last week. The slurring and shaking, Demopoulos stated, were part of a psychosocial response. "If the slurring were due to permanent damage, it would be there all the time."*

---

* In 1984, Muhammad Ali will be diagnosed with Parkinson's disease. The connection between boxing and Parkinson's had not been established at that time, but research has since shown a correlation. Dr. Samuel Goldman of the Parkinson's Institute and Clinical Center stated, "There's a good likelihood that his Parkinson's is a consequence of repetitive head trauma. It can really set off a degenerative cascade."

The fight promoter is Sports Internationale (Bahamas) Ltd., a dubious company on the verge of financial collapse. Indeed, Trevor Berbick was so sure that he would never see his payday that he demanded his $300,000 fee in advance. Ali is promised $3.5 million.*

The former champion is now thirty-nine years old and a rotund 236 pounds. His belly jiggles when sparring blows land. In one month, he will turn forty. He has been training in the Bahamas since September 21, intent on defeating the Jamaican and positioning himself for that elusive fourth title.

But Ali's definition of conditioning is not what it used to be. Instead of running every morning, he often only hikes or walks. He shadowboxes listlessly as he strolls. His hand speed is slow when he spars. The fight is scheduled for only ten rounds, which favors Ali, for he is hardly in shape to go fifteen.

The Bahamian venue is a dusty field in an unfinished sports arena where a sturdy ring has been constructed. A cowbell signals the rounds. A crowd of eight thousand, some of whom paid only $5 to get in, sit with anticipation. The fight is also being broadcast by SelectTV, a pay-per-view service. Announcer Don Dunphy calls the match and gives the first round to Ali, who has some pep in his step.

It will be the only round the ex-champ will win.

In the seventh, Berbick asks referee Zac Clayton to stop the fight, claiming his opponent is helpless. But Ali will not concede, causing Clayton to continue the bout.

It will go ten rounds.

✦ ✦ ✦

With forty-three seconds left in the final round, Berbick gets tired of hitting Ali and simply coasts to the bell. After 548 rounds, this will be the champ's final frame.

Everyone in the sports arena on this sweltering Friday night can

---

* He will receive only $1.1 million in the fight.

plainly see this is truly the end for Muhammad Ali. The cowbell ring is a signal of mercy.

After the unanimous decision for Berbick is announced, he turns to Ali and says, "You've inspired me since I was a kid."

✦ ✦ ✦

Back in the cramped dressing room, actor John Travolta consoles Muhammad Ali. Angelo Dundee and Drew Bundini Brown say little. Everyone knows Ali's twenty-one-year boxing legacy will endure, but the former champ is finished.

"I know it's the end. I'm not crazy," Ali tells the media. "I had excuses. I was too light. Didn't breathe right. No excuses this time. I'm happy. I'm still pretty. I could have a black eye. Broken teeth. Split lips.

"I think I came out all right for an old man."

CHAPTER THIRTEEN

JULY 19, 1996
ATLANTA, GEORGIA
12:30 A.M.

Years pass. Seasons change. So do circumstances.

It was back in 1984 that Muhammad Ali ran through the streets of Louisville, Kentucky, in white shorts and a singlet, carrying the Olympic torch as part of a nationwide relay to begin the games in Los Angeles. There, decathlon gold medalist Rafer Johnson would ascend to the top of the stadium and light the eternal flame that would burn throughout the sixteen days and nights of competition. It is part of Olympic lore that the identity of the person igniting the cauldron be kept secret. Only when Johnson stands in the spotlight will the world know he is that man.

Twelve years later, *Muhammad Ali* is the secret.

✦ ✦ ✦

Atlanta's Centennial Olympic Stadium is filled with eighty-five thousand spectators from around the world. The lavish opening ceremony has been rehearsed over and over before tonight. Nothing is left to chance as Atlanta welcomes the games. The performers entertaining the crowd have worked months to be here. As ten thousand athletes from 197 countries march into the stadium by nation, and the four-hour opening ceremony comes closer to the end, the question of the night is: Who will light the Olympic flame?

Shortly after midnight, President Bill Clinton formally declares the games open. The Olympic flag is raised over the stadium.*

Boxer Evander Holyfield emerges from a tunnel, bearing a torch with the Olympic flame. In a symbolic show, signifying that 1996 is the one-hundred-year anniversary of the first Olympic Games in modern history, held in 1896 in Athens, Greece, Holyfield is joined by Greek sprinter and 1992 gold medalist Voula Patoulidou. But the crowd knows that it is not these two elite athletes who will light the torch.

The relay continues as Holyfield hands off to Olympic gold medal swimmer Janet Evans, an American, who holds the torch high as she begins running up a long stairway toward the unlit Olympic cauldron.

Quickly, Evans finishes her climb and stands tall.

Suddenly, Muhammad Ali steps into the spotlight.

The crowd erupts. The champ is dressed all in white. He has been out of the public eye for more than a decade. Those in the stands and the worldwide television audience now see why: Ali is only fifty-four but appears years older. His hair is gray, his face frozen. The once-toned torso is puffy. Until now, few understood how debilitated Muhammad Ali had become.

Many things have happened to the champ. In December 1985, he and Veronica divorced. Eleven months later, he married Yolanda "Lonnie" Williams, whom he knew when she was a child in Louisville. Ali is also estranged from manager Herbert Muhammad, largely because his new wife is now handling his finances.

But most important of all, the fighter's health is declining drastically.

---

*The late hour allows viewers all over the world to more easily watch the event.

In fact, Janet Evans is afraid to hand the torch to the former fighter. During rehearsals last night, Ali dropped it twice. The swimmer has been told by organizers not to turn her flame off once she lights the fighter's torch with it, just in case he drops it again.

None of this is known by the crowd at Olympic Stadium. Just the sight of the world boxing champion sets off a nostalgic chant: "Ali, Ali, Ali!"

Despite his left arm visibly shaking, Muhammad Ali focuses, determined to light the cauldron. As Evans touches her flame to his, the champ grips his torch with both hands. This time, he does not let go.

For the first time in fifteen years, Muhammad Ali has the world spotlight again. Still clutching the now-lit torch, Ali bends and lights the device that will set fire to the cauldron. Balls of orange flame shoot into the dark Atlanta sky.

In this moment, the old Ali returns. He stares at the inferno he has just created. He knows how his presence is affecting the world. Then he vanishes.

"People say I had a good life. But I ain't dead yet," he has previously stated. "I want to live a good life, serve God, help everyone I can.

"And one more thing: I'm still gonna find out who stole my bike when I was twelve years old in Louisville. And I'm still gonna whup him. That was a good bike."

CHAPTER FOURTEEN

Muhammad Ali wants to come out of retirement.

He is almost sixty years old as he prepares for today's visitor. Oprah Winfrey will soon arrive for an exclusive interview for her magazine *O*. Ninety-five miles east of Chicago, the champ's eighty-eight-acre farm is his sanctuary—comprised of a pool, a bathhouse, an outdoor kitchen, two barns, a basketball court, an office, and a gym with a boxing ring, steam room, massage room, and hot tub spa. But the centerpiece is the four-thousand-square-foot home. The aroma of a hot cooked meal now permeates the house. Ali's chef is preparing chicken, salmon, and couscous. The interview will take place in the home office. A brown corduroy couch is in the center of the room. Photos of the champ's life line the walls: a framed *Sports Illustrated* cover with Ali in a tuxedo as "Sportsman of the Year," the fighter and Nelson Mandela making fists as if to box, and a poster of Ali with basketball legend Michael Jordan.

As Oprah's limousine pulls up the drive, the champ, dressed in a red button-down shirt, stands outside with Lonnie to welcome the forty-seven-year-old Winfrey into their home. Oprah, dressed in a light-blue sweater over dark-blue blouse, wears a silver bracelet and large earrings. Though Ali and Lonnie adopted a son in 1995 and are used to the ruckus of a six-year-old running through the house, it has been a long, quiet winter here on the farm, and Ali, a man who enjoys the limelight, is glad for Winfrey's star presence.

Media interviews like today's are rare for Ali, as Lonnie shields the fighter from outsiders. Lonnie Ali, fifteen years younger, with a master's degree in business administration, is a constant presence in her husband's life. But she trusts that Winfrey's interview will not harm Ali's image. A photographer will take pictures, but these will be carefully scrutinized before permission is granted to run them in the magazine.

Almost immediately, Ali delights Winfrey by performing a few magic tricks. He still enjoys making people laugh. However, "he shakes uncontrollably, speaks slowly, and slurs his words; you have to listen with your ear turned up," Oprah will state.

After the tour of the house comes a tour of the farm, during which Ali proudly shows off his favorite area: the boxing ring.

After which, it is off to the office for the Q and A. It is Oprah Winfrey's style to be not confrontational but nurturing. She begins with soothing questions, hoping to put the champ at ease. Fame is something both Oprah and Ali have in common. So she starts there.

✦ ✦ ✦

The interview starts.

Oprah: You are known as the most famous person on the planet. Do you feel like the most famous?

Ali: It's surprising, but I never realized why I was so famous.

Oprah: Nobody had ever heard of anyone like you.

Ali: I would say things like, "I am the greatest! I'm pretty! If you talk jive, you'll drop in five! I float like a butterfly, sting like a bee! I'm pretty!" When white people heard me talking like this, some said, "That Black man talks too much. He's bragging."

✦ ✦ ✦

Ms. Winfrey then takes the champ back to his childhood.

Oprah: Do you remember how you felt the first time, at the age of
    twelve, when you stepped into the ring?
Ali: I was nervous and scared. I was shaking.
Oprah: Did you go back the next night?
Ali: Yes—every night for a month. I loved it.

✦ ✦ ✦

Seasoned observers of the champ understand he was putting Ms.
Winfrey on with talk of making a boxing comeback. Even in his diminished state, Ali has a devilish sense of humor. But now, things turn
serious.

Oprah: The perception many people have is that you got hit too many
    times—that you're punch-drunk. Does the illness have anything
    to do with being hit in the head?
Ali: If that were so, then a million people must have gotten hit in
    the head! Joe Frazier got hit more than me—and he doesn't have
    Parkinson's. Sonny Liston got his hard, but he doesn't have it.
Oprah: Well, he's dead.
Ali: No boxer in the history of boxing has had Parkinson's. There's
    no injury in my brain that suggested that the illness came from
    boxing.

✦ ✦ ✦

The entire interview is published in June, including a photo showing
Winfrey hugging a smiling Ali. However, it is one thing to read
about the champ's physical decline but quite another to see it.

On June 7, shortly after *O* hits the newsstands, Oprah Winfrey
is interviewing actor Will Smith on the set of her television show
in Chicago. Smith is playing Ali in a movie about the fighter's life.
He has trained for two years to learn how to box and can mimic the

champ's voice so well that Lonnie Ali told Oprah the two men sound exactly alike on the phone.*

Now the studio audience will be shocked by two things. First, Winfrey suddenly announces that Muhammad Ali is in the house. The next surprise comes as the champ, dressed in a chalk-striped jacket, khaki pants, and a tie, walks onstage. Lonnie is in the front row wearing red. A section of the studio audience rises to give Ali a standing ovation. He is stooped and shaking all over.

Oprah gives him a warm kiss on the lips and leads him to a chair.

As Will Smith looks on, Oprah leans in toward Ali and asks, "What does having this film out now mean to you at this time in your life?"

Ali responds with a hard-to-hear whisper. "It means people who don't really know much about me, it will tell them more about who I am, and they'll understand more about the legend of Muhammad Ali. . . . It's a big honor. It makes me feel good, somebody takes the time to write a movie about my life. It makes me humble."

✦ ✦ ✦

Even though his ring comeback could have delivered a fatal blow years ago, Muhammad Ali—unlike his contemporaries Elvis Presley and John Lennon—is not destined to die young. But as he approaches age sixty, there is little quality of life for the champ. In his diminished state, he tries to be a good father to his adopted son, but he rarely sees his eight other children, who are scattered across the country. Lonnie Ali takes care of business and monitors her husband's physical status, but there is not much she can do about the illness destroying his once-magnificent body.

The old adage says, "Time heals all wounds."

Not in the case of Muhammad Ali.

---

* On March 27, 2022, Will Smith will apparently use his knowledge of boxing to hit comedian Chris Rock onstage at the Academy Awards ceremony.

CHAPTER FIFTEEN

APRIL 9, 2016
PHOENIX, ARIZONA
8 P.M.

Fifteen years have passed since Muhammad Ali's last major media exposure with Oprah Winfrey. He and Lonnie have moved to a place called Paradise Valley, in Arizona, so the champ can be closer to the Barrow Neurological Institute, which treats people with Parkinson's.

Ali is now seventy-four. He has survived Herbert Muhammad and Angelo Dundee, as well as many of his ring opponents. Lonnie Ali's gift for managing money means he no longer has financial problems—his net worth is roughly $80 million.

Now, as the champ prepares to make the last public appearance of his life—at a charity event in Phoenix—celebrities from the world of sports and entertainment have arrived to pay homage. Singer Carrie Underwood is determined to get her picture taken with the champ. Arizona Cardinals football coach Bruce Arians walks the red carpet, telling reporters that Muhammad Ali was the greatest of all time. "He was a hero of mine when I was a young man. That's where I got a lot of my swagger from, trying to copy him." In fact, most have come to this fund-raiser, dubbed "Fight Night," specifically to see the former champ. "When you hear the name Ali, it's a no-brainer," says comedian Sinbad. "It's easy. It's not a hard decision at all."

Once the audience settles into seats in the ballroom at the JW Marriott hotel, an emotional video tribute to Ali is shown on a big screen. After this, the crowd rises in a standing ovation as Muhammad Ali is helped to his seat.

It is a sad sight. The champ—wearing sunglasses with his tailored tuxedo—no longer speaks. His head is tilted forward. Ali has been hospitalized in recent years for urinary tract infections brought on by pneumonia and looks frail. He has lost a great deal of weight.

Lonnie Ali, dressed in a black formal gown, steps to the microphone to present this evening's awards. She starts by thanking the doctors who made her husband's appearance tonight possible. The evening is an enormous success, raising millions of dollars for Parkinson's research. Despite the pressure she is under with Ali's diminished condition, Lonnie is poised. She knows the end is near and has accepted it.

Two months later, she takes her husband to the hospital.

"A little cold," she tells Bob Gunnell, the family's official spokesman. "I just want to make you aware that Muhammad has got a little cold. It's nothing to worry about, but as a precaution, I'm going to take him to the hospital to get checked out."

✦ ✦ ✦

The "little cold" becomes worse. On June 3, 2016, Muhammad Ali dies. The time is 9:10 p.m. An imam stands at the former champ's bedside, singing the call to prayer. Ali's nine children, with a few grandchildren, surround his bedside. The ventilator keeping him alive was removed a half hour ago. Soon, darkness descends.

✦ ✦ ✦

The memorial service is held on June 10 in Louisville, Kentucky. Thousands of people attend. Ali's children take the lead.

"You have inspired us and the world to be the best version of ourselves," daughter Rasheda says. "May you live in paradise free from suffering. You shook up the world in life; now you're shaking up the world in death."

Laila Ali is next: "My whole outlook on life is my belief in myself, my belief in other people, my understanding of us all being connected, the humility that I have toward other human beings—that all really is ingrained in me from my father."

✦ ✦ ✦

As with Presley and Lennon, the world mourns the passing of Muhammad Ali. Words cannot accurately describe his legacy—other than to say this:

He earned the description "the Greatest."

EPILOGUE

Muhammad Ali was preceded in death by **Herbert Muhammad**, who passed away following heart surgery on August 25, 2008. Herbert's brother **Warith Muhammad** died of a heart attack just weeks later. Herbert and Ali battled in court during the 1990s, after Lonnie Ali took over the fighter's financial affairs. The champ sued Herbert, claiming he had forged a signature in fund-raising letters for a foundation promoting Islam. In 1999, Ali's lawyers requested that the court declare his business relationship with Herbert null and void. The manager had claimed he owned the rights to Ali's life story—and actually sold them to Columbia Pictures. The champ received no money from the deal. The lawsuits were settled before Herbert's death, and he and Ali reconciled. Herbert Muhammad is buried in Mount Glenwood Memory Gardens South cemetery in Glenwood, Illinois. For health reasons, Muhammad Ali could not attend the funeral.

✦ ✦ ✦

Sonji Clay-Glover (née Roi), married to Ali from 1964 to 1966, died in October 2005. Cause of death: a heart attack. She was fifty-nine years old.

Muhammad Ali's second wife, **Khalilah Ali** (née Belinda Boyd), still lives in South Florida. She appeared in the movie *The China Syndrome* and has been on the cover of *Ebony* magazine seven times.

Khalilah Ali remarried and divorced twice after splitting with the champ. She is seventy-two.

Veronica Ali (née Porché), the champ's third wife, remarried after their divorce. Her second husband died in 2004. Veronica made an appearance on *Dancing with the Stars* when daughters Hana and Laila performed on the television show in 2007. At the time of this writing, she is sixty-six and works as a psychologist in Southern California.

The champ's fourth wife, **Lonnie Ali**, still lives in Paradise Valley, Arizona. She is sixty-five and continues to manage the champ's estate.

✦ ✦ ✦

The boxers who fought Muhammad Ali are well known for those battles. **Joe Frazier** died of liver cancer in 2011 at the age of sixty-seven. **Ken Norton** passed in 2013 at the age of seventy after suffering a series of strokes. **Leon Spinks** fought until the age of forty-two but was beset by financial and health problems before dying in Las Vegas in 2021 at the age of sixty-seven. **Jimmy Young** died in 2005 of a heart attack; he was fifty-six. **Trevor Berbick**, the champ's final opponent, went on to become heavyweight champion of the world. His reign was brief; he was knocked out by a young fighter named Mike Tyson in 1986. Berbick was murdered by his nephew in 2006 after a dispute with the fighter over land; the young man struck Berbick four times on the head with a steel pipe.

Some of Ali's opponents are still living: **Larry Holmes** is seventy-two, retired, and living in Easton, Pennsylvania. **George Foreman**, who fought Ali in the "Rumble in the Jungle" in Zaire, is seventy-three. He is a successful entrepreneur, often seen in television commercials.

✦ ✦ ✦

Muhammad Ali fathered eight children from four women and adopted a ninth.

From Khalilah: **Maryum Ali**, fifty-three, is an activist and author.

Rasheda Ali, fifty-two, is an advocate for those with Parkinson's disease; **Jamillah Ali**, Rasheda's twin, is fifty-two and has dedicated her life to philanthropy. **Muhammad Ali Jr.**, who was never close to his father, is forty-nine and is involved with the Muhammad Ali Childhood Home Museum in Louisville, Kentucky.

Miya Ali, fifty, was born from a relationship with Patricia Harvell. Miya is an advocate for those with dyslexia.

Daughter **Khaliah Ali**, forty-eight, was born from a relationship with Aaisha Fletcher. She now serves on the board of the Philadelphia Juvenile Law Center.

From third wife, Veronica: **Hana Ali**, forty-six, writes books about her father. **Laila Ali**, forty-four, a former boxing champion, has retired from the ring and is raising five children with her husband, Curtis Conway, a former pro football player.

Asaad Amin Ali, twenty-seven, was adopted in 1995. He is a former baseball player and coach. He lives in Louisville and is involved with public speaking.

✦ ✦ ✦

One branch of the Nation of Islam changed its name to the American Muslim Mission in 1978. This was an attempt by Warith Muhammad to move the group away from its radical beliefs to a more traditional Islamic faith. Warith stepped down in 1985 and dissolved the organization, but the other branch of the Nation of Islam was soon reborn under the leadership of Louis Farrakhan, who advocates many of the same hateful racist and anti-Semitic beliefs once propagated by Elijah Muhammad. The Nation of Islam is headquartered in Chicago and has an estimated membership of fifty thousand followers.

AUTHORS' NOTE

The three men we have featured in this book each had a colossal influence on the United States and on world culture, much of it positive but some of it the opposite. In that sense, Elvis Presley, John Lennon, and Muhammad Ali are similar to presidents and other cultural icons. Politics, global exploration, war, and natural disasters dominate historical renderings. But cultural achievements shape the country as well, sometimes in lasting ways.

Fame changes those who receive it. It is not a natural condition for anyone. What binds together our three subjects is how their fame overwhelmed them. Unable to deal with the pressure that comes from intense public notoriety and scrutiny, each of them withdrew, allowing others to dictate how their lives would evolve.

Elvis Presley was one of the most charismatic singers in history. From the very beginning of his career in the mid-1950s, he mesmerized his audience. Yes, the United States was ready for something new (rock 'n' roll), and many young people were attracted to personal rebellion against the conformity of the Eisenhower years—and Elvis's good looks and sensual moves certainly played into this. He was blessed with a magnificent voice and personal magnetism above anything ever seen onstage before.

You can't learn that.

When Bill O'Reilly spoke with Ann-Margret, a charismatic person herself, she had trouble articulating her assessment of Elvis. But while discussing him, her face transformed into a wide-eyed glow of admiration. After all these years, her memories of the man were communicated not just with words but by the smile on her face.

Elvis was not a social crusader or an especially introspective person. He lived largely from day to day, never forming a big-picture philosophy. Thus, he was easy to exploit—and much of that was his own fault. Despite knowing he had a responsibility to his young daughter, who adored him, he lacked the discipline to wrest the reins of control of his career from a self-interested handler or to stop his own destructive behavior. (We included the suicide of Elvis's young grandson in this book to emphasize how fragile family lines can be.)

Music can bring joy and solace to a world that badly needs those things. Presley's entertainment legacy is simply unmatched. Along with Muhammad Ali, he remains a worldwide icon decades after his death. His talent and creative accomplishments changed music forever.

As a historical figure, Elvis Presley did far more good than harm, but he paid an enormous price for his success. Not only did he destroy himself, but his excesses prevented him from accomplishing so many more positive things. He did not understand the lethal danger that accompanied his massive fame, and he was not receptive to instruction. Therefore, his slide into self-destruction continued unimpeded. He had to know the damage he was doing to his once-strong body. Still, though the sycophants around him hastened his demise, the primary blame lies with him. He had a native intelligence beyond most performers, so he understood his personal madness, but he could not stop it and totally surrendered himself and his career to a reckless, greedy business manager.

And so the King left the proverbial building far too soon. The world was stunned when he died at age forty-two. His physical decline was public, but his private demons were not. And it is the demons that are remembered most.

✦ ✦ ✦

Not since King George III and his Green Dragoons in the American War of Independence has a group of Englishmen so heavily influenced the landscape of America. Beginning in 1964, the Beatles propelled American culture through a decade of turbulence and dramatic change. As the most outspoken member of the group, John Lennon drove the narrative. It went like this: from clean-cut young men with catchy tunes, to worldwide phenoms, to counterculture celebrants of the recreational drug scene. Peace, love, and rock 'n' roll.

Unlike his bandmates, Lennon was always subversive and relatively unstable. But the public saw only the witty, nonconformist side of the man. Two days before he was murdered, *Playboy* magazine published an interview with Lennon in which he admitted to being violent toward women, including his first wife. Today, his words would have gotten him canceled.

Like Elvis, but to a lesser extent, John Lennon oozed charisma. However, his overall vision guided the Beatles into the world's consciousness. Their music remains legendary today.

Also like Presley, Lennon eventually became an isolated man. His estrangement from his friends and bandmates must be considered a historical tragedy. Had the lads stayed together, the world would have been a better place. But that was impossible because of Lennon's desperate search for escape and emotional comfort. Once a human being succumbs to a powerful narcotic like heroin, their historical course is dramatically altered for the worse. In addition, Lennon became almost totally dependent on Yoko Ono for his life direction. He ceased to chart his own destiny. Someone else's view of life is *not* yours. If you cede decision-making to another person, disaster often follows.

John Lennon had another thing in common with Elvis Presley: lack of big-picture awareness. Here was a son of Liverpool influencing tens of millions of young people the world over. Did he respect that? The evidence says no. He lived primarily for himself, often acting impulsively and callously.

The Lennon-McCartney creative collaboration was far more sophisticated than anything Elvis put out. But, again, Lennon did not seem to understand this. His dismissal of McCartney from his life is actually shocking. The pair had accomplished so much. No band has ever had more influence than the Beatles.

With a strong native intelligence, Lennon had to know that becoming inebriated to the extent that he did was going to cause pain for the people around him. And it did. But as he approached forty, he seemed to wake up—too late, as it turned out, because evil stalked him.

Many Americans vividly remember the Beatles on *The Ed Sullivan Show*, in *A Hard Day's Night*, and rolling out the "Magical Mystery Tour." Their records and performances are indelible to this day. We *listen* to the lyrics.

Did John Lennon understand his place in cultural history? Debatable. He rode many waves in his career, some of which had a fierce undertow. The fact that Lennon did not want anyone to know about his heroin addiction demonstrates that he knew right from wrong. But he wasted many years in his prime. As did Elvis Presley.

The historical legacy of John Lennon and the Beatles, at least in America, is undeniable. They provided their fans with lifelong positive memories. That overrides any controversy or what might have been. John Lennon is remembered fondly.

And he should be.

✦ ✦ ✦

Muhammad Ali stands apart from Presley and Lennon because of the race factor. Once again, we are confronted with an incredibly charismatic human being. Ali was an amazing athlete, but his persona overshadowed his boxing success. "Larger than life" is the cliché. It fits Muhammad Ali perfectly.

But as with Presley and Lennon, Ali did not control his great gifts—or his own life, for that matter. Others dealt the cards, and Muhammad played them. But putting his fate in the hands of a controversial business manager led directly to many years of impairment and, finally, death.

Along the way came cruelty as well as kindness, hatred and love—much of it in public. Others felt as Smokin' Joe did, but in the everyday world, Muhammad Ali was largely revered, especially by the poor and marginalized. Just a glimpse of the man could bring joy.

In 1979, while working for KMGH-TV in Denver, Bill O'Reilly did a walking interview with Ali at Stapleton Airport—just a Q and A about Leon Spinks, who defeated Ali for the title in a shocking upset and then lost the rematch to Ali. The boxer was low-key that day, but everyone he passed stopped cold.

Like Elvis and John Lennon, Muhammad Ali had a keen native intelligence. However, he willingly allowed himself to be manipulated, especially financially. Why? We don't know. How could he have agreed to continue taking senseless beatings? We don't know.

But he did.

Muhammad Ali's place in history is obvious. He was the greatest prizefighter of all time, as he loudly proclaimed. But it's more than that—Ali remains a modern contemporary hero alongside Martin Luther King Jr. and Barack Obama.

It was Ali's presence that spurred the massive admiration. His private life was a mess, yet his children revere him. His philosophy on race was deeply flawed, a product of indoctrination by Elijah Muhammad. But when he died, America and the world mourned. And when he lit the Olympic torch in 1996, millions felt personal pain at seeing his diminished state.

✦ ✦ ✦

It is unknown whether Muhammad Ali understood his historical position. He glided through life a contradiction, dispensing both kindness and cruelty. Despite a massive amount of reporting on him, the true nature of Ali remains largely shrouded in mystery.

Which brings us to the issue of historical judgment.

The United States is populated with heroic and inspiring people. That's the legacy of the most powerful nation on earth. Yet our society often denigrates historical figures to a shocking degree. Cancel culture has gravely damaged the United States, casting fear throughout the land, assassinating people's characters with sadistic glee. When school board members in a major city like San Francisco demand that the names "Abraham Lincoln" and "George Washington" be banished from high schools, you know things are out of control.

Human beings can never live up to expectations of perfection. Thomas Jefferson was obviously a flawed man who exploited his slaves at a time when enslavement was an industry virtually unchallenged in Jefferson's South. Yet he built a foundation of freedom for his country that eventually afforded billions of people a pathway to prosperity.

So do we cancel Thomas Jefferson? He certainly harmed people for selfish pursuits, but he also helped countless human beings.

Judeo-Christian philosophy, which was embraced by America's founding fathers, affords forgiveness and requests humility. None of us is without sin. Yet the cancel culture fanatics gladly throw the first stone.

The subjects of this book should not be judged. They should be appreciated for their extraordinary talents and for their positive contributions to this country and the world.

And the thing is, they were all in the arena at the same time—an amazing display of cultural history within a short time frame, perhaps never to be seen again.

It was our privilege to write about Elvis Presley, John Lennon, and Muhammad Ali in a way that makes them real, for better or for worse.

But please know that both of us side with the better.

Thanks for reading our book.

BILL O'REILLY
MARTIN DUGARD
May 2022

ACKNOWLEDGMENTS

From Bill O'Reilly: The following greatly assist me in my literary and journalistic endeavors: Makeda Wubneh, Jonathan Leibner, Nicole Casey, Taylor Casey, Victor Garcia, Fred Newman, and Edgar Royce.

✦ ✦ ✦

From Martin Dugard: Thanks to Bill O'Reilly, Makeda Wubneh, and Eric Simonoff. And as always, to Calene: You are my sunshine.

INDEX

ABOUT THE AUTHORS

Bill O'Reilly is a trailblazing TV journalist who has experienced unprecedented success on cable news and in writing eighteen national number-one bestselling nonfiction books. There are more than eighteen million books in the *Killing* series in print. He lives on Long Island.

Martin Dugard is the *New York Times* bestselling author of several books of history, among them the *Killing* series, *Into Africa*, and *Taking Paris*. He and his wife live in Southern California.